Corporate Social Development

A Paradigm Shift

countries also face the barrier that funders want to see immediate results, even though experience has taught us that in reality there must be preparation and building over time before impact becomes evident.

In Germany, large social development agencies run the institutions, and it has been difficult for grassroots organizations to create a public identity that would attract support and funding. [illegible] Organizations have been able to use the media effectively to establish their own identity and are now able [illegible]

In the Philippines, [illegible] disability organizations, [illegible] Denmark. Over three years, [illegible] successful and proven [illegible] funding for the [illegible]

[illegible]

[illegible] training to Russian disability groups. In 1995, the Federal Law on the Social Protection of Persons with Disabilities was enacted, requiring that assistance be provided to disability organizations, though very little of this law has been implemented.

Corporate Social Development

A Paradigm Shift

Rajanikant Verma

MD PUBLICATIONS PVT LTD
NEW DELHI
www.mdppl.com

Published by :

MD Publications Pvt Ltd
"MD House", 11, Darya Ganj,
New Delhi-110 002
Phone : +91-11-41563325 (Customer Service)
+91-11-41562846 (Editorial)
E-mail (orders) : order@mdppl.com
Website : www.mdppl.com

ISBN : 978-81-7533-226-3

Published and Printed by Mr. Pranav Gupta on behalf of **MD Publications Pvt Ltd** at Printext, New Delhi.

PREFACE

Corporate development refers to the planning and execution of a wide range of strategies to meet specific organizational objectives. The kinds of activities falling under corporate development may include initiatives such as recruitment of a new management team, plans for phasing in or out of certain markets or products, establishing relationships with strategic business partners, identifying and acquiring companies, securing financing, divesting of assets or divisions, increasing intellectual property assets and so on.

One of the more common manifestations of corporate development has to do with reshaping the management arm of the corporation. This may involve a process of phasing certain management positions out of the existing structure or creating new positions in an effort to strengthen the management team. As part of this type of approach, corporate development may also demand that one or more current managers are released from the company and replaced with people who possess skills required to move the company forward. When this is the case, the corporate development team will handle the functions of recruitment and evaluation of potential hires.

There is no one tried and true formula for the process of corporate development. The actual structure of the corporate strategy will depend greatly on the current circumstances of the company and the area where the development is desired. In most cases, the process will not be of short duration; corporate development is usually a process that takes place over an extended period of time and may be adjusted or refined as the project moves forward.

Just as a management team may be revamped, corporate development may also be employed to change the current focus for clients. This may mean looking into the potential for breaking into new markets with existing products or developing complimentary products that will allow this type of expansion. Depending on the status of the base market, corporate development may also look at shifting away from a shrinking consumer market while seeking market share in a different consumer market with newer products.

A social development approach is grounded in recognising the value of partnership working towards positive outcomes. Social development professionals emphasise the importance of building up an in-depth understanding of institutional contexts – both formal and informal structures, processes and practices – that determine the 'rules of the game'. Without such understanding, technical advice alone is likely to be less effective. Similarly, discussion, negotiation and achieving consensus require an appreciation of other stakeholders' perspectives.

I am very grateful to Mr. Pranav Gupta, Director of MD Publications Pvt Ltd, New Delhi, for his kind cooperation and support for this book.

Rajanikant Verma

Contents

1

Corporate Social Development

An Introduction

Corporate Development refers to the planning and execution of a wide range of strategies to meet specific organizational objectives. The kinds of activities falling under corporate development may include initiatives such as recruitment of a new management team, plans for phasing in or out of certain markets or products, establishing relationships with strategic business partners, identifying and acquiring companies, securing financing, divesting of assets or divisions, increasing intellectual property assets and so on. There is no formula for "corporate development" and the activities encompassed are often the role of the CEO or other executives. However, particularly in larger companies, corporate development is provided as a charter for a particular executive or team. In these cases, the opportunities and initiatives are numerous enough to justify specialists, instead of being delegated to the office of the CEO and line of business executives. Often the corporate development executives come from a legal background, due to the complex contractual issues associated with many transactions. When focused on product or financial issues, corporate development executives often have MBA or CPA credentials.

For example, if a company is looking towards non-organic growth expansion, a corporate development group will evaluate potential target companies. The acquisition of small or private companies by a large corporation is usually not conducted with the assistance of investment bankers, but executed by the corporate development team themselves. *Corporate development* is a term that references the variety of planning options and strategies that can help to move a company toward its goals. The process of this type of strategic development can be applied to just about any facet of the corporation's organizational structure. In actual structure, corporate planning can involve finding ways to fine-tune the existing structure of the company or expanding the company's interest through acquisitions or mergers.

One of the more common manifestations of corporate development has to do with reshaping the management arm of the corporation. This may involve a process of phasing certain management positions out of the existing structure or creating new positions in an effort to strengthen the management team. As part of this type of approach, corporate development may also demand that one or more current managers are released from the company and replaced with people who possess skills required to move the company forward.

When this is the case, the corporate development team will handle the functions of recruitment and evaluation of potential hires. Just as a management team may be revamped, corporate development may also be employed to change the current focus for clients. This may mean looking into the potential for breaking into new markets with existing products or developing complimentary products that will allow this type of expansion.

Depending on the status of the base market, corporate development may also look at shifting away from a shrinking consumer market while seeking market share in a different consumer market with newer products. For example, many typewriter manufacturers during the 1980's and 1990's slowly phased out their core business and began to focus more on computer parts and accessories as a way to continue operations. The process of corporate development can also be applied to the task of growing the company through mergers and acquisitions. In this scenario, the project development will involve identifying potential target companies for acquisitions or unions resulting in a new and more aggressive corporation. The team will consider all possible outcomes from any given potential merger or acquisition and attempt to project if the action is likely to result in positive growth or could possibly impair the company permanently.

There is no one tried and true formula for the process of corporate development. The actual structure of the corporate strategy will depend greatly on the current circumstances of the company and the area where the development is desired. In most cases, the process will not be of short duration; corporate development is usually a process that takes place over an extended period of time and may be adjusted or refined as the project moves forward. It may be fashionably financial, and often perfectly legal, to ask why at all corporations should be involved in development, if the business of business is business. There are at least two reasons 'why,' argues Michael Hopkins in *Corporate Social Responsibility and International Development*. One, almost half the world's population lives on less than $2 a day. And two, businesses need to work with others to create the capacities and conditions which sound governance requires, to ensure the sort of functioning society in which business can be done.

The book concludes with forceful suggestions, both for implementation within and outside the company. In the first category are the following: developing a CSR (corporate social responsibility) strategy; paying a 'living wage' and also paying suppliers properly, on time; maintaining safety and environmental standards; and monitoring the company's anticorruption policy. Development actions outside the company include collaboration with the government in antipoverty initiatives; lending in-house training skills to a wider public; advising SMEs; and mentoring entrepreneurs. Recommended read for those in corporate governance.

INSTITUTION-BUILDER

He could have been a greater economist, with contributions

to match those of Sir Richard Stone, who was awarded the Nobel Prize in economic sciences for his empirical work on national income estimation. But he chose the path of an institution builder. It was through these institutions that he wanted the social science profession to contribute to the country. Thus reminisces Vinod Vyasulu in one of the essays included in *A Passionate Humanitarian: VKRV Rao*. Unfortunately, his time in politics was that of Indira Gandhi, who was fond of him as a person, but who had no use for his values and skills in her politics, continues Vyasulu. He did not become Finance Minister or even Deputy Chairman of the Planning Commission. The Professor, an institution builder par excellence, accepted that with grace and retired to Bangalore. And ISEC came to be. Indira Gandhi visited the campus, had breakfast with the Professor and dedicated it to the nation. Poignant accounts.

To construct a 'storm free institution' that would restore the faith of the common people in banking, and stem the panic in Bengal, was formed the UBI in December 1950, by amalgamating four banks. "During the Second World War, when the money market got artificially inflated and business seemed unlimited, crisis was already being anticipated," recount Indrajit Mallick and Sugata Marjit in *Financial Intermediation in a Less Developed Economy: The History of the United Bank of India*. "Amongst the 15 scheduled banks in Bengal, four went into liquidation, two had to go for reconstruction, the fate of two others was undecided and one was forbidden from accepting any more deposits; 11 non-scheduled banks too failed."

The small middle-class depositors lost faith in local banking as a system and flocked to only the large banks, the authors add. "This hurt not only the medium banking establishments, but Bengal's economy and industry in general. It was this which forced banks with proud individual histories to merge with each other and become a single large banking establishment." Corporate Social Responsibility is the voluntary role and contribution on the part of the business community towards a better social and environmental development, which is beyond their investment to organizational development. The business organisations can be lead by large multinationals and for small, locally based businesses.

While the actions on the part of business organisations are ethically bound to its stakeholders, who include customers, owners/investors, government, suppliers and competitors. Corporate Social Responsibility consists of a wide-range activities and programs that involve businesses looking at how to improve their social, environmental and local economic impact, their influence on society, social cohesion and human rights, and fair trade. Key areas of concern are environmental protection and the well being of employees, the community and civil society in general, both now and in the future. It refers to the comprehensive approach that a corporation takes to meet or exceed stakeholder expectations beyond measures of revenue, profit and legal obligation.

NGOs AND CORPORATE SOCIAL RESPONSIBILITY

How far the Non Governmental Organisations in the nation can join hands with the corporate in their effort to social and environmental development is the prime concern of this chapter. The corporate social responsibility blends the objective of social development and environmental protection thorough ethical effort. Many non-governmental organizations in India are engaged in social development and environmental development activities. These organisations are good enough to support the industrial development by ensuring community participation the developmental process. The concept of corporate social responsibility is underpinned by the idea that corporations can no longer act as isolated economic entities operating in detachment from broader society. Corporate Social Responsibility to be looked upon as mutual support programs that ensure development of community near by the industrial area with the expansion and development of the industrial organisations.

The community today needs external agency intervention in the alleviation of many social problems like poverty, health, unemployment, community education, homelessness and eco development programs. By looking upon the needs of the community, the organisation gets an opportunity to understand the social needs of the people and it will enable them to intervene into such social issues and finding solution to the many basic needs. It develops greater trust and confidence on the community on the business organisation effort in their real development. Integrated community investment strategies align internal community-related issues and link business goals with community needs. Here the role of Non Governmental Organisations can be better realized. The Non Governmental Organisations existing within the industrial location and closer to the community can better act as moderators and facilitators in the realization of their social need and better environmental protection.

The industrial expansion is a threat to the people living near by and it invites protest from many like consumer, investors, activist groups, government regulators and other stakeholders. To develop a better rapport with the community in the implementation of the developmental activities the Non Governmental organisations can play better role with the industry and community. They can help the industrial management in convincing the expansion program to the community and there by develop a proactive and social environmental and industrial development policy. Lower operating costs, Enhanced brand image and reputation, reduced regulatory oversight, Product safety and decreased liability, improved financial performance etc. are the benefit to the organisation.

The benefit of Corporate Social Responsibility is not only for the community and organisation but also for the employees. The Research demonstrates Corporate Social Responsibility initiatives have a positive impact on employee morale, motivation, commitment, loyalty, training, recruitment and turnover. Benefits in these areas have been found to improve the bottom line of companies. Three surveys across Europe, the USA and a survey involving 25 countries found employees felt greater loyalty, satisfaction and motivation when their companies were socially responsible. The impact of these HR initiatives gives better brand image to the organisation in the labour market and it in turn help the HR department to get potential employees who believe in similar values system.

The ultimate goal of such effort is the development of an 'organisational culture which establishes harmonious relationship with the Community-Employee and Organisation at large. This establishes that fact that many Corporate Social Responsibility initiatives reflect the essence of Human Resource Management activities.

ROLE OF HUMAN RESOURCE MANAGERS

If Non Governmental Organisations can play better role in the corporate social responsibility, the question here is who can play better role in linking industry with community. The answer here is Human Resource Management Department of the industry. The HR managers should take lead in its effort to make a linkage between community and the industry. To develop better rapport with the people, HR managers have to make use of their Strategic Relationship Management Skills. They should interact with the community by establishing better linkage with the Non Governmental Organisations Working there in the locality. The HR managers can initially conduct Focus Group Discussion (FGD) with the community and community leaders with the help of Non Governmental Organisations and need evaluation and need prioritization is to be conducted. Here HR managers can act as facilitators in the Corporate Social Responsibility initiatives.

The community may have unlimited social needs. It is the responsibility of the HR managers to intervene into those needs and give a realistic perception to the community members related to their unlimited and unrealistic needs. The needs of the community are to be segregated into important and important needs, to unimportant and unimportant needs. Both short-term goals and long-term goals are to be segregated. The discussion to be entertained and the need categorization and finalization should come from the community itself. The HR managers who act as the implied leaders should lead the community towards realistic goal perception that integrates the goals and objectives of Corporate Social Responsibility programme initiated by the organisation.

This indicates that as leaders of the Corporate Social Responsibility programme HR managers should integrate the needs of the community and that of the organisation. The list of social development needs and the environmental protection needs to be discussed soon after the Focus Group Discussions, with the top management in order to ascertain whether all those needs can be met with the budget allotment for the developmental programs. A multi level discussion, with members of the NGO's, HR managers and representative of the Top Management, is to be initiated for the finalization of the social intervention programme. Corporate Social Responsibility offers the HR community opportunities to demonstrate its strategic focus. The relationship with the community and Non Governmental Organisations indicates the level of HR manager's success role in the Corporate Social Responsibility effort.

Corporate social responsibility is most frequently used to describe a company's relations with its wider community. CSR is on the boundary of HR and PR. There are dangers for companies and for the HR function if it is allowed to slide too far towards PR. More than excessive use of relationship management techniques they should make use of strategic relationship management approaches. This strategic relationship management approaches includes the relationship development, maintenance and separation factors. After the goal attainment the HR managers should be able to separate themselves from the community and Non Governmental Organisations and lead them to new interventions and action programmes where the organisations development and Social Development can be better integrated. If HR managers are not orienting and experimenting them with innovative areas the Human Resource Management don't have better role in the industrial sector. HR has a role in demonstrating the benefits of workplace practices that both reflect CSR and at the same time, contribute to organizational efficiency and success.

2

Historical and Contemporary Context of Corporate Social Development

The interest in Corporate Social Responsibility (CSR), which recognizes that companies have obligations that extend beyond short-run profit maximization to include notions of social and environmental concern, has increased considerably in recent decades. The Globalisation of the world economy and the related trade liberalization has brought forward a discussion of the importance of business as an actor in the development of society. The aim of this is to analyze the effectiveness of the CSR strategies of international companies in terms of their impact on development in the host country. This will be performed as a case study of CSR in India. India constitutes a location with significant potential for international companies to contribute to development through CSR since it is an open nation with substantial international presence but still faces challenges regarding poverty alleviation and inequalities.

Very little academic literature examines the development effects of CSR. In order to undertake this analysis, an analytical tool will be established that will present key characteristics of efficient CSR in terms of its impact on development. These key characteristics will be derived from the theory of new institutional economics, and will primarily argue that in order for CSR strategies to achieve the greatest efficiency, they must adhere to the institutional framework of the host context. The case study of the thesis will outline the nature of the international companies' CSR strategies in India and evaluate them according to this analytical framework. The findings of the thesis indicate that the development effects of the contemporary CSR strategies in India are modest. However, CSR is a relatively recent amendment to the corporate agenda and it has potential to increase in efficiency and importance in the future.

Neighbourhood organizing has a history as old as the neighbourhood concept itself. It is certainly not simply a product of sixties dissent. New Social Movement theory argues that community-based resistances – around geographic communities such as a neighbourhood or communities of cultural identity such as the black or women's community – have become the dominant form of social action since the 1960s, replacing more class and labor based organizing. Unlike other commentators who propose that neighbourhood organizing is disappearing, little more than a vestige of earlier urban spatial relations in an industrial society, new social movement theorists argue that community-based resistances, such as neighbourhood organizing, become in a post-industrial order the primary means of social change. While this theory has much to contribute to our understanding of the contemporary salience of community-based organizing and the importance of this collection of essays, it tends to overlook the rich and significant history prior to the 1960s that undergirds current efforts.

To illustrate the point, this essay begins with a discussion of the varied types of neighbourhood organizing that have persisted since the late nineteenth century and the lessons to be learned from them. It follows with a discussion of neighbourhood organizing in the 1980s, arguing that the political economy of the larger historical context is fundamental to understanding the nature and potential of neighbourhood organizing in any historical period.

TYPES OF NEIGHBOURHOOD ORGANIZING

Since the 1880s, there have been three main types of neighbourhood organizing. The social work approach is best characterized by the social settlement movement, which began in the United States in 1886, and by contemporary social service delivery at the neighbourhood level, such as neighbourhood centers or health clinics. The political activist approach is best reflected in the work of oppositional efforts which see power as the fundamental issue. These date back to the ward-based political machines of the nineteenth century, but as social efforts are best reflected in the efforts of the Communist Party in the 1930s, the efforts of Saul Alinsky and followers since the late 1930s, New Left neighbourhood organizing in the 1960s, and a host of current neighbourhood based grouping since then, perhaps most notably in African-American and gay male communities.

The neighbourhood maintenance approach also originated in the late 19th century, when more middle class residents sought to defend their neighbourhood against change and perceived threats. The ongoing history since the 1920s of neighbourhood protective associations, whose primary concern is maintaining or improving property values, is the classic example.

LESSONS FROM THE PAST

Simply stated, there have been a number of key lessons from the past of neighbourhood organizing that should inform the study of contemporary efforts.

Neighbourhood organizing has a long and important history. As neighbourhood organizing is not simply a product of the past generation, not a transitory phenomenon. It is a means of democratic participation, a means of extra-political activity, a way to build community, obtain resources, and achieve collective goals.

Neighbourhood organization has been an integral, ongoing, and significant basis of civil life in the United States for more than a century. Whereas people continually choose in astounding numbers not to participate in the electoral process, underscoring both the inability of politicians to galvanize the electorate and the alienation of citizens from the political process, this is not true for participation in neighbourhood organizations. Americans have always turned most easily to organizations at the grassroots level to build community, meet individual and collective needs, and participate in public life. This is as true today as it was one hundred years ago.

Neighbourhood organizing cuts across the political spectrum. While all neighbourhood organizing is a public activity, bringing people together to discuss and determine their collective welfare, it is not inherently reactionary, conservative, liberal, or radical.

Nor is it inherently inclusive and democratic, or parochial and authoritarian. It is above all a political method, an approach used by varied segments of the population to achieve specific goals, serve certain interests, and advance clear or ill- defined political perspectives. Organizations can be creative efforts open to innovation and supportive of progressive struggles as well as defensive responses to external pressures. The form an organization takes depends on a number of factors, especially the ideology and goals of its leadership, constituency organized, and local context.

Neighbourhood organizing efforts develop in a larger context that transcends local borders and determines the dominant form of neighbourhood organizing in any era. Conditions at the local level directly spawn and nurture neighbourhood organizing projects. The organizers, residents, local conditions, and many other factors at the grassroots level combine to forge consistently unique neighbourhood organizing experiences.

But while neighbourhood organizing projects do have a significant origin, nature, and existence of their own at the local level, they are also the products of national and even international political and economic developments. To no small degree, the larger political-economic context determines the general tenor, goals and strategies, even the likelihood of success, of local efforts.

It was the liberal reform political economy of the Progressive Era, the period frôm approximately 1900 through 1917, that responded positively to the social settlement idea and that legitimated the first era of neighbourhood organizing. While other types of neighbourhood organizing existed in this period, it was the social work approach, best exemplified in the social settlements and the Cincinnati Social Unit Plan, which dominated the era. In the depression era of the 1930s the social work approach had much less salience and support. As capitalism collapsed, as one reform solution after another failed to halt the economic depression, the political activist type of neighbourhood organizing, most notably the radical efforts of the Communist Party in many cities and the urban populist work of Saul Alinsky in the Back of the Yards neighbourhood in Chicago, personified grassroots activity.

The hotly debated and precarious political economy of the era legitimated citizen action and political ferment at the grassroots level. In the post World War II era the conservative cold war economy stifled the political activist approach of the depression era and nurtured the neighbourhood maintenance type of neighbourhood organizing. Of course, homeowners' and property associations had been strong in the United States since the 1920s.

The business of protecting property values was important especially in the United States, where homes were economic investments and where the lack of government protection and support for maintaining communities put the onus of neighbourhood maintenance and development on property owners.

The conservative eras of the 1920s and 1950s, however, tied this necessity for neighbourhood associations to a reactionary politics. Segregationist goals became quite typical of neighbourhood associations, interconnecting the protection of property values with a politics of neighbourhood exclusion. Of course the relationship between the national political economy and neighbourhood organizing is not a one way street where the dominant form of neighbourhood organizing is determined by the national political economy of an era. The historical process is much more complex, more of a dialectical interaction between the national political economy and grassroots resistances and initiatives.

In the 1960s and the first part of the 1970s, when the political activist type of neighbourhood organizing came to dominate again, the national political economy both produced the change and was the product of it. It was the grassroots resistance of the southern civil rights movement, the student New Left, and the rebellion in black urban slums that pushed the national political economy left, that expanded the political discourse to legitimate grassroots resistance, that demanded the passage of social policy to address the needs of the poor and people of color. The shift in political economy at the national level, expanded with LBJ's Great Society and War on Poverty programs, developed in response to these challenges. These legitimated further the political activist approach, so much so that a heyday of political activist neighbourhood organizing continued well into and through the 1970s, causing some commentators to herald a "backyard revolution" in the making. It is this interpenetration between the national political economy and community organizing that comes across so vividly in the history of neighbourhood efforts.

NEIGHBOURHOOD ORGANISING IN THE 1980s

The importance of the national, even global, political economy in shaping the nature of neighbourhood organizing is especially evident in the 1980s, in the increasing importance of CDCs and the widespread adoption by most neighbourhood organizations of more moderate strategies. In the 1980s, as we know all too well, the United States made a clear turn to rightwing politics at the national level.

The twelve years of Reagan/Bush policy from 1981-1993 promoted a neoconservative agenda grounded in rightwing programs, policies, and political discourse. Responding to the heightened demands of an emerging global economy and the challenged status of U.S. corporations in it, neoconservatives sought to cut social costs.

They went after labor unions, government programs, and claimant movements; they shifted even the limited political dialog about human needs completely to corporate needs; they delegitimized the public sector and public life and pushed people into increasingly private spheres and private conceptions of the good life. In the neoconservative 1980s, the impact of national context on local organizing was enormous. While a wide variety of efforts continued, promoting democratic resistance and left insurgency, it was the neoconservative political economy that largely determined the direction of most community organizing during the decade, pushing them into community economic development and moderate strategies.

COMMUNITY ECONOMIC DEVELOPMENT

In general during the 1980s concern with broader social issues and social action receded. In the economic crisis of the past few decades, economic survival became the paramount issue for most individuals, organizations, businesses, and cities. As economic support for social services and solving social problems declined due to opposition at the federal level and shrinking tax bases at the local, and as political discourse in the nation revolved around free market solutions to all problems, neighbourhood organizing efforts moved into the business of economic development.

This trend is nowhere more evident than in the rapid growth and spread of community development corporations (CDCs) in the 1980s. CDCs first sprang up in the 1960s, when they were tied to the civil rights and anti-poverty movements of the period, and were funded by a few foundations and Great Society programs. In this first wave were only about a 100 organizations, but among them were such well-funded, significant efforts such as The Woodlawn Organization and the Bedford-Stuyvesant Restoration Corporation. For its multitude of important projects the Bed-Stuy CDC received about $4 million in federal support annually. The second wave of community development organizations came in the 1970s, when the number of development projects increased tenfold. These were smaller efforts that began in opposition to urban renewal, redlining, factory closings, or the lack of tenant rights.

For those involved in community economic development, most funds came from foundations, primarily The Ford Foundation, and federal sources, such as the Community Services Administration and the Office of Neighborhood Development. The idea of community economic development caught on in the Carter Administration, and by the late 1970s, CDCs, with all their virtues and drawbacks, were central components of the limited but significant, federally- assisted neighbourhood development movement. Beginning around 1980, however, CDCs found government support drastically cut. The new, third wave of CDCs that developed in the privatization campaigns of the Reagan years were forced into becoming much more businesslike than their predecessors. They had to exhibit "business talent and development skills once thought to be the exclusive province of the for-profit sector," as one report put it.

The Community Services Administration and the Office of Neighbourhood Development were dismantled. Other sources of federal funds were dramatically cut back. The bottom line for CDCs, as with seeming everything else in the decade, was economic success. The primary goal, as Benjamin Marquez argues in an astute analysis of CDCs role, was to "correct the market's failure to provide jobs and services to the community." Added to this, for the CDCs in minority neighbourhoods, was to help build a non-white middle class by developing highly specific and measurable development projects in which neighbourhood people could work for their own economic betterment.

The new CDCs became less like community organization and more like small businesses and investment projects, evaluated on their economic success. Most avoided political controversy, were dominated by professionals with a technical orientation, had narrow memberships bases, and rejected social action activity.

While market demands forced most CDCs to become so oriented to economic success that they were not able to sustain their work for community empowerment, they did not always give up on these goals by choice. They were forced into it.

The absence of public support, newly rigid interpretations of IRS restrictions on political activity of nonprofit groups, the necessity of seeking funds from and joining in partnerships with private sector leaders, and the orientation of the CDC approach to economic investment and development decisions, all pushed CDCs away from politics and an analysis of power. "This lack of fiscal and political support," Marquez concludes, "has forced CDCs to accommodate themselves to rather than redirect the course of the free market."

Economic development has become a central issue for progressive organizing efforts that formerly spurned or discounted the strategy. Many older, prominent community organizing efforts now do community economic development, from ACORN to NPA (National People's Action) and IAF (Industrial Areas Foundation). To their credit, these political activist projects see community economic development as part of a much larger program of community work that also includes organizing, empowerment, advocacy, and social action. Still, community economic development has become virtually synonymous with neighbourhood organizing, as if organizing and empowerment were rooted in economic development issues, as if neighbourhood struggles were always the same as community economic development, as if working in partnership with local banks and putting in "sweat equity" were the answers to urban poverty and housing shortages.

It has not quite worked out that way. "If the primary success story of the last 25 years has been the development of a legitimate, skilled nonprofit development sector with the proven capacity to create and preserve housing, jobs and businesses," Bill Traynor of the Community Training and Assistance Center in Boston sums up the problem, "the major failure has been the proliferation and dominance of a narrowly focused – technical – production related model of community development which is estranged from strong neighbourhood control or direction and which does not impact the range of issues which affect poor neighborhoods."

MODERATE STRATEGIES

Most activists promoting community economic development would probably defend their consensual approach as appropriate for the Reagan-Bush years. To have a chance at community development, efforts must be in tune with capitalist economic development and have a working relationship with the powers that be in the public and private sector. Given the shift in the national political economy, organizers think they must now be more community economic development minded. Neo-Alinsky organizer Shel Trapp sees a natural progression in his work. First, organizations defend the neighbourhood; then they take an "offensive" stance. "That's when you start to link development with organizing," he argues. Robert Rivera, an IAF organizer, puts it similarly: "There are two types of organizing. One that is for, the other is against. Now you have to be for something. It's a different style of organizing."

But at play in the 1980s was more than a "life cycle" of organizing. Community economic development and building community partnerships with local economic and political elites became the dominant form of neighbourhood organizing because of the demands and constraints of organizing in a neoconservative political economy. Organizers were willing to rewrite history (good organizing has always been for things) in an effort to distance themselves from the radicalism of the past, maintain current support, and legitimate their efforts in a context hostile to social action. The changes that took place in community development corporations are emblematic of the way organizing responded to the conservative context of the '80s, but moderate strategies during that period were by no means limited to CDCs.

Most neopopulist, political activist neighbourhood organizing efforts during the 1980s and early 1990s adopted more moderate strategies, and a more moderated version of oppositional politics. Battle lines shifted. "To a surprising extent, claim M. W. Newman and Lillian Williams in a recent Chicago Sun Times article, "the grass roots no longer 'fight the power.' They fight for a share of the power. Sometimes they win a sizable share.... [Sometimes they] team up with the established elite that they once derided and that once spurned them." Even National People's Action (NPA), criticized by some organizers as too confrontational, opposed being "out in the streets making symbolic statements, when you can be in the boardroom negotiating specific agreements that win for neighbourhoods."

Consider the evolution of the Industrial Areas Foundation, the direct descendant of Alinsky organizing, over the past decade. IAF currently has 28 organizing projects in New York, New Jersey, Maryland, Tennessee, Arizona, California, and Texas, but it is in Texas, where the IAF network includes 10 organizing efforts, that it is the strongest. Throughout the state, in San Antonio, Houston, El Paso, Austin, Fort Worth, and in the Rio Grande Valley, IAF organizers and active members struggle for utility reform, improved public education, government accountability, healthcare for the indigent and basic public services, including water and sewers for the "colonias".

Most visibly they organize "get out the vote" efforts to promote bond packages to help IAF neighbourhoods, hold "accountability sessions" to keep politicians publicly in line with IAF objectives, encourage voter registration, and work to improve schools by halting the drop out rate, stopping drug use and violence, and getting parents more involved. More quietly, in the day in and day out practice of community organizing they serve as "schools of public life," empowering neighbourhood residents by giving them "an opportunity to do something about things that [they] have been frustrated all their lives."

IAF organizations do all this remarkably well, as many commentators have noted. Peter Applebome in the New York

Times proposed that the IAF Network is "in ways large and small... changing politics in Texas." And Mary Beth Rogers, ex-Chief of Staff to Texas Governor Ann Richards, concludes in her study of Texas IAF that these "are virtually the only organizations in America that are enticing working poor people to participate in politics." While still following much of the Alinsky style of organizing, in the 1980s IAF made some significant changes in their organizing method to meet the needs of new constituents and adapt to the demands of a new conservative context. The major change in IAF organizing is a shift from a radical politics to a strategy of moderation. Where CDCs look for consensus, IAF groups focus on the importance of "standing for the whole."

Of course, many in power still see IAF as a radical protest group, and even during Alinsky's lifetime some IAF projects, such as The Woodlawn Organization, shifted from "conflict to coexistence." In the 1980s, however, this developed into an organizing credo.

Now, IAF seeks to organize "community sustainers" and "core moderates," especially women in mainline religious congregations and civic organizations. They want the civic volunteers who already work tirelessly for the PTA or church group – the folks, IAF says, who already protect the community and stand for the whole. The strategy of moderation pushes IAF organizers to distance themselves from radicals and social movements. Whereas Alinsky took pride in being a radical, in the current IAF radicals are seen as alienated outsiders. "IAF now almost makes a fetish of its commitment to moderates," notes organizer trainer Mike Miller in a recent article in Christianity and Crisis. "Will the next book be Reveille for Moderates?"

Standing for the whole seeks to legitimize grassroots organizing in the eyes of both the powerless and the powerful, both of whom IAF assumes, as do CDC proponents, to be fundamentally moderate in outlook. It seeks to create a working relationship between those with and without power in order to promote the interests of its members. In the 1980s confronting government officials became – according to IAF – less and less productive. Even when local government officials were sympathetic with the issues, they felt they did not have the resources to address them.

So "standing for the whole" now includes developing working relationships with business and government leaders in order to further the goals of both IAF constituents and the larger community. The strategy of moderation, the commitment to moderates, the grounding of IAF efforts in mainstream religious institutions, and a definition of power which emphasizes building relationships leads, however, to a politics which limits the parameters of IAF's work, and excludes alliances with other movement activists and organizations, as Mike Miller and others persuasively argue.

It encourages IAF to work alone with its constituency and mainstream allies, and to avoid confronting the harsh realities of power that oppress their constituents. The moderate strategy, for all its short-term gains, is fraught with traps. Most important, the emphasis on moderation and negotiation and a more interest group style of politics changes the role of the organizer. Standing for the whole moves IAF away from the Alinsky idea of the organizer being in the background working his or her way out of a job focusing primarily on developing community residents to lead the organization.

The more IAF gets involved in negotiating with government officials and corporate executives, the more the organizers have come to the center stage to be the brokers and spokespersons for the organization. And the more the organizer becomes the broker, the more potential, as in all interest group organizing, to be both co-opted and, worse, ignored. Moderate strategy ultimately bargains away the tactic of radical protest. The American Medical Association and other powerful interest groups can afford to be moderate; poor and working people must always fight for power.

NEIGHBOURHOOD ORGANIZING IN THE '90s

The responses of grassroots efforts to shifts in the national political economy always produce strategies that both replicate and challenge existing power relations. For all its obvious limitations, a focus on community economic development has built a broad base of real technical expertise and created innovative projects which in a limited way help meet the dire need for housing and in poor neighbourhoods. The politics of moderation gives up on more radical change but it helps build the capacity for governance, gets advocates to the bargaining table, and wins modest victories. Given the dramatic tensions and shifts occurring worldwide, both in the global economy and in national political struggles, we can expect in the near future to see the political economy encourage more of the same: continued proliferation and preference for grassroots efforts, continued focus on community economic development as global competition remains heated and as nation- states and corporate-elites persist in avoiding domestic social needs, and continued diverse strategies with most funding and support going to moderate approaches which are willing to work with business and government leaders.

Current events will likely continue to overwhelm such neighbourhood efforts. It is much more difficult to be optimistic now about the prospects of neighbourhood organizing than it was just 15 years ago. It is no paradox neoconservatives call for neighbourhood-based solutions and "empowerment" of citizens; they know well that these are less expensive strategies for problems that require costly national and global solutions and neighbourhood- based initiatives. Without the existence of a social movement able to push the national political discourse left, win funding for social programs and redistributional policies, and struggle for state power, we can expect, at best, incremental change from the top and important but modest victories at the grassroots. Whatever the context ahead, neighbourhood organizing, even with its limits, will remain essential: as schools of democracy and progressive citizenship, as seeds of larger resistance efforts, as demonstrations of the persistence of public life in an increasingly private world, as the vehicles of struggle in which we win victories, develop skills, forge identity, and legitimate opposition, and as potential grassroots components of the next major social justice movement.

To play such roles, however, neighbourhood organizing must both build on and go beyond the contemporary context. It must benefit from the new skills and strategies learned in the 1980s and challenge the neoconservative political economy which heavily shaped organizing in the past decade. While the history of neighbourhood organizing makes clear that national context is fundamental, it also instructs that conflict – ideological and direct action challenges – is essential to push the context, policies, and programs towards meeting basic human needs and implementing more democratic processes.

THE CONTRIBUTION OF SOCIAL POLICY TO DEVELOPMENT

In the era of globalisation, neoliberal reform and the post-Washington Consensus. What does this jargon mean for social policy and social service provisioning? For many developing countries it means that governments are being urged by northern governments, international financial institutions and capital markets to:

- Target the poor and provide safety nets;
- Reduce or keep a tight rein on government expenditures;
- Restructure the tax system, favouring regressive over progressive taxation and reducing corporate and trade-related taxes; and
- Flexibilise labour markets and sideline certain aspects of labour market policy.

It also means a reconfiguration of the relative roles and responsibilities of international organisations, central and local governments, non-governmental organisations (NGOs), trade unions and the private sector, through the privatisation of public services, corporate social responsibility, decentralisation and the channelling of development assistance through NGOs (UNRISD 2000). Such developments also involve the strengthening of technocracy and bypassing some democratic institutions in decision-making processes. In addition, they alter the roles and responsibilities of women and families in both the social and economic domains.

These policy prescriptions and trends have profound implications for social policy and provisioning, some of which are quite worrying. The starting point for UNRISD's work was the recognition that social policy is a key dimension of government policy not only for social protection, but also for equity and economic development. (UNRISD 2006).

- It must protect people from the perverse, unstable and inequitable effects of markets, and the changes in circumstances that occur with ageing, unemployment, maternity and disability.
- It must enhance the productive potential of members of society, through health and education services that enhance human capital. It can also contribute to growth by increasing consumption or demand related to low-income groups.
- It must assist families, households and women with reconciling the burden of social reproduction and care, with that of other roles and tasks, and it must be concerned with how the burden of reproduction is shared both institutionally and from a gender perspective.
- It also has a crucial role to play in securing and realising social rights and in reinforcing national and social cohesion, particularly in post-conflict societies or multi-ethnic societies.

Social policy - in theory and historically under the different welfare regimes that characterised, for example, the late industrialisers of northern Europe, East Asia and some Latin American countries - has been concerned with social protection, redistribution, production and reproduction, as well as social rights, social cohesion, political stability and regime legitimacy.

However, different welfare regimes have placed different weights on each of these aspects. A policy focus that gives excessive weight to distributive aspects will likely prove economically unsustainable, as in the case of several "populist regimes"; while one that over-emphasises productivist aspects of social policy, as occurred to some extent in East Asia, would likely encounter political opposition. A purely "protectivist" approach would likely fail on both counts (UNRISD 2006).

This analysis suggests the following:

- if the goal of development is to build societies that are socially inclusive and economically and democratically robust, then social policy has a key role to play in relation to all three of these aspects;
- contemporary approaches to social policy that focus narrowly on poverty reduction, safety-nets and targeting are problematic;
- social policy serves multiple purposes associated with protection, redistribution, production, reproduction, social rights and cohesion;
- there are crucial connections, complementarities and synergies between these different functions; and neglecting one can affect others;
- social policy is not something that should be determined on the basis of top-down technocratic decision-making and standardised policy prescriptions; its content and sustainability will depend very much on institutional, political and historical factors.

CONTEMPORARY ISSUES IN SOCIAL POLICY REFORM

Two of the most prominent areas of social policy reform of the past two decades relate to targeting and the role of the private sector in social provisioning. Both these developments raise important questions about the effectiveness of contemporary policy approaches and the roles and responsibilities of public and private institutions and actors. Private enterprises, and more specifically transnational corporations, are far more active in the social policy arena. Historically, the social role of business was limited primarily to philanthropy, and complying with labour market policies. In some countries, notably in East Asia, there emerged what is called the corporate social welfare model where large national corporations assumed important responsibilities for social welfare as part of a social pact in which they received incentives from the state, as well as labour peace for relatively long periods of time.

Today, we see two new developments associated with what can be called the privatisation of social policy. First, large enterprises are engaging directly in providing essential public services. Second, companies are engaging in public-private partnerships and corporate social responsibility by adopting a variety of voluntary initiatives to improve working conditions and support local communities and social development programmes, such as HIV/AIDS. More recently, large national and transnational corporations are being urged to play a more proactive role in poverty reduction and the Millennium Development Goals (MDGs). What should we make of these developments?

COMMERCIALISATION AND PRIVATISATION

As regards the commercialisation and privatisation of social services, UNRISD work on heath care provisioning and urban water services suggests the following:

- Privatisation programmes that proliferated in the 1990s were heavily influenced by ideological considerations that prioritised goals associated with efficiency and neglected aspects associated with equity.
- Privatisation has often had perverse effects in terms of equity. Research that UNRISD is currently conducting in seven countries to determine how access to water and affordability have been affected, shows a very mixed record in terms of urban access to clean water, and a generally worsening situation in terms of affordability for low-income groups.
- Early on in the privatisation process, giving priority to efficiency concerns often meant that regulatory dimensions were marginalised. Sometimes this was

apparent in regulatory design, but it was more evident in terms of not having in place the institutional capacity to implement regulations that may have existed on paper.

- And, what is clear from the radical response to privatisation in many countries, policy makers fundamentally ignored the political economy of privatisation and how local responses and social contestation would ultimately undermine the sustainability of this policy approach.

CORPORATE SOCIAL RESPONSIBILITY

As regards corporate social responsibility (CSR), it is apparent that the discourse and rhetoric of CSR is running well ahead of the reality, in terms of significant transformations in social practice. Nevertheless an increasing number of corporations are adopting a variety of initiatives in the social arena, and the CSR ethos and agenda is being institutionalised through the formation of new entities such as the UN Global Compact and NGO or multi-stakeholder standard-setting, monitoring and certification organisations. Apart from the limited evidence of significant improvements in social performance of companies, there are other major concerns with the CSR agenda.

First, while an increasing number of large corporations are taking initiatives in relation to one or a few specific aspects in the social domain, simultaneously they tend to engage in practices that have perverse effects, through for example, relying more and more on subcontracting, which often implies a deterioration in labour standards, or engaging in forms of transfer pricing, tax avoidance and lobbying that ultimately reduce corporate tax contributions, which of course are important for funding social and other government expenditures. The mainstream CSR agenda often ignores such contradictory practices.

Second, CSR involved the privatisation of regulatory authority related to social or labour market policy. Increasingly organised business interests and NGOs are taking up functions that were previously associated with the state. In some cases, such developments may mean that the institutional capacity to regulate markets and minimise perverse effects is being enhanced, along the lines suggested by the proponents of "embedded liberalism". But in other cases, it means a further weakening of the roles and responsibilities of both the state and trade unions, which is problematic from the perspective of governance and equitable development.

TARGETING AND POVERTY REDUCTION

Since the late 1980s, social policy in many developing countries has been particularly concerned with "targeted" protection, i.e., channelling aid and social spending first and foremost to "the poor" or particular "vulnerable" groups. This approach characterised the social funds that emerged as a palliative for structural adjustment programmes, and has evolved through broader-based programmes and schemes associated with conditional cash transfers or primary education for girls. Such an approach can be praised for having refocused attention on "the social", and indeed, in various countries social spending has increased. It has also been useful from the point of view of mobilising political will to address poverty issues. And it has placed time-bound targets on the rhetorical goals that were set at various World Summits in the 1990s. But this approach also needs to be handled with caution for the following reasons.

First, targeting has often been pursued not so much as a way of reaching or reinforcing universalism but as part of broader policy approach associated with the unravelling of universalism. Second, too narrow a perspective on targeting, such as that which has characterised many social funds related to structural adjustment programmes, seems to run counter to what we know about successful approaches to poverty reduction.

Few countries or regions that have advanced in terms of poverty reduction, whether in East Asia, states like Kerala, Africa in the 1960s and 70s, or in some Latin American countries like Costa Rica and Chile, have had explicit poverty reduction policies. Successful regimes generally adopted a more balanced approach, i.e. one that was also concerned with growth and redistribution, and they also placed greater emphasis on universalist policies, or at least what is called stratified universalism, where social policy favoured large social groups, such as formal sector workers.

Third, targeting is administratively quite complex. It is not easy to identify or reach the poor, particularly when they constitute the majority of the population, are part of the so-called informal sector and often undocumented, and are highly mobile. Moreover, the administrative capacity of the state to target is often limited in contexts where the civil service has been weakened through budget cuts, lay-offs and corruption.

Fourth, targeting can undermine the functioning of complex systems, which are crucial in the case, for example, of health and education. Research on gender dimensions of social policy carried out in India found that targeting primary education for girls did boost enrolment rates but also involved a trade-off with secondary and tertiary education. This is extremely problematic as it is these parts of the system that produce teachers, provide parents with the incentive to send children to school in the first place, and provide girls with the skills needed to access employment, obtain contraception, and negotiate intra-household relations.

Fifth, targeting is risky and may backfire from a political economy perspective, in that by making the middle classes pay for privatised social services, they have one less reason to pay taxes to finance social and other policies. Finally, social policy needs to be motivated and sustained by a powerful coalition of social and political forces or social pacts involving state, political parties, business, labour and other social groups.

The politics of targeting and the Poverty Reduction Strategy Papers (PRSPs) look quite different, involving primarily donors, selected ministries and selected civil society organisations. This combination of donor, techno-ratic and NGO interests is very different to the types of political coalitions that underpinned social policy in the past.

More recently we see a shift to what may either be considered "smart targeting" or smart universalism, depending on one's perspective, in the form of large programmes involving conditional cash transfers to children and others.

While several such programmes have been regarded as success stories, they also need to be looked at carefully. Does the expenditure involved detract from other areas of social spending? Are they complementary to, rather than a substitute for other universal features of social policy? Do they lean towards universalism by urging, for example, parents to realize certain universal rights? And how sustainable are they both financially and politically?

SOCIAL POLICY AND DEMOCRATISATION

The relationship between social policy and democratisation is a crucial issue given the wave of political reform that has enveloped many countries in the past two decades, as well as our host country, Nepal, in recent weeks. According to textbook political theory, democratisation should improve the well-being of the poor as political leaders and representatives become more responsive or accountable to citizens. In countries where there is a strong association between democracy and social policy the following conditions generally exist:

- Highly competitive political systems,
- An informed electorate,
- Relatively high levels of interest group organisation, in particular, unionisation,
- Pro-welfare political parties that win elections, and
- Social pacts where organised or corporatist interests, including business, support or at least do not resist social reform.

Also welfare development is generally related to economic development although economic development is not a sufficient condition for effective social policy. The relationship today between social policy and democratisation is far more complex and uncertain than theory and history suggest. Even when the poor are in the majority, democratisation has not necessarily spurred income distribution or extensive social provisioning in favour of the poor. Research at UNRISD has examined why this has occurred. Key reasons include the following (Bangura and Hedberg forthcoming):

- Electoral competitiveness and the responsiveness of leaders to the needs and demands of the poor can be undermined through inadequate information, lack of credibility of leaders and programmes, and ethnic diversity.
- Parliamentary competitiveness can also be undermined. In democracies, parliaments are expected to aggregate voters' choices as well as scrutinise government policies. However, the ability of parliaments to perform these roles very much depends on the nature of the party systems and legislative distribution of power.
- Trends associated with technocratic governance, promoted by the IFIs, also weaken the role of traditional policy makers and shield certain policy institutions from democratic oversight and bargaining processes.
- The ability of low-income voters to extract responsiveness from governments through interest group pressure has also changed, with the weakening of unions and peasant organisations, the rise of the unorganised informal sector, and NGOs.
- Corporatist arrangements and social pacts, where elite interests historically went along with universalist approaches to service provisioning, in return for social or labour peace or other incentives from government, have also broken down.

In fact, what we see today is that many new democracies, even those dominated by left of centre political parties have adopted fairly orthodox neoliberal policies as, for example, in South Africa or Brazil. In regions such as Latin America and Africa, some parties have tried to distance themselves from interventionist and populist policies of the past that were associated with macroeconomic failure. What is also apparent is that governments or parties in power do not necessarily implement a standardised set of social policies throughout their tenure. Rather, the content and quality of social policy often varies according to the political electoral cycle with social expenditures increasing during election years.

In the context of globalisation, parties are also subjected to the pressures and conditionalities of the international market, IFIs and bilateral agencies, and must signal markets and donors accordingly with orthodox policies. In addition, technocrats within Central Banks, and economics and finance ministries, are often ideologically and academically in tune with such policy approaches.

INSTITUTIONAL AND POLITICAL REFORMS

All these factors and trends can result in what Thandika Mkandawire has referred to as "choiceless democracies". Recently, though, we see several developments that may alter this scenario. In the past, left wing parties could rely to some extent on an alternative ideology and a rearguard of support from the socialist bloc. During the 1980s and 1990s such alternatives collapsed. Now in some Latin American and Middle Eastern countries we see the resurrection of populist alternatives to neoliberal orthodoxy which assign a high priority to social policy. In a few countries, this approach is fuelled not only by alternative globalisation ideologies but also large state-sector revenues from the extractive industries. Such scenarios and possibilities, however, are few and far between, although they sometimes have spill-over effects in other countries. However, in regions like Latin America, we also see a more general resurgence of social democratic parties and governments.

A more widespread development concerns the increasing attention to "good governance", and issues of transparency, participation, decentralisation, accountability and anticorruption. Such institutional reforms could potentially translate into positive gains as far as social policy is concerned. In practice, however, the way powerful actors and entrenched institutions interpret and apply such reforms often renders them far less effective than the rhetoric and analytical foundations of good governance might suggest. But perhaps the major problem with the good governance agenda is that it has tended to let neoliberal reform off the hook. Development failures are largely understood as failures of domestic institutions in developing countries, rather than macroeconomic conditionality or unjust North-South and power relations.

The third development relates to a more recent shift in thinking within some mainstream international develop-ment institutions, most notably the critique of neoliberal orthodoxy and conditionality. In 2005, the UN finally broke its silence as regards neoliberalism and policy conditionality through the publication of at least four reports that critique neoliberalism head on. These include the Human Development Report, UNRISD's report on Gender Equality, UNCTAD's report on Rethinking the Role of FDI, and UNDESA's Report "The Inequality Predicament". The World Bank also focused its attention on equity and acknowledged the important role of "some forms of redistribution" in the 2006 World Development Report.

What remains to be seen is how this intellectual shift is translated into policy change. Potentially, one of the positive policy implications relates to the emphasis being placed on concepts such as "policy coherence" and "policy space".

These concepts not only highlight the contradictions between social development and neoliberal macroeconomics, but also the fact that democratic institutions and processes in developing countries should enjoy a greater say in determining development priorities. Calls for greater policy coherence and policy space derive from both the heightened critique of neoliberal policies and conditionality, as well as the historical experience of some Asian and other countries that pursued a very different policy approach. Potentially policy space means:

- Policies that are more in tune with domestic needs, priorities and realities;
- That governments can rely on a broader range of policy instruments, including social policy;
- The possibility for governments to correct imbalances that have arisen in state-market relations and to re-embed

markets.

However, converting policy space into either greater policy coherence or a more universalist and transformative social policy will require not only top-down institutional reforms but also changes in power relations. Here the contemporary focus on participation is potentially important, but the type of selective and sanitised participation that often characterises, for example, poverty reduction strategy processes, is limited in its transformative potential. The increasing attention to granting the excluded and disempowered greater "voice" may help in the design of more inclusive social policies and programmes, but voices not only need to be heard - those with voices need to become "players".

This requires more than dialogue; it requires organization, mobilisation and strategic alliances. Developments associated with the consolidation of NGO networks, transnational activism, the revival of trade unions and cooperative organisations in some countries, the organisation of informal sector workers, and the emergence and strengthening of certain multi-stakeholder institutions, and of new social pacts involving sectors of business negatively affected by neoliberal restructuring are relevant in this regard. Another development relates to the regulatory role of the state and other institutions vis-à-vis corporations that have become increasingly engaged in social policy in the past decade. Companies that are involved in both the provisioning of social services, and in corporate social responsibility initiatives, are coming under closer scrutiny from both state and civil society actors. Increasing attention is focusing not only on CSR but also "corporate accountability", a concept that implies not only that companies must answer to different stakeholders, but also enforceability, i.e. that agreed standards, regulations and laws must be complied with and non-compliance must incur some form of penalty.

3

Corporate Social Responsibility as Business Strategy

CORPORATE SOCIAL RESPONSIBILITY

Hardly a day goes by without some mention in the media of corporate social responsibility and its growing significance on good business practices. CSR, as it is commonly known, is becoming increasingly important to us all, both as individuals and in our professional lives. Despite much public focus on large multinationals, it is the changing behaviour of the privately held business sector that is likely to make the greatest impact on global corporate social responsibility. Privately held businesses have always been the economic engine of the world, but in recent years their voice has been lost under the clamour of the large multinationals.

Privately held businesses may not be conducting the expensive campaigns that catch the public's attention, but they are making changes which affect their bottom line. Whether changes are made to be more attractive employers, a more appealing supplier to a large multinational or simply because of the ethical desire of the owner, all the evidence in this survey points to privately held businesses becoming more socially responsible. Whatever the reason, the survey results reflect an increasingly competitive and constantly changing business environment. As for the rest, it is surely only a matter of time before all privately held businesses have to adhere to greater pressure to do business in a more socially responsible and transparent manner. The businesses that are responsive, quick and innovative will be the ones who not only survive the change, but emerge as winners.

Corporate Social Responsibility (CSR), also known as corporate responsibility, corporate citizenship, responsible business and corporate social opportunity is a form of corporate self-regulation integrated into a business model. Ideally, CSR policy would function as a built-in, self-regulating mechanism whereby business would monitor and ensure their adherence to law, ethical standards, and international norms. Business would embrace responsibility for the impact of their activities on the environment, consumers, employees, communities, stakeholders and all other members of the public sphere. Furthermore, business would proactively promote the public interest by encouraging community growth and development, and voluntarily eliminating practices that harm the public sphere, regardless of legality. Essentially, CSR is the deliberate inclusion of public interest into corporate decision-making, and the honoring of a triple bottom line: People, Planet, and Profit.

The practice of CSR is subject to much debate and criticism. Proponents argue that there is a strong business case for CSR, in that corporations benefit in multiple ways by operating with a perspective broader and longer than their own immediate, short-term profits. Critics argue that CSR distracts from the fundamental economic role of businesses; others argue that it is nothing more than superficial window-dressing; others argue that it is an attempt to preempt the role of governments as a watchdog over powerful multinational corporations.

DEVELOPMENT

Business ethics is one of the forms of applied ethics that examines ethical principles and moral or ethical problems that can arise in a business environment. In the increasingly conscience-focused marketplaces of the 21st century, the demand for more ethical business processes and actions (known as ethicism) is increasing. Simultaneously, pressure is applied on industry to improve business ethics through new public initiatives and laws (e.g. higher UK road tax for higher-emission vehicles).

Business ethics can be both a normative and a descriptive discipline. As a corporate practice and a career specialization, the field is primarily normative. In academia, descriptive approaches are also taken. The range and quantity of business ethical issues reflects the degree to which business is perceived to be at odds with non-economic social values. Historically, interest in business ethics accelerated dramatically during the 1980s and 1990s, both within major corporations and within academia. For example, today most major corporate websites lay emphasis on commitment to promoting non-economic social values under a variety of headings (e.g. ethics codes, social responsibility charters). In some cases, corporations have re-branded their core values in the light of business ethical considerations (e.g. BP's "beyond petroleum" environmental tilt).

The term CSR came in to common use in the early 1970s although it was seldom abbreviated. The term stakeholder, meaning those impacted by an organization's activities, was used to describe corporate owners beyond shareholders from around 1989. Whilst there is no recognized standard for CSR, public sector organizations (the United Nations for example) adhere to the Triple Bottom Line (TBL). It is widely accepted that CSR adheres to similar principals but with no formal act of legislation.

In comparison to PHBs, large multinationals have a far more powerful stakeholder group to consider and have, in many cases, adopted an holistic approach to CSR. Many businesses have signed up to the United Nation's voluntary framework, The Global Compact, a cross-cultural ethical practice for businesses who are prepared to commit to principles in the following four main areas:

- Human rights
- Labour standards
- The environment
- Anti-corruption.

The United Nations Global Compact is not a regulatory instrument, but relies on public accountability and the self-interest of companies to further its aims without enforcing or measuring business actions.

GOVERNMENTS

While corporate responsibility principles are developed within companies and often fostered by non-governmental organisations, national governments have a major role to play. They can set reference frameworks, encourage action and promote dialogue but crucially can enforce action through legislation.

Governments can use taxation to encourage 'green' practices, set minimum wages and impose restrictions on working hours. In many countries targets are set on businesses to reduce greenhouse emissions. Yet many businesses stress that government incentives, rather than punitive taxes, would do more to encourage ethical behaviour, especially on 'green' issues. We all have a personal responsibility to each other and the world around us.

Everything we do has an effect on other people. It is the same for businesses, large and small, public or private, that their actions affect a large number of stakeholders. Such stakeholders include customers, shareholders, employees, suppliers and society in general. With growing scrutiny of business operations, organisations are increasingly being driven to satisfy the expectations of opinion formers, governments and customers in order to thrive. In essence, businesses adopting CSR principles believe that by operating ethically and responsibly, they have a greater chance of success.

For privately held businesses (PHBs), with fewer stakeholders to satisfy, their greatest concern appears to be their customers and their own ability to satisfy the demand for products effectively. Businesses are demonstrating that well managed corporate responsibility actually supports business objectives, especially amongst large corporates where improved compliance, reputation and relationships have been shown to increase shareholder value and profitability.

For privately held businesses, the pressure to act can stem from the demands of the supply chain; with large multinationals increasingly demanding that suppliers conform to ethical business practices. Incorporating corporate responsibility into a business's core strategy can also enhance its attractiveness as an employer. Nevertheless, many PHBs are adhering to the highest ethical standards - why? In order to answer this question we need to understand what is driving business ethics amongst PHBs and what initiatives they are implementing. Although PHBs perhaps face the greatest challenge, it is these businesses that could make the greatest impact on global corporate social responsibility.

WHAT ARE PRIVATELY HELD BUSINESSES DOING

PHBs are 'the economic engine of the world'. Although public attention is often focused on large multinationals and how ethical their business practices are, PHBs are expected to adhere to the same ethical practices. However, the two sets of businesses differ greatly in terms of size and structure. When adopting more ethical business practices, PHBs are at a distinct disadvantage to their multinational counterparts. Primarily due to lack of resources, but PHBs also lack experience or peers in their industry group to develop examples of 'best practice'. PHBs also are not subject to the weight of expectation and attention which falls on multinationals who impact our daily lives.

COST MANAGEMENT

Maintaining strict cost control encourages careful management of resources whose use can contribute to CO2 levels and environmental degradation. The IBR results show widespread agreement that the need to control costs encourages ethical behaviour amongst PHBs. Only in a few countries did 50 per cent or fewer respondents cite this issue. It was considered as the leading driver in eleven countries, led by Brazil (87 per cent) and India (85 per cent).

The International Business Report (IBR) 2008 results

emphasise a key point - that the adoption of ethical business practices is fundamental to the success of privately held businesses. The main factor driving corporate responsibility is the need for PHBs to attract and retain high quality staff to meet current and future demands. This was identified by 65 per cent of respondents in our survey. Closely behind was cost management (63 per cent) reflecting the recognition that controlling costs is good for business and the environment?

The need to establish confidence and loyalty among customers led 56 per cent of respondents to cite public attitudes/building brand as an important driver. Employment Recruitment/retention of staff was a driver of social responsibility in all countries - and the main factor in almost half of surveyed countries. The proportion of respondents citing this driver as important varied from 53 per cent in Hong Kong to 89 per cent in Denmark. Unemployment in Denmark is amongst the lowest in the world, perhaps explaining respondents' concern with labour recruitment/ retention.

Labour market considerations also seem to lie beneath the high proportion citing this factor in Turkey (86 per cent) and Vietnam (85 per cent), where skills shortages in certain sectors are acute and some employers have great difficulties with staff retention. Business ethics is a key factor for recruitment and retention in Denmark's tight labour market. Privately held businesses ignoring CSR issues are facing future skills shortages that will threaten their global competitiveness."

TAX RELIEF

Taxation reasons are perceived as the most important driver of business ethics in only one country, Thailand, cited by 94 per cent of respondents. Nevertheless, tax measures were cited as important incentives by a large percentage of respondents in Brazil and Vietnam, both at 79 per cent. In Brazil this seems to reflect taxation reductions introduced to encourage businesses to standardise employment practices. Tax transparency is also a prerequisite to public listing - a desire for many privately held businesses in Brazil.

Taxation is one area that governments can use to force businesses to change their actions. However, it is not evident from the IBR results that any CSR related taxes are having a strong effect on PHBs, which poses a question: Have governments around the world utilised taxes or tax breaks effectively enough to positively affect global business ethics?

PUBLIC ATTITUDES/BUILDING BRAND

While they may not be under the same scrutiny as multinationals, PHBs still identify responsible behaviour as being integral to reputational management and long-term strategy. Public attitudes/building brand is cited by 56 per cent of respondents globally as a key driver of ethical business behaviour. Mexico (89 per cent) and Greece (85 per cent) top the list while France lies at the other extreme at only 27 per cent, a long way behind the next lowest country - Belgium at 39 per cent. It is interesting to note that for PHBs, public attitudes/building brand comes after employee and cost management issues. It suggests that individuals are driving PHBs towards more ethical business practices. As organisations grow in size, the level of scrutiny under which they operate also grows with large multinationals having to give greater consideration to public attitudes/building brand.

'Saving the Planet' and 'Government Pressure'

Neither option was considered the 'most' important driver of corporate responsibility in any country. But saving the planet was cited as an important factor by three quarters (or more) of respondents in Brazil (84 per cent) and India (75 per cent). At the other extreme is the United States with just 21 per cent of PHBs identifying saving the planet as a driver for social responsibility and in many other mature economies less than a third of respondents identified this as a key issue.

Government pressure was considered an important driver by just 38 per cent of respondents, the lowest of the seven issues which the IBR presented. It featured most prominently in Italy (67 per cent) and least in Denmark (16 per cent). There is no doubt that governmental pressure can generate positive action. The question is whether governments are doing enough in the PHB sector for the level of change needed?

Investor Relations: Only in Vietnam are investor relations considered the prime incentive to adopt a more ethical business practice. Vietnamese PHBs appear to be benefiting from structural reforms to modernise the economy and boost more competitive, export-driven industries, but this modernisation is very recent and companies appear to be striving to impress both local and overseas investors.

This also seems to be a feature of emerging markets in general with India (75 per cent of respondents), the Philippines (71 per cent), Brazil (64 per cent) and Turkey (63 per cent) leading the emerging economies citing this factor.

By contrast, in more mature economies, where investor relations have been managed for decades, it is seen as less of a driver. Throughout the EU and in Singapore, the proportion of respondents identifying investor relations is 35 per cent; 32 per cent in the United States and just 9 per cent in Japan. These figures are perhaps unsurprising considering that PHBs have fewer external investors to satisfy compared to public listed companies.

INTERNSHIPS AND WORK EXPERIENCE

Businesses offering internships and work experience are often best placed to identify the market's finest talent and are in prime position to recruit them to permanent positions. Among the global regions, the practice was most prevalent in the EU (83 per cent of respondents) but two Latin American countries -Mexico (95 per cent) and Argentina (87 per cent) - recorded higher proportions.

The bottom eight countries in this context are all in Asia, with very low proportions in India (35 per cent), Japan (40 per cent) and Vietnam (41 per cent). Businesses in industries particularly challenged by skills shortages have shown that by using internships and work experience initiatives effectively, they can help to find the right talent to build a stable future for their business.

IMPLEMENTING CORPORATE RESPONSIBILITY

When privately held businesses were asked what they had done in the past year to manage their corporate responsibility, workforce related matters topped the list. This complemented the result which showed staff attraction/retention as a key driver of ethical behaviour. Four of the top five initiatives were directly associated with people and their workplace - active promotion of workforce health and well-being (71 per cent of respondents); provision of apprenticeships and work experience (67 per cent); promotion of diversity/equality in the workplace (64 per cent) and allowing flexible working (62 per cent). These all have an important role in the context of social responsibility, though the initiatives also play a key role in human resource management.

HEALTH AND WELL-BEING

Measures to improve workforce health and wellbeing are in place at most PHBs surveyed - over 80 per cent in many countries and over 90 per cent in Malaysia, South Africa, the United States and New Zealand. They are clearly seen as vital to attract and retain staff in a tight labour market, with skills shortages pressurising production and growth. Even in emerging markets at the other end of the scale - Thailand, India, Armenia and the Philippines - 35 to 45 per cent were undertaking such measures. Employee health is essential to the morale of the workforce. Such incentives demonstrate an employer's concern about the individuals it employs.

However, it is also increasingly important to manage costs encountered through time lost from long-term absenteeism - a huge issue for private businesses in some more mature economies. Private businesses in Malaysia are being forced to change their products and services to reduce their environmental impact. Businesses satisfying the global demand for more ethical production and delivery are best placed to capture the rapidly growing market generated by discerning consumers and multinationals."

FLEXIBLE WORKING

In today's increasingly demanding society, employers have to become more flexible to accommodate family-friendly work practices. The IBR survey found that action to promote flexible working has been widespread over the past year, notably in Germany, where 90 per cent of PHBs adopted such measures. There is a spread of countries across the globe among the most vigorous promoters of flexible working, but those least likely to adopt flexible working are all in Asia. This suggests that working practices such as home working or flexi-time are yet to reach private businesses in some of the emerging markets. However, the rate of growth and the increased maturity of such economies seem likely to lead to the rapid modernisation of working practices in the near future.

DONATING TO GOOD CAUSES

This is the third most popular action in managing social responsibility in our survey, and the only one in the top five not concerned with human resource issues. International practice shows very marked divergences reflecting cultural and fiscal differences, strongly affecting individual country results. In Thailand, for example, donating to worthy causes is a strictly personal and religious matter, rather than a business issue and thus only 11 per cent of respondents' record donations to community causes/charities. Similar cultural factors also affect corporate donations in France, where only 31 per cent of privately held businesses donate.

The Philippines (22 per cent), Japan (27 per cent) and India (33 per cent) also have very low percentages in this area. Countries with tax concessions, no cultural inhibitions and where useful publicity can accrue push up the global average to 65 per cent. The highest proportions are in the United States (94 per cent), New Zealand (91 per cent), and Botswana, Ireland and South Africa (all 88 per cent).

DIVERSITY/EQUALITY IN THE WORKPLACE

The culturally diverse economies of Malaysia (91 per cent), South Africa (90 per cent) and the United States (84 per cent) lead the way on implementing policies to promote equality in the workplace. In most other countries this figure falls to between 60 and 80 per cent, but there are some major exceptions - Japan (28 per cent), Singapore (21 per cent) and Thailand (15 per cent).

WASTE MANAGEMENT AND ENERGY EFFICIENCY

Improved waste management and energy efficiency are strongly correlated. In many countries, led by Ireland, Malaysia and Taiwan, a large proportion of respondents say they have taken action on waste management and have also acted to improve energy efficiency. In general, countries at this end of the scale have matured but resource poor economies, so there is a strong incentive for energy and related efficiency. At the other end of the scale, in Armenia and Vietnam, relatively few companies have acted on energy efficiency and waste management.

These countries are newcomers to the global marketplace and at present, amid their very rapid progress, waste management and energy efficiency appear to have a relatively low priority.

However, as frameworks and policies become increasingly global and universally accepted, emerging markets may have difficulties reaching any potential levels driven by their more mature counterparts. Such global policies appear inevitable in the long term and for some privately held businesses, falling behind in implementing waste management and energy quotas may become a concern. They may wish to act now to avoid being crippled by daunting targets over the coming decades.

Many privately held businesses in Argentina are experiencing pressure from their multinational customers to become a more ethical supplier. As a result, CSR credentials are becoming a priority for Argentine businesses as they compete in the global marketplace."

A FORMALISED STRATEGY

We asked privately held businesses whether corporate responsibility policies were incorporated into a written document or strategy. Amongst all businesses, 56 per cent said they had a formalised programme. However, the proportion in individual countries showed marked variations from the global average, ranging from 74 per cent in mainland China to 29 per cent in Vietnam.

Yet neither at the top or bottom of the range was a pattern discernable among the countries included, from a geographical, development status or political perspective. However, the appearance of countries such as mainland China, Mexico and Brazil at the top suggests that PHBs in these countries have come under the greatest pressure to formally adopt a strategy to comply with the CSR frameworks of their large corporate customers.

The IBR survey shows that privately held businesses appear more likely to adopt ethical business practices for practical commercial reasons than any other. Although unsurprising, it offers an insight into ways in which organisations and governments can improve global corporate social responsibility. While 'saving the planet' is a concern, by far and away the main drivers for action on corporate social responsibility are recruitment and retention issues followed closely by cost management. This highlights the power of the individual. Privately held businesses are having to take notice of individuals and install CSR initiatives because it is being demanded by their workforce through recruitment and retention issues.

THE DEMAND FOR ACTION

Another factor is the demand of the large corporate. CSR frameworks are filtering down the supply chain, influencing the business practices of privately held businesses. Such businesses are often able to change the direction of their business more efficiently due to the ability of the owner to individually alter the business's operations. Corporate social responsibility is no longer the domain of the large corporate and is now a necessity rather than a choice. Those privately held businesses adopting ethical business practices quickly and efficiently will survive. These are the businesses who will secure the skilled workers and the contracts with the large multinationals. Those failing to act now face an uncertain future.

APPROACHES

Some commentators have identified a difference between the Continental European and the Anglo-Saxon approaches to CSR. And even within Europe the discussion about CSR is very heterogeneous. An approach for CSR that is becoming more widely accepted is community-based development projects, such as the Shell Foundation's involvement in the Flower Valley, South Africa. Here they have set up an Early Learning Centre to help educate the community's children, as well as develop new skills for the adults. Marks and Spencer is also active in this community through the building of a trade network with the community - guaranteeing regular fair trade purchases. Often alternative approaches to this are the establishment of education facilities for adults, as well as HIV/AIDS education programmes.

The majority of these CSR projects are established in Africa. A more common approach of CSR is through the giving of aid to local organizations and impoverished communities in developing countries. Some organizations do not like this approach as it does not help build on the skills of the local people, whereas community-based development generally leads to more sustainable development.

SOCIAL ACCOUNTING, AUDITING AND REPORTING

Taking responsibility for its impact on society means in the first instance that a company accounts for its actions. Social accounting, a concept describing the communication of social and environmental effects of a company's economic actions to particular interest groups within society and to society at large, is thus an important element of CSR.

A number of reporting guidelines or standards have been developed to serve as frameworks for social accounting, auditing and reporting:

- Account Ability's AA1000 standard, based on John Elkington's triple bottom line (3BL) reporting
- Accounting for Sustainability's Connected Reporting Framework.
- Global Reporting Initiative's Sustainability Reporting Guidelines
- Good Corporation's Standard developed in association with the Institute of Business Ethics
- Green Globe Certification / Standard
- Social Accountability International's SA8000 standard
- The ISO 14000 environmental management standard
- The United Nations Global Compact promotes companies reporting in the format of a Communication on Progress (COP). A COP report describes the company's implementation of the Compact's ten universal principles.
- The United Nations Intergovernmental Working Group of Experts on International Standards of Accounting and Reporting (ISAR) provides voluntary technical guidance on eco-efficiency indicators, corporate responsibility reporting and corporate governance disclosure.
- Verite's Monitoring Guidelines

The FTSE Group publishes the FTSE4Good Index, an evaluation of CSR performance of companies. In some nations legal requirements for social accounting, auditing and reporting exist (e.g. in the French bilan social), though agreement on meaningful measurements of social and environmental performance is difficult. Many companies now produce externally audited annual reports that cover Sustainable Development and CSR issues ("Triple Bottom Line Reports"), but the reports vary widely in format, style, and evaluation methodology (even within the same industry). Critics dismiss these reports as lip service, citing examples such as Enron's yearly "Corporate Responsibility Annual Report" and tobacco corporations' social reports.

Organisations of the 21st century can no longer limit themselves to producing and marketing products or services without any concerns for the impact they have on society. If they want to be trusted by their customers, employees and the public at large, they have to be more socially responsible. One key issue of Corporate Social Responsibility (CSR) which needs to be addressed is the integration of ethnic minorities in the workplace and the community.

DEMOGRAPHIC CHANGES

The lack of proper governmental strategies following the demographic changes of the 50's and 70's has left many British companies struggling to this day to deal with the problem themselves. Many organisations have played a passive role in this integration process by staying within the legal boundaries and are now experiencing difficulties in that area.

A LACK OF CONSIDERATION OF DIFFERENCES

One of the major reasons behind these integration problems is the lack of awareness and consideration for cultural differences. People from different cultural backgrounds have different sets of norms, different sets of values and different assumptions. This means that we all have different ways of reacting to events, different ways of communicating and different behaviours. We judge the others from our own frame of reference and tend to think that "our way is the right way". In a multicultural workforce, this can lead to misinterpretation, misunderstanding, incomprehension, mistrust and disrespect.

As a result, rather than getting closer, people distance themselves from those they consider different and groups are formed on the basis of commonalities, whether it is ethnicity, colour, language etc. "Departmental ghettos" start to appear. Often, there are rivalries and tensions. In some instances, these situations can degenerate into discrimination, bullying or racist behaviours.

THE LAW IS NOT ENOUGH

Staying within the letter of the law is not enough for organisations experiencing these situations. It is imperative for them to resolve these issues if they want to retain a stable and productive workforce and be regarded as good "corporate citizens". Organisation can be more socially responsible by contributing to a smooth cultural integration of ethnic minorities into the workplace.

BEING MORE SOCIALLY RESPONSIBLE

Integration does not mean imposing one way. It means harmonising and synergizing differences. Having a clear and unbiased understanding of the context is the first step toward formulating proper integration strategies. The second step is to develop cultural awareness. Being open to differences, understanding and respecting the other's cultural background are the key elements in preparing the ground for integration. The third step is to build or rebuild trust. Finally, only when trust has been demonstrated from all sides, solutions can be discussed.

It is the step where different norms and values are reconciled and tangible and intangible elements of integration are defined. Building shared ownership of the solutions is at that stage essential to reinforce trust and guarantee implementation. These steps can take different forms; for example interviews with the various groups involved for step one, training programmes at the levels concerned in the organisation for step two and facilitated workshops for steps three and four involving all concerned or a limited number of influential representatives of each group, who can then intervene as mentors to their members.

Being proactive in the integration process of ethnic minorities is a corporate social duty which can strongly impact the community and contribute to a much more committed workforce. During the last few months Farnham has been working with a number of clients in the development of programmes, using a training approach normally associated with supporting the integration of home and foreign workforces, to address the growing issue of multicultural tension within the domestic workforce. Because of the sensitivity of the issue, each programme has to be very carefully designed and often involves a number of programmes each with a different perspective at each level. The need to exercise corporate social responsibility is evolving in many different guises, in light of recent events; perhaps this one in particular needs our attention now.

POTENTIAL BUSINESS BENEFITS

The scale and nature of the benefits of CSR for an organization can vary depending on the nature of the enterprise, and are difficult to quantify, though there is a large body of literature exhorting business to adopt measures beyond financial ones (e.g., Deming's Fourteen Points, balanced scorecards). Orlitzky, Schmidt, and Rynes found a correlation between social/ environmental performance and financial performance. However, businesses may not be looking at short-run financial returns when developing their CSR strategy.

The definition of CSR used within an organization can vary from the strict "stakeholder impacts" definition used by many CSR advocates and will often include charitable efforts and volunteering. CSR may be based within the human resources, business development or public relations departments of an organisation, or may be given a separate unit reporting to the CEO or in some cases directly to the board. Some companies may implement CSR-type values without a clearly defined team or programme. The business case for CSR within a company will likely rest on one or more of these arguments:

- ***Human resources:*** A CSR programme can be an aid to recruitment and retention, particularly within the competitive graduate student market. Potential recruits often ask about a firm's CSR policy during an interview, and having a comprehensive policy can give an advantage. CSR can also help to improve the perception of a company among its staff, particularly when staff can become involved through payroll giving, fundraising activities or community volunteering.

- *Risk management:* Managing risk is a central part of many corporate strategies. Reputations that take decades to build up can be ruined in hours through incidents such as corruption scandals or environmental accidents. These events can also draw unwanted attention from regulators, courts, governments and media. Building a genuine culture of 'doing the right thing' within a corporation can offset these risks.
- *Brand differentiation:* In crowded marketplaces, companies strive for a unique selling proposition that can separate them from the competition in the minds of consumers. CSR can play a role in building customer loyalty based on distinctive ethical values. Several major brands, such as The Cooperative Group, The Body Shop and American Apparel are built on ethical values. Business service organizations can benefit too from building a reputation for integrity and best practice.

License to Operate

Corporations are keen to avoid interference in their business through taxation or regulations. By taking substantive voluntary steps, they can persuade governments and the wider public that they are taking issues such as health and safety, diversity or the environment seriously, and so avoid intervention. This also applies to firms seeking to justify eye-catching profits and high levels of boardroom pay. Those operating away from their home country can make sure they stay welcome by being good corporate citizens with respect to labour standards and impacts on the environment.

CRITICISMS AND CONCERNS

Critics of CSR as well as proponents debate a number of concerns related to it. These include CSR's relationship to the fundamental purpose and nature of business and questionable motives for engaging in CSR, including concerns about insincerity and hypocrisy.

Corporate social responsibility (CSR) is a major buzzword within academic circles, politics, activist groups, and the business community. There are many definitions of CSR which emphasize different areas, but the most contemporary and most applicable to the majority cases, is defined by the World Bank Group's Corporate Social Responsibility Practice, as a department of Foreign Investment Advisory Service (FIAS): "Corporate social responsibility is the commitment of businesses to contribute to sustainable economic development by working with employees, their families, the local community and society at large to improve their lives in ways that are good for business and for development" (World Bank Group's).

However, there is no set definition of CSR to which all agents follow, and this has led to confusion regarding what, if anything should be expected of companies in the area of social responsibility. Whatever way it is defined, it assumes that a company is responsible for its wider impact on society, not merely the return to stockholders. The question of whether or not companies *should* do CSR is a normative statement. Its answer is highly dependent on the ideological viewpoint from which the respondent is replying from.

Most of the research and debate about CSR has been centered on the positive benefits to the community, of which there are many, and which also seems to find much agreement among academics and business executives. The new direction is relating CSR to profitability. Here the literature is more divergent. Therefore, in an effort to provide some practical examples and substance to the debate, this chapter will focus on studying the dynamics of the relationship between CSR and profitability, by enabling a case study of three companies.

The direction of this chapter will unravel some of the mystery about CSR, and then study its relationship to the financial performance of companies, show the debate between the positive and negative effects of doing or not doing CSR, illustrate some of the socially responsible accounting measures available, and provide a more effective way for companies to accrue the benefits of CSR. I will be utilizing a case study of three companies; two that do use variant forms of CSR, and another that does not.

The companies chosen will be The Body Shop, Starbucks, and Sara-Lee respectively. The Body Shop and Starbucks have developed rather large positive brand images from their CSR campaigns. The purpose of the chapter will be to see if each of these firms CSR policies (or lack thereof) influences their bottom line.

These companies were selected because they illustrate a cross-representation of the types of firms that exist in the global economy, as it relates to CSR: on one side, firms that are immersed in the CSR dialogue and practices (in one form or another), and at the other end, firms which do not engage CSR at all, or very little. I believe it will be useful to categorize the three firms using Sethi's 'Level of Social Commitment' table: ranked from lowest to highest, the categories are 1) Social Obligation (Sara-Lee), 2) Social Responsibility (Starbucks), and 3) Responsiveness (The Body Shop).

The categorization of these three companies as either supportive or non-supportive of CSR policies (or a mix of both) can be determined by several factors: the level of space provided to demonstrating the firms supportiveness of CSR, either on their website or annual reports, the type of rhetoric used to indicate their support of CSR, and financial commitments to CSR policies (although this should be qualified to recognize that small to medium firms should not be expected to contribute on the same level as large MNEs).

CSR does not just involve spending money to become socially responsible; it can also involve a change in accounting practices. Verification and reporting can also be important for obtaining and maintaining a firm's license to operate, improving internal operations and building relationships. Communities, customers, investors, employees and their representatives, regulators and non-governmental organizations wishing to know about a firm and its activities are likely to consult the firm's CSR verification reports.

However, verification activities and reporting not done in a rigorous, professional manner, and not seen as credible, will undermine a firm's credibility and reputation, thereby shutting doors to opportunities and diminishing profitability.

Opinion and research has been divided regarding the relationship between CSR and financial performance. On the one had, conventional wisdom would assume that CSR has been considered as a zero-sum tradeoff with profitability: more money spent on CSR means less spent on increasing market share, or re-investment. Conversely, academic thought has also suggested that those companies, who appear to be more responsible in the areas of environment and societal behavior, would more attractive for investors, and therefore perform better financially.

An increasing number of firms have responded to these concerns by devoting more resources to CSR. However, some companies' managers have resisted, arguing that additional investment in CSR is inconsistent with their efforts to maximize profits. Investment in CSR promotes product differentiation at the product and firm levels. Some firms will produce goods or services with attributes or characteristics that signal to the consumer that the company is concerned about certain social issues. Also, many companies will try to establish a socially responsible corporate image. Both of these strategies will encourage consumers to believe that, by consuming the product, they are directly or indirectly supporting a cause.

The real question is not that all firms should do CSR in the same form, but rather that firms should tailor certain specificities of CSR to their business strategy, to become more competitive. Rather than trying to connect CSR to short-term profitability, a better estimate of the benefits of CSR need to be taken into a long-term account.

CSR is about looking at the relationship of a firm's activities on society and the environment. It would not be out of line for a firm to introduce more environmentally friendly measures as their approach to CSR. "For example, several companies have reported enhanced productivity and reduced costs from introducing new technologies aimed at reducing pollution". Although there has been much work in the field, the empirical data is scattered, and provides no definitive conclusions on the relationship between CSR and a firm's performance, whether it is positive or negative. "Anecdotal evidence certainly suggests that investment in corporate ethics and social responsibility, as well as avoiding negative consequences, can often lead to positive payoffs".

It is also important to acknowledge that while positive or neutral correlations between social and environmental responsibility and superior financial performance have generally been supported by the evidence, conclusive causal links have not. Many studies are being undertaken, with varying conclusions. Suffice it to say that research is continuing on this issue. While empirical research is ongoing, the correlation between CSR and profitability can be found to be the strongest in the long-term benefits of proactive CSR performance, with respect to brand name recognition and customer loyalty, rather than immediate returns to investors.

Traditional methods of the studying the performance of firms, within accounting, have been measured in financial terms, looking at profit and loss accounts, the balance sheet and the cash flow statement. These tools are used to maximize shareholder wealth within the firm. However, new streams of thought have emphasized the need for a more holistic approach to the study of firms, and their role in society. "Effectively the line of reasoning is that a better informed society will be empowered to ensure that the organizations operate to the benefit of that society by ensuring that organizations are accountable to society for their actions so those actions can be changed to the benefit of that society".

This is the essence of the stakeholder approach. In his seminal text 'Strategic Management: A Stakeholder Approach', "Freeman defines stakeholders in numerous ways, but the most commonly quoted definition is: any group or individual who can affect or is affected by the achievement of the organizations objectives". While mostly coming out of the theoretical background of social contract theory, most often associated with Hobbes (1651) and Rousseau (1762), stakeholder theory, as a type of social accounting of corporations, has roots within the field of political economy as well:

Political economy is the study if the interplay of power, the goals of power wielders and the productive exchange system. As a framework, political economy does not concentrate exclusively on market exchanges. Rather it first of all analyses in whatever institutional framework they occur and, second, analyses the relationship between social institutions such as government, law and property rights, each fortified by power and the economy. In this sense, political economy serves to create a space for discussion and dialogue on the potential benefits and consequences of CSR.

So where do these three firms fit? Sethi's Three-Stage Schema will be useful to determine and evaluate the types and levels of social commitment, and therefore the classification of the selected firms into the appropriate categories in table 1.0:

Social Obligation Low	*Social Responsibility*	*Responsiveness High*
Reactive Proscriptive	Prescriptive Does more than required by law	Proactive Anticipates and prevents problems
Adheres to legal requirements	Does than required by economic considerations	Searches for socially responsible acts
Adheres to economic considerations	Avoids public stands on issues	Takes public stands on issues

These categories can be described as "adaptive, proactive, and interactive", and apply to the companies Sara-Lee, Starbucks, and The Body Shop respectively. *Social Obligation* is corporate behavior in response to market forces or legal constraints.

These managers confine their responses to social issues

to those mandated by prevailing laws and the operation of the economic system.

Social Responsibility is when the organization's approach to social responsibility acknowledges the importance of ethical and socially responsible behaviors. Frequently seen as good corporate citizens, socially responsible organizations are willing to assume a broader responsibility than that prescribed by law and economic requirements. Finally, *Social Responsive* firms say what is important is not how corporations should respond to social pressure but what should be their long-run role in a dynamic social system. Managers in socially responsive firms are proactive (leaders) in their dealing with social issues.

My reasoning for placing these firms within their specific category was to illustrate the wide array of responses to the CSR debate and social issues. There is also some overlap between the products created by these firms, for continuity. It made more sense to compare and contrast three somewhat similar firms, than three widely different ones. The Sara Lee Corporation is a global consumer products company with food, beverage, and household and body care businesses. With powerful brands, such as *Ambi Pur, Ball Park, Douwe Egberts, Hillshire Farm, Jimmy Dean, Kiwi, Sanex, Senseo* and its namesake, *Sara Lee,* the company has leading positions in numerous categories in the more than 180 markets in which it competes. Due to the lack of CSR discourse and activities, they fit within Sethi's 1st category: social obligation.

The firm places the most emphasis first on working within, and obeying the limits of the law. Little more is said about going beyond and doing more than what the legal framework requires, for both the company and the individual. Their website only makes mention of two charities within the firm through which employees can donate their own personal funds. The firm is distinct from the other two selected, in that its first objective, as made obvious to anyone that visits their website, is that their business is brands, and this objective is made explicit in their everyday practices. Looking through their *Winning through Integrity: Global Business Standards* document, Sara-Lee only spends 129 and 101 words talking about their commitment to the environment and communities respectively, in which it operates.

The rest of the document is devoted to respecting individual workers rights, and installing a sense of integrity within the workers to do the "right thing" in every situation, for the benefit of the firm. Starbucks was selected because of its specific brand appeal, and because of the large amount of information regarding its CSR programs.

The company tries to portray itself, quite successfully, as a socially responsible citizen; a social environment for people to come together to exchange ideas and create networks, and on the side, enjoy a cup of coffee, to experience the full "flavor" of the Starbucks experience. "Starbucks' efforts towards social responsibility are also carefully crafted to be in cohesion with the brand's image.

The company formed the Starbucks Foundation in 1997 with an initial $500,000 contribution from the company founder and CEO Howard Shultz, with literacy as its main focus". This is why they are classified in Sethi's second category, social responsibility. Starbucks sees that the traditional method of coffee production can be exploitative, and attempts to counteract this through its line of socially responsible coffee brands (Fair Trade, Organic, etc), but this has been caused by intense public scrutiny and interest. Another reason for placing Starbucks in this category is found within the Starbucks' internal handbook given to new employees, *Starbucks Standards of Business Conduct*:

Starbucks reputation for integrity flows from our steadfast commitment to our core values and guiding principles - values and principles which require compliance with the law and ethical conduct. Starbucks depends on its partners to follow the law and to make the right decisions. However, we recognize that Starbucks operates in a complex and dynamic world and that what's "right" may not always be obvious. Starbucks Standards of Business Conduct ("Standards") provide practical overviews of some of the legal and ethical standards that we all must follow on a day-to-day basis.

Starbucks recognizes that they exist in, and are part of a dynamic and complex world, and as a result, the firm must follow legal and ethical standards on a day-to-day basis. This recognition is an important part of their social responsibility categorization. Finally, the last firm chosen was The Body Shop.

Their website maintains that "The only thing that will stay the same at The Body Shop is what we believe in - *Profits with Principles*. We strive to change everything else to maintain creative positive change. We at The Body Shop will continue to challenge ourselves, our industry, our staff and our customers". The whole way they do business is dedicated to creating "profits with principles". And this is why I fit them in Sethi's 3rd category, "responsiveness". On their website, it reads, "At the Body Shop, we believe business is about more than just the exchange of products and money. It's about an exchange in experience, community action, and knowledge too because business is ultimately about human relationships."

While there is obvious overlap in the goods produced by the firms, it is also recognized that there is overlap within Sethi's Three-Stage Schema. For example, all three firms meet the characteristics of the first column, social obligation. However, Sara-Lee does not try to anticipate and prevent social problems, as characterized by The Body Shop, but the firm does avoid public stands on issues, and therefore could be seen to fit partially with the social responsibility category. It was necessary to place the firms within the prescribed categories, but overlap is present.

From a more objective viewpoint, there are several reasons why firms should practice CSR, many of which will be touched upon in this chapter, such as: to balance corporate power with responsibility; discourage creation and imposition of government regulations; to help correct negative externalities, many of which are created by corporations; and a sense of moral obligation of firms to help society deal with its problems and to contribute to its welfare. In a world where 51 of the 100 largest economies in the world are corporations, it behooves these corporations to take on responsibilities that are similar to those of governments.

The business case for CSR is certainly difficult to present, but the debate and arguments are hard to ignore. Like-minded companies can form profitable long-term business relationships.

Larger firms can stimulate smaller firms with whom they do business to implement a CSR approach. For example, some large automakers insist their suppliers be certified to environmental management systems standards. Other examples: Starbucks only purchases Fair Trade coffee from cooperatives that pass certification; The Body Shop does not test on animals, nor engages with suppliers that do animal testing, so to be a supplier of the Body Shop, requires a more socially responsible friendly approach.

Some firms have responded to these concerns by devoting more resources to CSR. Other companies' managers have resisted, arguing that additional investment in CSR is inconsistent with their efforts to maximize profits. Investment in CSR promotes product differentiation at the product and firm levels. Some firms will produce goods or services with attributes or characteristics that signal to the consumer that the company is concerned about certain social issues. Also, many companies will try to establish a socially responsible corporate image. Both of these strategies will encourage consumers to believe that, by consuming the product, they are directly or indirectly supporting a cause. Mainstream economists would support that market failure occurs due to an inefficient allocation of resources, or where public sector services would be more efficient.

However, the term can also refer to instances where the market does not adequately reflect the desires of the general public. Remembering the example of the Exxon oil spill in Alaska, it is interesting to note that the GDP for the USA increased that same year.

The oil that was spilled, required workers to clean up the Alaskan coast, contain the oil, among a myriad of other disaster cleanup duties. While this was good for GDP, the oil spill was still a massive environmental disaster, spilling somewhere between 10-30million gallons of oil into fragile ecosystems and environments. The US Environmental Protection Agency writes, "The spill posed threats to the delicate food chain that supports Prince William Sound's commercial fishing industry. Also in danger were ten million migratory shore birds and waterfowl, hundreds of sea otters, dozens of other species, such as harbor porpoises and sea lions, and several varieties of whales."

Critics of CSR can stem largely from the neoclassical side of economics. Many would argue that CSR is a zero-sum trade off with profit; that by spending money on CSR philanthropy and "goodwill", the company will have less money to reinvest in the growth of their firm, will potentially lose market share.

It can be argued that firms are already benefiting society. Milton Freidman would say that the only responsibility of a corporation to society is to maximize its profits, and operate within the legal framework of that society. However, the new business climate does not allow firms to escape socially irresponsible behaviour. NGOs and social activist watchdogs are constantly vigilant of any irresponsible corporate behaviour, and it has become a standard business practice for many firms to engage in more socially responsible behaviour, beyond being merely law-abiding, such as CSR.

Freeman and Liedtka illustrate seven reasons why CSR is something that should not be followed:

1. The origins of the concept are suspect, as they derive primarily from the field of economics, and fail to include, among others, history, religion, and culture.

2. The different models of CSR all accept the terms of the debate as set forth by Milton Friedman's argument that sees corporations only as profit maximizers.

3. Corporate social responsibility accepts the prevailing business rhetoric of "capitalism: love it or leave it."

4. CSR is inherently conservative–it starts with the standard received wisdom and then attempts to "fix" its unintended consequences.
5. CSR promotes incompetence by leading managers to involve themselves in areas beyond their expertise-that is, repairing society's ills.
6. CSR accepts a view of business and society as separable from each other, each with a distinct ethic, linked by a set of responsibilities.
7. The language of rights and responsibilities is, itself, both limiting and often irrelevant to the world of the practicing manager.

However valid these arguments may be, they have been silenced by the overwhelming majority of those in favor of CSR (NGOs, businessmen and academics), and the benefits it can provide to society.

Sometimes, organizations which advocated CSR or certain major events can push firms to implement CSR practices before they intended too. In April of 2000, a large non-profit organization dedicated to social justice and a major voice in anti-Globalisation movement called the Global Exchange, threatened to boycott many Starbucks stores and operations in Seattle and across the country. "Global Exchange is a membership-based international human rights organization dedicated to promoting social, economic and environmental justice around the world".

The enormous media attention created by such an event forced Starbucks to concede some of the grass-roots organization's demands, creating an alliance with Trans Fair USA, to begin selling Fair-Trade Certified coffee in their 2,300 stores nationwide.

Now, Starbucks is proud of their relationship with TransFair USA, and is the largest seller of fair-trade certified coffee in the world. This has had serious positive implications for the coffee growers in Latin America, from which Starbucks purchases its fair-trade certified coffee. Alternative, or fair, trade is a movement that is attempting to make the social and environmental conditions in which commodities are produced a very visible part of the product.

The goal is to improve the livelihoods of low-income producers by increasing the income from their products and by improving other social conditions such as health and education.

This is accomplished by attempting to distinguish alternative-trade products from other commodities at the retail level by explicitly advertising their conditions of production. At the point of exchange between producers and importers, alternatives trade insists on a relationship based on more than the self-interest of both parties. Importer criteria for participation in a fair-trade labeling scheme are geared at promoting longer, closer relationships between buyers and sellers and making sure tat a greater proportion of the final price reaches the farmer. Importers must purchase coffee directly and exclusively from small producers' organizations listed in the production registry. They must pay a minimum price to the grower, regardless of the current world market, creating a type of basic social security net.

Starbucks' participation meant the largest increase to the success of the Fair Trade movement in recent history. The United States consumes one-fifth of the worlds coffee supply, and Starbucks has obvious advantages to tap into the American coffee market. In fiscal 2005, Starbucks significantly increased its purchases of fair trade certified coffee. The Company purchased 11.5 million pounds of Fair Trade Certified coffee, exceeding its goal of 10 million pound, representing approximately 3.7% of Starbucks' total coffee imports.

This represents approximately 10 percent of global fair trade certified coffee imports. Twenty-one percent of the fair-trade certified coffee imported into the U.S. in fiscal 2005 was purchased by Starbucks, making it the largest purchaser of fair trade certified coffee in North America.

Here are some of Starbucks' financial highlights for the 2006 fiscal year: "Record worldwide store openings of 2,199;

consolidated net revenues of $7.8 billion for the full fiscal year, an increase of 22 percent; Net earnings of $564 million, compared to $494 million in fiscal year 20053. The Body Shop is an example of a firm that is completely immersed in the socially responsible corporation style. The Body Shop is a firm that makes their business decisions predicated on their "Profits with Principles" mentality:

The way we trade creates profits with principles. We aim to achieve commercial success by meeting our customers' needs through the provision of high-quality, good-value products with exceptional service and relevant information which enables customers to make informed and responsible choices.

Our trading relationships of every kind - with customers, franchisees and suppliers - will be commercially viable, mutually beneficial and based on trust and respect.

The table 1.1 shows the financial performance of The Body Shop, according to their 2006 annual report:.

Summary	2005	2006	Change
Retail Sales	724.0	772.0	+7%
Turnover	419.0	485.8	+16%
Operating Profit	39.2	41.5	+6%
Earnings per share (pence)	13.8	13.6	–1%
Dividend per share (pence)	5.7	6.6	+16%
Net debt	19.8	12.7	–?7.1m

*Figures are in British pounds (£) unless otherwise stated

*The Body Shop Annual Report, 2006

Of significant importance is the recent takeover of the company by L'Oreal, the French cosmetics group, for the sum of £652 million. Many critics are concerned what this will mean for the high social responsiveness image of The Body Shop. Naturewatch is an organization committed to campaigning against animal cruelty, has been boycotting L'Oreal for some time, and now boycotts against The Body Shop as well, since the stores resources and profits are now at L'Oreal's disposal. Other organizations however, such as PETA, continue to support The Body Shop, in the hopes that its positive CSR approach policies will spread throughout L'Oreal.

Sara-Lee is a company that has large market-share, but has been experiencing a slump from July 2005, to July 2006. During that time, net sales dropped from $16, 029M, to $15,944M. Also during this time, Sara-Lee has seen drops financially across the board, in other areas such as Net Income (from $719M to $555M). Looking at the Market Value per Share at Year-end, for 2005 and 2006, the value has dropped from just under $20, to just barely above $16. It is recognized that without holding constant for other factors, it is difficult to tell how much this drop in sales may be attributable to their ineffectual CSR policies.

However, it would be premature to not assume that a more proactive CSR policy, could have done much to improve brand image and retain customer loyalty, thus increasing net sales for those years. Still, Sara-Lee is a very competitive firm, so how can firms remain competitive given their lack of CSR policies? That being said, the profitability of a firm nowadays is strongly related to the success of its brand. The power of the brand has the ability to make or break firms in the global economy, and has become so important, that many firms are being judged, traded and criticized, based largely on their brands reputation. The success and appeal of the firms brand goes far in explaining, and influencing the success of the firm's reputation, and therefore, the firm's profitability.

"This has lead to a rise in cause related marketing (CRM), also known as societal marketing-a strategic positioning and marketing tool that links a company or brand to a relevant social cause or issue, for mutual benefit. Consumers are known to be anthropomorphic about brands, attaching emotional and practical aspects to them". For example, although they have made some attempt to clean up their supply chain recently, it is nothing new or shocking to state that Nike produces much of its product in "sweatshop" conditions overseas. However, the success of Nikes brand, the way the firm positions and presents themselves to consumers in the global market, mitigates what would initially seem to be a devastating situation. Since Nike is still one of the most successful firms, due in no small part to the firms branding success, it would stand to reason that a positive firm brand is essential to the success of the firm. CSR has come about as a new way for companies to protect, and enhance their firm's brand, and reputation, through many types of policies and practices. Consequently "many products have labels that indicate the use of certain ingredients and production methods that promote CSR...Labels that refer to CSR attributes also create new (socially responsible) product categories in the perception of the consumers".

This next section will look at the particular aspects of each companies brand used in this case study, to see how the success of each firms individual brand influenced their firms reputation. Starbucks was selected in part because of its specific brand appeal. "Starbucks efforts towards social responsibility are also carefully crafted to be in cohesion with the brand's image. The company formed the Starbucks Foundation in 1997 with an initial $500,000 contribution from the company founder and CEO Howard Shultz, with literacy as its main focus". The company tries to portray itself, quite successfully, as a socially responsible citizen; a social environment for people to come together to exchange ideas and create networks, and on the side, enjoy a cup of coffee, to experience the full "flavor" of the Starbucks experience. As their website states, "The Company's objective is to establish Starbucks as the most recognized and respected brand in the world.

To achieve this goal, the company plans to continue to rapidly expand its retail operations...and selectively pursue opportunities to leverage the Starbucks brand..." This will be accomplished by new product innovation, but also through brand name differentiation to remain competitive. Starbucks has been attacked by anti-Globalisation activists (literally and academically) for exploiting Third-world coffee farmers, although indirectly, through its supply chain. Starbucks has responded by revamping part of its supply-chain process by rewarding producers who demonstrate environmental and social responsibility. "In so doing, it has strengthened its *values integrity* - an important concept for Passionbrands".

Whatever the case is for Starbucks having promoted CSR activities, it has seem to have had a positive effect on the firms image, and financial performance. Consumers would be most dismayed if Starbucks began treating its workers less favorably than it already does, or took less public stands on important issues, such as selling fair-trade coffee. The Body Shop also has a large, easily recognizable brand image, and is continually innovating and improving upon this image. As stated in their most recent annual report, "In order to deliver this 'masstige' experience for our customers, we have continued to focus on product innovation, the roll out of our new store design and the development of improved customer service programs for our sales associates and The Body Shop At Home™ consultant".

Brand image and placement is important to all companies in order to be successful, and "masstige" (a blend between 'mass' and 'prestige') is an attempt by The Body Shop to market its product as a high quality purchase, available to people of all classes. It would appear this new brand image has served The Body Shop well financially, but how can these improvements also be measured? This leads us to new, positive methods by which to calculate the benefits of CSR. A unique method of measuring the social responsibility empirically has been created by the FTSE4Good Index. FTSE, an independent company that provides independent market information says, "Our sole business is the creation and management of indices and associated data services, on an international scale".

Unfortunately, the results of those findings are no longer made publicly available. In 1995, the company created FTSE4Good, as a means to of indicating to the public that that the firm carried out its business practices in a socially responsible manner; but:

The launch of the FTSE4Good series was also in response

to growing investor demand for Socially Responsible Investment (SRI) indices and products. This growth is fuelled by investors seeking to capitalize on the long-term benefits of good corporate social responsibility (CSR) and sustainability performance, recognizing that good CSR practice mitigates risk and goes hand in hand with good company management.

The selection of which companies make the FTSE4Good Index is based upon three classifications: Environmental sustainability, human rights, and stakeholder relations. This serves to create a global standard for which firms can be judged on their commitment to social responsibility. Firms that are not found on the index are deemed to be socially irresponsible. Each year, the FTSE increases the selectivity of their criteria, as an attempt to be a catalyst for the continual promotion and enhancement of CSR policies and activities.

As stated earlier, previous studies have attempted, and failed to find a positive relationship between social responsibility and financial performance. This was mostly due to a failure within the methodology of the studies itself. The nature of the relationship between CSR and financial performance is more complex than simply stating 'A affects B'. This has led to more studies being done to look at the more complex relationship between the two.

A more recent methodology, outlined by Lee Burke and Jeanne M. Logsdon, emphasizes the use of the concept of strategic CSR, which is useful because it provides an opportunity to measure the benefits of CSR in a broader context than simple correlations between philanthropic contributions and profits. "Corporate social responsibility (policy, program or process) is *strategic* when it yields substantial business-related benefits to the firm, in particular by supporting core business activities and thus contributing to the firm's effectiveness in accomplishing its mission".

It does so by emphasizing the new idea that the purpose of CSR within firms is for value creation. "The question that is addressed here is: under what conditions does a firm jointly serve its own strategic business interests and the societal interests of its stakeholders". In their study, value creation is most prevalent when the following categories are taken into consideration, when contemplating which CSR policy to move forward on:

- *Centrality:* Closeness of fit to the firm's mission and objectives
- *Specificity:* Ability to capture private benefits by firm
- *Pro-activity:* Degree to which the program is planned in anticipation of emerging social trends and in the absence of crises
- *Voluntarism*: The scope for discretionary decision-making and the lack of externally imposed compliance requirements
- *Visibility:* Observable, recognizable credit by internal and/or external stakeholders for the firm
- *Value creation:* Identifiable, measurable economic benefits that the firm expects to receive
- In the end, according to Burke and Logsdon, when value creation occurs, it is most like to take the following forms in table 1.2:

	Centrality	Specificity	Pro-activity	Voluntarism	Visibility
Value Created	Customer loyalty Future purchasers	Productivity gains	New products or markets	New product or geographic market opportunities	New product on new markets Edge in meeting emergency needs

This is important for firms to recognize, if they wish to garner the most positive benefits to be gained from CSR. This could go a long way in helping a firm such as Sara-Lee improve its socially responsible image, and could serve to improve upon Starbucks' and The Body Shops CSR strategy. In the end, from the study done of the three firms selected, all of which are still very profitable and competitive in their industries, the initial conclusion is that the positive relationship between CSR and profitability is more anecdotal than it is empirical. A firm that doesn't have CSR policies, can balance that out, and still remain competitive, by having an aggressive brand marketing strategy, such as Sara-Lee.

However, CSR may affect a firm's performance in more than one way. A more effective way for firms to approach CSR is through analyzing what gains can be made by strategically emphasizing a firms comparative advantages in some sectors over others. Other studies have attempted to empirically measure certain specific aspects of CSR and other facets of corporate and consumer behaviour.

In a study done by Brown and Dacin, "...our results also suggest that CSR associations have a significant influence on consumer responses to new products. The results of all three studies demonstrate that negative CSR associations ultimately can have a detrimental effect on overall product evaluations, whereas positive CSR associations can enhance the product evaluations".

It is a tricky position for CEOs of companies to decide whether or not they should do CSR, and it is a difficult business decision to anticipate a consumer's reaction to such practices. More and more, companies have to deal with the prevalence of CSR advocates, and to take their responsibility and role in society seriously. Perhaps this is the most conclusive argument that can be made in favor of CSR at this time. Ergo, firms that avoid this new business reality, do so at their own peril. If the arguments for a socially responsible approach were widely accepted, nobody would even use the label "CSR" because everyone would be doing it. Those of us who spend our time marshalling the case for would do well to spend a little time hearing the case against, and considering what should be the response.

Of course, one of the challenges in considering cases "for" and "against" CSR is the wide variety of definitions of CSR that people use. We assume here we are talking about responsibility in how the company carries out its core function

- not simply about companies giving money away to charity. Below are some of the key arguments most often used against CSR and some responses.

- Businesses are owned by their shareholders - money spent on CSR by managers is theft of the rightful property of the owners
- The leading companies who report on their social responsibility are basket cases - the most effective business leaders don't waste time with this stuff
- Our company is too busy surviving hard times to do this. We can't afford to take our eye off the ball - we have to focus on core business
- It's the responsibility of the politicians to deal with all this stuff. It's not our role to get involved
- I have no time for this. I've got to get out and sell more to make our profit line.
- Corporations don't really care - they're just out to screw the poor and the environment to make their obscene profits

Businesses are owned by their shareholders - money spent on CSR by managers is theft of the rightful property of the owners. This is the voice of the laisser-faire 1980s, still being given powerful voice by advocates such as Elaine Sternberg. Sternberg argues that there is a human rights case against CSR, which is that a stakeholder approach to management deprives shareholders of their property rights. She states that the objectives sought by conventional views of social responsibility are absurd. Not all aspects of CSR are guilty of this, however. Sternberg states that ordinary decency, honesty and fairness should be expected of any corporation.

RESPONSES

In the first instance, this case strongly depends on the model of social responsibility adopted by the business being a philanthropic one. The starting point assumption is that, through CSR, corporations simply get to "give away" money which rightfully belongs to other people. If CSR is seen as a process by which the business manages its relationships with a variety of influential stakeholders who can have a real influence on its licence to operate, the business case becomes immediately apparent. CSR is about building relationships with customers, about attracting and retaining talented staff, about managing risk, and about assuring reputation.

The market capitalisation of a company often far exceeds the "property" value of the company. For instance, as much as 96% of Coca Cola is made up of "intangibles" - a major part of which rests on the reputation of the company. Only a fool would run risks with a company's reputation when it is so large a part of what the shares represent.

In any case, if shareholders are to be accorded full property rights one would expect to see the balancing feature of responsibility for the actions taken by the enterprises they often fleetingly own. Since most shareholders remain completely unaware of any such responsibility, it can only fall to the management - the "controlling mind" of the company, to take that responsibility on. The leading companies who report on their social responsibility are basket cases - the most effective business leaders don't waste time with this stuff.

When surveys are carried out of the "Most Respected Business Leaders" you will often find names there, such as Bill Gates of Microsoft, a few years ago Jack Welch of GE, who have not achieved their world class status by playing nice. Welch is still remembered for the brutal downsizing he led his business through, and for the environmental pollution incidents and prosecutions. Microsoft has had one of the highest profile cases of bullying market dominance of recent times - and Gates has been able to achieve the financial status where he can choose to give lots of money away by being ruthless in business. Doesn't that go to prove that "real men don't do CSR"?!

Response II

There is no denying the force of this argument. We do not live in a Disney world where virtue is always seen to be rewarded, and that's a fact. Nevertheless, the picture is not as simple as the above argument makes out. In the first instance, very few businesses operate in a black or white framework, where they are either wholly virtuous or wholly without redemption. There are many aspects in the way Jack Welch restructured General Electric which would play to the kind of agenda recognisable to advocates of social responsibility - in particular that of employee empowerment. Welch has gone on record as saying that he believes the time has passed when making a profit and paying taxes was all that a company had to worry about. And since Welch moved on, General Electric has been busy catching up big time with its EcoMagination initiative.

Also, many of the leading companies with regard to their social responsibility are equally successful companies. The same "Most Respected" surveys will usually provide other names at, or near, the top such as IBM and Motorola - and these are companies that have been much more strongly associated with the CSR movement. Coca Cola achieved its place partially because of its profile in social responsibility. When still in charge, Sir John Browne of BP was widely respected as having led BP into a strong position as one of the world's leading companies whilst also showing environmental leadership. The events that latterly tarnished that reputation simply show that the skill in execution is the key to success - but even those events don't disprove the fact that success in business and commitment to responsibility can go hand in hand.

Our company is too busy surviving hard times to do this. We can't afford to take our eye off the ball - we have to focus on core business. It's all very well for the very big companies with lots of resources at their disposal. For those fighting for survival, it's a very different picture. You can't go spending money on unnecessary frills when you're laying people off and morale is rock bottom. And the odd bit of employee volunteering won't make any difference to our people when they feel cynical and negative about how the company operates.

Response: Managing your social responsibility is like any other aspect of managing your business. You can do it well, or you can do it badly. If the process of managing social responsibility leads you to take your eye off the ball and stop paying attention to core business, the problem is not that you're doing it at all - it's that you're doing it badly. Well managed CSR supports the business objectives of the company, builds relationships with key stakeholders whose opinion will be most valuable when times are hard, and should reduce business costs and maximise its effectiveness.

If you don't believe, ask yourself if the following statements make sense:

- Times are hard, therefore it is in my interest to pollute more and run an increased risk of prosecutions and fines, not to mention attracting the attention of environmental pressure groups
- Times are hard; therefore can afford to lose some of my most talented people - serving or potential - by erecting barriers on the basis of race, gender, age or sexual orientation. And it doesn't matter if employment tribunals occur as a result of my poor employment practices.
- Times are hard; therefore need to ignore changing values in my customer base towards socially responsible goods and services can keep making things just the way I always have.
- Times are hard, so can ignore the fact that the local communities around my plant are poor living environments with low education achievement, meaning that my best staff won't want to live in them and our future staff will need supplementary training in basic skills such as literacy which they should be getting at school. Our company can be an island of prosperity in a sea of deprivation.

It's the responsibility of the politicians to deal with all this stuff. It's not our role to get involved. Business has traditionally been beyond morality and public policy. We will do what we're allowed to do. We expect governments to provide the legal framework that says what society will put up with. There's no point, for instance, allowing smoking to remain legal - even making large tax receipt from it - and then acting as though tobacco companies are all immediately beyond the pale. If you think it's so dreadful, you should make it illegal. If not, then let us get on with the job of meeting the demand out there of adults who can choose for themselves.

Response III

In some areas, this is right - albeit that it is getting increasingly difficult to sustain. If you consider that of all the institutions which are currently getting more powerful in the world, they are essentially the global players - the multinational corporations and the non-governmental organisations. The institutions which are decreasing in power and influence are those tied to the jurisdiction of the nation state - governments first and foremost. It is tempting therefore to look towards the multinationals to take a lead in creating solutions for global problems where the governments seem incapable of achieving co-operative solutions. The interest of Unilever in sustainable fisheries comes to mind. However, there is a strong case that says that the democratic deficit created by such a process is too important to ignore. To whom are the multinational corporations accountable?

Outside of that "macro" scale, the argument holds up less well. Many companies actually spend considerable time and money seeking to influence the formation of public policy in their area of interest. And since that area of interest can range far and wide - from international treaties on climate change, through to domestic policy on health (such as that relating to smoking) or transport - the fact is the lobbying activities of companies show that they have a role like it or not. And if that lobbying has involved blocking legislation that serves a social end purely in order to continue to profit in the short term, then the company is on very dodgy ground.

If CSR is simply about obeying the law and paying taxes, then perhaps the above statement is fair comment. If it is about managing the demands and expectations of opinion formers, customers, shareholders, local communities, governments and environmental NGOs - if it is about managing risk and reputation, and investing in community resources on which you later depend - then the argument is a nonsense.

CSR AND THE NATURE OF BUSINESS

Corporations exist to provide products and/or services that produce profits for their shareholders. Milton Friedman and others take this a step further, arguing that a corporation's purpose is to maximize returns to its shareholders, and that since (in their view), only people can have social responsibilities, corporations are only responsible to their shareholders and not to society as a whole. Although they accept that corporations should obey the laws of the countries within which they work, they assert that corporations have no other obligation to society. Some people perceive CSR as incongruent with the very nature and purpose of business, and indeed a hindrance to free trade.

Those who assert that CSR is incongruent with capitalism and are in favor of neoliberalism argue that improvements in health, longevity and/or infant mortality have been created by economic growth attributed to free enterprise. Critics of this argument perceive neoliberalism as opposed to the well-being of society and a hindrance to human freedom. They claim that the type of capitalism practiced in many developing countries is a form of economic and cultural imperialism, noting that these countries usually have fewer labor protections, and thus their citizens are at a higher risk of exploitation by multinational corporations. A wide variety of individuals and organizations operate in between these poles.

For example, the REALeadership Alliance asserts that the business of leadership (be it corporate or otherwise) is to change the world for the better. Many religious and cultural traditions hold that the economy exists to serve human beings, so all economic entities have an obligation to society (e.g., cf. Economic Justice for All). Moreover, as discussed above, many CSR proponents point out that CSR can significantly improve long-term corporate profitability because it reduces risks and inefficiencies while offering a host of potential benefits such as enhanced brand reputation and employee engagement.

CSR AND QUESTIONABLE MOTIVES CSR

Some critics believe that CSR programs are undertaken by companies such as British American Tobacco (BAT), the petroleum giant BP (well-known for its high-profile advertising campaigns on environmental aspects of its operations), and McDonald's to distract the public from ethical questions posed by their core operations. They argue that some corporations start CSR programs for the commercial benefit they enjoy through raising their reputation with the public or with government. They suggest that corporations which exist solely to maximize profits are unable to advance the interests of society as a whole.

Another concern is when companies claim to promote CSR and be committed to Sustainable Development whilst simultaneously engaging in harmful business practices. For example, since the 1970s, the McDonald's Corporation's association with Ronald McDonald House has been viewed as CSR and relationship marketing. More recently, as CSR has become mainstream, the company has beefed up its CSR programs related to its labor, environmental and other practices All the same, in McDonald's Restaurants v Morris & Steel, Lord Justices Pill, May and Keane ruled that it was fair comment to say that McDonald's employees worldwide 'do badly in terms of pay and conditions' and true that 'if one eats enough McDonald's food, one's diet may well become high in fat etc., with the very real risk of heart disease.'

Shell has a much-publicised CSR policy and was a pioneer in triple bottom line reporting, but this did not prevent the 2004 scandal concerning its misreporting of oil reserves, which seriously damaged its reputation and led to charges of hypocrisy. Since then, the Shell Foundation has become involved in many projects across the world, including a partnership with Marks and Spencer (UK) in three flower and fruit growing communities across Africa. Critics concerned with corporate hypocrisy and insincerity generally suggest that better governmental and international regulation and enforcement, rather than voluntary measures, are necessary to ensure that companies behave in a socially responsible manner.

THE PROFIT IMPERATIVE

Because maximizing return to shareholders is legally required of corporate officers, profit must be the ultimate measure of all corporate decisions. Profit necessarily takes precedence over community well-being, worker safety, public health, peace, environmental preservation, and national security.

The primacy of profit over ethics may have moderately destructive impacts, as with Enron's manipulation of electricity markets to maximize profit on the backs of California citizens. In other instances, it can mean the deaths of many innocent people, as when Ford and Firestone executives continued selling a product combination that they knew was killing many of their customers, while withholding the danger from the public. Their decision stemmed from a "rational" cost-benefit analysis which indicated that settling lawsuits resulting from fatal accidents was less costly than a recall.

If you were to knowingly withhold such information when selling your personal vehicle, you could be convicted of manslaughter in the event of a fatality; yet those executives will never see the inside of a prison cell because they effectively enjoy corporate immunity.

In both of these examples, the natural human reaction is outrage toward the decision-makers, but we should work past our visceral response. A thoughtful analysis that recognizes the profit imperative tells us that we can best prevent future harm by focusing on restoring citizen control over corporations systemically, not tackling one offender or harm at a time.

Consider this: the much-publicized financial fraud cases have occurred in (by far) the most highly scrutinized and regulated realm of corporate behavior. What might be unearthed if we adequately staffed and funded investigations into other areas where the profit imperative has more serious consequences, such as violations of workplace safety or compliance with laws to keep our drinking water and air free of toxins?

THE GROWTH IMPERATIVE

Corporations live or die by whether they grow. For a publicly-traded corporation, there is no such thing as "big enough." The growth imperative fuels the corporate drive to continually pursue new resources and markets around the world. As natural resources are depleted, new frontiers continually are sought. The effects of this imperative are now visible, as more of the world's few remaining pristine places are targeted for commercial exploitation.

Corporate planners relentlessly lure "less-developed societies" into the global corporate economy to tap new sources of consumers and cheap labor while institutions like the World Trade Organization and International Monetary Fund supplement enticements with coercive power.

Corporations generate propaganda, claiming that global corporatization (promoted as "free trade") raises living standards. But this story is contradicted by global economic data (documented extensively by the Center for Economic and Policy Research, which demonstrate that corporate colonialism—the siphoning of profit from the country or region of production—is having a debilitating impact on many developing countries.

STRUCTURAL AMORALITY

Corporations are artificial creations, shielded from obligations of personal morality and responsibility by their very design. As a result, decisions that may be antithetical to community interests, workers' welfare, or public and environmental health are made without risk of personal liability. Furthermore, having no real commitment to a particular locale, corporations can relocate easily to escape taxes, unionized employees, and environmental protection laws. In light of growing public awareness and resistance to environmental and societal harm, more corporations are seeking to veil their amorality and appear altruistic.

This practice of "greenwashing" is intended to coax more people to buy their products, services or stock, but if corporate benefits do not accrue, altruistic poses are dropped. For example, when Exxon Corporation executives realized that their spending to mitigate damage to Alaskan shores after the Valdez oil spill was not swaying public opinion enough to benefit the company's bottom line, they dropped the pretense of moral obligation and stopped the cleanup.

QUANTIFICATION

Corporations require subjective values to be translated into objective quantities that are easily tallied on balance sheets. Forests, for example, are valued only in terms of "board feet." Their immense value in sustaining life or providing clean water and spiritual nourishment goes uncounted. This carries over to government institutions that are heavily influenced by industry; hence the U.S. Forest Service considers trees worth thousands of dollars to timber companies as economically worthless unless they are cut down.

Such accounting without human values allows corporate cost/benefit analyses to be the measuring stick for many public health policies. The resulting policy of "risk-assessment" inflicts sickness and death from easily preventable pollution or toxic pesticides to avoid the "excessive" costs of healthier alternatives. Corporate political powers succeeded in pushing Congress to effectively abandon the Precautionary Principle (addressing or preventing probable health hazards proactively, rather than waiting for definitive scientific proof of public harm) when it repealed the Delaney Amendment in 1996. Delaney simply required that our food be free of proven carcinogens.

EXPLOITATION AND HOMOGENIZATION

Corporate profit depends not only on minimizing employee compensation but also on shifting costs created by business onto society as a whole, commonly called externalization. We all foot the bill for such externalized costs of pollution, illness, health care, public infrastructure to support corporate expansion, and much more. Corporate employees often are dehumanized—seen as replaceable parts in a machine. For managers in the corporate workplace, personal morality must not interfere with profit-based decision making, though these decisions often carry deep personal, community, or environmental consequences. A CEO who resists moving a factory overseas to evade environmental regulations or refuses to cut workers' pay soon will be replaced if these actions result in an unexploited opportunity for profit.

Corporations have a tremendous stake in fostering homogeneous consumers and conformity. Consumption accelerates as more people believe that certain commodities bring material satisfaction. Inner satisfaction, self-sufficiency, and contentment in nature are subversive to corporate goals. As transnational chains increasingly dominate commerce, native societies are pressured to give up their traditional ways and join the corporate global culture—uniqueness is gradually vanquished.

LACK OF LIMITATIONS

Our country's founders and many subsequent generations recognized the danger in allowing corporations to grow in size and power. Corporations initially were given a limited lifespan, barred from engaging in any activity not expressly permitted, and relegated to a narrow range of permissible actions. Corporations were deemed appropriate tools to serve a public benefit through engaging in commerce but were fully subordinate to democracy and prohibited from legally attempting to influence elections, education, public policy, and other realms of civic society.

But it's easy to forget lessons not learned through personal experience. For more than a century, we have permitted corporations to elude democratic control and escape our limitations on their lifespan, size, and activities. We have yielded to them immense power to weaken citizen sovereignty over business and to shape our laws and government. As a result of vast political power, the majority of harms caused by corporations are perfectly legal, rendering even rigorous enforcement of the laws governing corporate actions inadequate. Banishing corporations from political participation is a necessary first step to reclaiming our democracy.

We must abandon the absurd notion that corporations can reform themselves. Such notions deceive and distract us from our fundamental work. This does not mean we should fail to support the efforts of those working to improve corporate actions from within; but merely asking for greater "corporate responsibility" makes little more sense than asking a bulldozer to act responsibly. Even *Business Ethics* magazine founder Marjorie Kelly now writes "it won't be enough to rely on voluntary initiatives, codes of conduct, enlightened leadership...we must change the fundamental governing framework for all corporations in law."

It is we the people who must be responsible, as we have not been for over 100 years, and relegate corporations to their proper role—a tool for serving the public interest. Only by disillusioning ourselves can we hope to see the roots of our problems and recognize our responsibility: to restore our authority over corporations as citizens and re-program the machine.

DRIVERS

Corporations may be influenced to adopt CSR practices by several drivers.

Ethical Consumerism

The rise in popularity of ethical consumerism over the last two decades can be linked to the rise of CSR. As global population increases, so does the pressure on limited natural resources required to meet rising consumer demand. Industrialization in many developing countries is booming as a result of technology and globalisation. Consumers are becoming more aware of the environmental and social implications of their day-to-day consumer decisions and are beginning to make purchasing decisions related to their environmental and ethical concerns. However, this practice is far from consistent or universal.

GLOBALISATION AND MARKET FORCES

As corporations pursue growth through globalisation, they have encountered new challenges that impose limits to their growth and potential profits. Government regulations, tariffs, environmental restrictions and varying standards of what constitutes labour exploitation are problems that can cost organizations millions of dollars. Some view ethical issues as simply a costly hindrance. Some companies use CSR methodologies as a strategic tactic to gain public support for their presence in global markets, helping them sustain a competitive advantage by using their social contributions to provide a subconscious level of advertising. Global competition places particular pressure on multinational corporations to examine not only their own labour practices, but those of their entire supply chain, from a CSR perspective.

SOCIAL AWARENESS AND EDUCATION

The role among corporate stakeholders to work collectively to pressure corporations is changing. Shareholders and investors themselves, through socially responsible investing are exerting pressure on corporations to behave responsibly. Non-governmental organizations are also taking an increasing role, leveraging the power of the media and the Internet to increase their scrutiny and collective activism around corporate behavior. Through education and dialogue, the development of community in holding businesses responsible for their actions is growing.

Ethics Training

The rise of ethics training inside corporations, some of it required by government regulation, is another driver credited with changing the behaviour and culture of corporations. The aim of such training is to help employees make ethical decisions when the answers are unclear. Tullberg believes that humans are built with the capacity to cheat and manipulate, a view taken from, hence the need for learning normative values and rules in human behaviour. The most direct benefit is reducing the likelihood of "dirty hands", fines and damaged reputations for breaching laws or moral norms.

Organisations also see secondary benefit in increasing employee loyalty and pride in the organization. Caterpillar and Best Buy are examples of organizations that have taken such steps. Increasingly, companies are becoming interested in processes that can add visibility to their CSR policies and activities. One method that is gaining increasing popularity is the use of well-grounded training programmes, where CSR is a major issue, and business simulations can play a part in this.

LAWS AND REGULATION

Another driver of CSR is the role of independent mediators, particularly the government, in ensuring that corporations are prevented from harming the broader social good, including people and the environment. CSR critics such as Robert Reich argue that governments should set the agenda for social responsibility by the way of laws and regulation that will allow a business to conduct them responsibly. The issues surrounding government regulation pose several problems. Regulation in itself is unable to cover every aspect in detail of a corporation's operations. This leads to burdensome legal processes bogged down in interpretations of the law and debatable grey areas.

General Electric is an example of a corporation that has failed to clean up the Hudson River after contaminating it with organic pollutants. The company continues to argue via the legal process on assignment of liability, while the cleanup remains stagnant.

The second issue is the financial burden that regulation can place on a nation's economy. This view shared by Bulkeley, who cites the Australian federal government's actions to avoid compliance with the Kyoto Protocol in 1997, on the concerns of economic loss and national interest. The Australian government took the position that signing the Kyoto Pact would have caused more significant economic losses for Australia than for any other OECD nation. Critics of CSR also point out that organisations pay taxes to government to ensure that society and the environment are not adversely affected by business activities.

CRISES AND THEIR CONSEQUENCES

Often it takes a crisis to precipitate attention to CSR. One of the most active stands against environmental management is the CERES Principles that resulted after the Exxon Valdez incident in Alaska in 1989. Other examples include the lead poisoning paint used by toy giant Mattel, which required a recall of millions of toys globally and caused the company to initiate new risk management and quality control processes. In another example, Magellan Metals in the West Australian town of Esperance was responsible for lead contamination killing thousands of birds in the area. The company had to cease business immediately and work with independent regulatory bodies to execute a cleanup.

STAKEHOLDER PRIORITIES

Increasingly, corporations are motivated to become more socially responsible because their most important stakeholders expect them to understand and address the social and community issues that are relevant to them. Understanding what causes are important to employees is usually the first priority because of the many interrelated business benefits that can be derived from increased employee engagement (i.e. more loyalty, improved recruitment, increased retention, higher productivity, and so on). Key external stakeholders include customers, consumers, investors (particularly institutional investors, regulators, academics, and the media).

LATIN AMERICA AND THE CARIBBEAN

The move towards CSR is relatively new in Latin America and the Caribbean and is gaining ground as companies are pressed to adapt to the demands of the global economy. For small and medium enterprises (SMEs) in this region, adopting

CSR practices can open doors to new market opportunities and bring a number of other benefits including reduced costs, improved bottom lines and public image, and greater opportunities to do business with other SMEs or larger firms.

The levels of corporate citizenship are corporate governance law, corporate philanthropy and corporate social responsibility. Corporate citizenship means adhering to laws, and complying with some standards. Corporate philanthropy means helping communities via social investments. Corporate social responsibility requires performance of one's obligations to stakeholders

In addition to these benefits, adopting responsible management practices can also help smaller businesses access the capital they need to grow.

To further promote the expansion of CSR among small and medium enterprises in the region, there are a number of obstacles to overcome: the lack of understanding among SMEs about CSR; the scarcity of trained experts in the region to build business capacity in this area; and insufficient shareholder or government pressure on companies to make their management records public. The Multilateral Investment Fund is working to address these challenges through projects aiming to raise awareness among SMEs in Latin America and the Caribbean about the benefits of CSR and to support smaller companies in their efforts to implement CSR measures.

MIF also partners with large companies, foundations and universities interested in building awareness and spreading CSR knowledge to businesses throughout the region.

4

Social Development Theory

Social development is a process which results in the transformation of social structures in a manner which improves the capacity of the society to fulfill its aspirations. Society develops by consciousness and social consciousness develops by organization. The process that is subconscious in the society emerges as conscious knowledge in pioneering individuals. Development is a process, not a programme. Its power issues more from its subtle aspects than from material objects. Not all social change constitutes develop-ment. It consists of four well-marked stages – survival, growth, development and evolution, each of which contains the other three within it.

The quantitative expansion of existing activities generates growth or horizontal expansion. Development implies a qualitative change in the way the society carries out its activities, such as through more progressive attitudes and behavior by the population, the adoption of more effective social organizations or more advanced technology which may have been developed elsewhere. The term evolution refers to the original formulation and adoption of qualitative and structural advances in the form of new social attitudes, values, behaviors, or organizations.

While the term is usually applied to changes that are beneficial to society, it may result in negative side-effects or consequences that undermine or eliminate existing ways of life that are considered positive. The formulation of valid theory possesses enormous power to elevate and accelerate the expansion and development of human capabilities in any field, leading to fresh discoveries, improvement of existing activities and capacity for greater results. Science is replete with examples of theoretical formulations that have led to important breakthroughs, such as the discoveries of Neptune and Pluto, electromagnetic waves, subatomic particles, and new elements on the periodic table.

Today scientists are discovering new substances on computer by applying the laws of quantum mechanics to predict the properties of materials before they synthesize them. In fact, a broad range of technological achievements in this century has been made possible by the emergence of sound theoretical knowledge in fields such as physics, chemistry and biology. As management expert Peter Drucker put it, "There is nothing more practical than a good theory." Valid theory can tell us not only what should be done, but also what can be done and the process by which it can be achieved. Social development can be summarily described as the process of organizing human energies and activities at higher levels to achieve greater results. Development increases the utilization of human potential.

In the absence of valid theory, social development remains largely a process of trial and error experimentation, with a high failure rate and very uneven progress. The dismal consequences of transition strategies in most Eastern Europe countries, the very halting progress of many African and Asian countries, the increasing income gap between the most and least developed societies, and the distressing linkage between rising incomes, environmental depletion, crime and violence reflect the fact that humanity is vigorously pursuing a process without the full knowledge needed to guide and govern it effectively. Advances in development theory can enhance our social success rate by the same order of magnitude that advances in theoretical physics have multiplied technological achievements in this century. The emergence of a sound theoretical framework for social development would provide the knowledge needed to address these inadequacies. It would also eventually lead us to the most profound and practical discovery of all – the infinite creative potentials of the human being.

HIERARCHY OF LEARNING

Social development consists of two interrelated aspects – learning and application. Society discovers better ways to fulfill its aspirations and it develops organizational mechanisms to express that knowledge to achieve its social and economic goals. The process of discovery expands human consciousness. The process of application enhances social organization. Society develops in response to the contact and interaction between human beings and their material, social and intellectual environment. The incursion of external threats, the pressure of physical and social conditions, the mysteries of physical nature and complexities of human behavior prompt humanity to experiment, create and innovate.

The experience resulting from these contacts leads to learning on three different levels of our existence. At the physical level, it enhances our control over material processes. At the social level, it enhances our capacity for effective interaction between people at greater and greater speeds and distances. At the mental level, it enhances our knowledge. While the learning process takes place simultaneously on all these planes, there is a natural progression from physical experience to mental understanding. Historically, society has developed by a trial and error process of physical experimentation, not unlike the way children learn through a constant process of physical exploration, testing and even tasting.

Physically, this process leads to the acquisition of new physical skills that enable individuals to utilize their energies more efficiently and effectively. Socially, it leads to the learning and mastery of organizational skills, vital attitudes, systems and institutions that enable people to manage their interactions with other people and other societies more effectively. Mentally, it leads to organization of facts as information and interpretation of information as thought. The outcome of this learning process is the organization of physical skills, social systems, and information, which are then utilized to improve the efficiency and effectiveness of human activities. It is a cyclical process in which people are continuously learning from past experiences and then applying that learning in new activities.

This learning process culminates in a higher level of mental effort to extract the essence and common principles or ideas from society's organized physical experiences, social interactions and accumulated information and to synthesize them as conceptual knowledge. This abstract conceptual knowledge has the greatest capacity for generalization and application in other fields, times and places. The conceptual mind is the highest, most conscious human faculty. Conceptual knowledge is the organization of ideas by the power of mind. That conceptual knowledge becomes most powerful when it is organized into a system. Theory is a systematic organization of knowledge.

A comprehensive theory of social development would provide a conceptual framework for discovering the underlying principles common to the development process in different fields of activity, countries and periods. It would also provide a framework for understanding the relationships between the accumulated knowledge generated by many different disciplines. If pursued to its logical conclusions, it would lead to not just a theory of social development, but a unifying theory of knowledge—which does not yet exist in any field of science or art.

SEARCH FOR A SOCIAL OPERATING SYSTEM

Rapid advancement in computer technology and application has primarily been the result of dramatic progress in two parallel but interrelated fields - development of the processing capacity of the silicon chip and development of more advanced operating systems that enable users to utilize the chip's greater computing power. Chip development increases the *potential power* of the computer. Development of more powerful, intuitive and easier to use operating systems increases the *practical power* of the technology. As a parallel, advances in scientific and technical knowledge have vastly increased the potential productivity and developmental achievements of society. But full utilization of this potential requires the capacity to consciously direct and accelerate social development processes.

The discovery of methods to genetically engineer improved varieties of food crops or to control population growth through improved medical devices would have little practical value unless we also possessed the know-how to promote dissemination and adoption of these advanced technologies. Historically, advances in our understanding of material and biological process have far outstripped advances in our understanding of social processes. As a result, vast social potential has been created, but society has not yet acquired the capacity to fully utilize it for its own development. A theory of development should aim at a knowledge that will enable society more consciously and effectively to utilize its development potentials.

Why a Framework has not yet Emerged

A question naturally arises. If such a framework is possible, why with all the attention focused on development for so many decades has it not yet emerged? Social development theory has been elusive for several reasons. First, because of the very practical importance of this issue, attention in this field has very largely focused on the material results of development and on those strategies that have proven most effective for achieving those results, rather than on abstract principles or theoretical concepts. Rapid economic progress in North America and Europe after the Second World War, which was followed by even more stunning achievements in Japan and other East Asian nations, imbued governments and the international community with the confidence that development was primarily a question of money, technology, industrialization and political will.

Confident that the lessons of early achievers provided all the knowledge necessary for those that were to follow, there was an urge for concerted action and an expectation of results, rather than a quest for theoretical knowledge. In most discussions, development was conceived in terms of a set of desirable results—higher incomes, longer life expectancy, lower infant mortality, more education. Recently emphasis has shifted from the results to the enabling conditions, strategies and public policies for achieving those results—peace, democracy, social freedoms, equal access, laws, institutions, markets, infrastructure, education and technology. But still little attention has been placed on the underlying social process of development that determines how society formulates, adopts, initiates, and organizes, and few attempts have been made to formulate such a framework.

Second, a very large number of factors and conditions influence the process. In addition to all the variables that influence material and biological processes, social processes involve the interaction of political, social, economic cultural, technological and environmental factors as well. Development theorists have not only to cope with atoms, molecules, material energy and various life forms. They must also cope with the near infinite variety and complexity of human beliefs, opinions, attitudes, values, behaviors, customs, prejudices, laws, social institutions, etc. Third, the timeframe for social development theory cannot be confined to the modern day or even the past few centuries. Human development has been occurring for millennia. The basic principles of development theory must be as applicable to the development of early tribal societies as they are to the emergence of the post-modern global village. Development theory must be a theory of how human society advances through space and time.

LOOKING BEYOND THE INSTRUMENTS

Fourth, the instruments of development—science and technology, capital and infrastructure, social policies and institutions—are so compellingly powerful in their action, that they are often mistaken for its cause and source. Most efforts to understand the development process have focused on the central importance of one or a few of these instruments—primarily on money, markets, the organiza-tion of production and technological innovation. Some efforts have also been made to describe what has been learned about the contribution of education, skills, laws, public policies, strategies, social systems and institutions.

While it is evident that all of these instruments can and do play an important role in social development, it has not been adequately explained what determines the development of these instruments themselves or the extent to which they are utilized by society or the process by which they can be made to generate maximum results. Obviously, the ultimate determinants of development cannot be the instruments themselves, for none of them exists independently from society. To understand the central principles of development, we must look beyond these instruments to the creator of the instruments. Human beings fashion technology, invent money, erect infrastructures, establish policies, build institutions and adopt values to serve their needs and aspirations.

Although humanity exhibits a strong tendency to mistake these instruments for primary determinants rather than created products of its own initiative, the ultimate power of determination must lie with the human beings who create and use these instruments, rather than with the instruments themselves. Money and technology do have useful power, including a power of organization and efficiency, a power to increase the velocity of production and transactions. But they do not possess an intrinsic living power for growth or development, a source of aspiration or energy that compels their own advancement. Moore's Law describing advances in the speed of microprocessors is not driven by material forces—the microprocessor does not increase its own speed—it is driven by humanity's quest for greater productive power.

The surge in value of financial markets is not driven by impersonal physical or mathematical laws governing the growth of money, but by the quest of human beings for greater material prosperity. This self-existent power for growth is an endowment of human beings, living organisms compelled to develop by a pressure within themselves, which in turn gives life and energy to the growth of the instruments and systems they create. What has been lacking is an organized theoretical framework that describes the role of each of these instruments as aspects of a greater whole and shows each in its proper relation to the others or the greater whole of which they are all parts.

To arrive at such a framework, we have to shift our focus from the instruments of development to their creator; from the role of money and technology to the role of human beings that invent new forms of money and technology and harness them for productive purposes. The theory has to place human beings at the center and view all other aspects of development from the perspective of and in relation to human motivation and action. This conceptual knowledge of the development process should enable every society to better utilize the available instruments better, in order more fully to tap its developmental potential.

DEVELOPMENT AS A SPHERICAL WHOLE

A theory of social development should generate a framework around which all knowledge of the factors, instruments, conditions, agencies and processes of development can be integrated. Rather than singling out a specific set of determinants or giving primacy to a limited set of instruments, it would reveal the nature of the relationships and processes that govern the interaction of all these elements to generate developmental results. Rather than generate a linear formula or 'right' perspective, it would make it possible to view the whole field and phenomenon of development from multiple perspectives that are integrated and unified ways of knowing the whole, rather than divided and separate ways of viewing the parts.

The modern tendency to divide scientific inquiry into an increasing number of specialized fields of study has made the emergence of an integrated perspective very difficult.

Philosopher Stephen Toulmin mourns the absence of broader conceptual thinking in physics over the past few centuries and argues the need for grand cosmological visions of the universe to unify and integrate the discoveries of many different disciplines. Comparatively, the need for synthesis is even greater for the study of human social development than for understanding the physical and chemical evolution of the universe.

For in human development, we must not only grapple with four material dimensions in space and time that preoccupy the physicist and chemist, but also integrate the dimensions of life and mind—including physical, genetic and biological determinants; social behaviors, skills, attitudes, customs, traditions, systems, formal organizations, non-formal institutions, and cultural values; and linguistic determinants, data, facts, information, beliefs, opinions, systems of thought, ideas, theories, and spiritual values—all of which interact and influence each other to impact the course of human development.

The quest for theory in social development cannot lead to any linear or logarithmic equation that adequately explains and predicts human progress. The reality we seek to understand is not of that type. It is not linear or unidimensional or evens a combination of several dimensions. It is a complex, many-dimensional whole that evolves in many interrelated directions simultaneously. The development of society is best represented to our minds as an expansion from a point to a sphere, rather than as movement along a single line or along multiple lines of progress. Social development is the gradual discovery and unfolding of the potential of a complex, integrated whole, a living organization, a living social organism.

From Unconscious Experience to Conscious Knowledge

Finally, social development theory remains elusive because the very nature of social learning is a subconscious seeking by the collective that leads ultimately to conscious knowledge. We experience first and understand later. Our mental comprehension perpetually lags behind physical experience and struggles to catch up with it. Our view is that the very intensive, concentrated global experience of the past five decades provides fertile soil for the formulation of a more synthetic conceptual framework for social development. Such a framework can vastly accelerate the transfer and replication of developmental achievements around the world and make possible more conscious and rapid progress even for the most advanced societies in the world.

Basic premises

These observations suggest a starting point for formulation of a comprehensive conceptual framework:

- Social development theory should focus on underlying processes rather than on surface activities and results, since development activities, policies, strategies, programs and results will always be limited to a specific context and circumstance, whereas social development itself encompasses a potentially infinite field in space and time.
- The theory should recognize the inherent creativity of individuals and of societies by which they fashion instruments and direct their energies to achieve greater results. It should view development as a human creative process, rather than as the product of any combination of external factors or objective instruments that are created and utilized as the process unfolds and whose results are limited to the capacity of the instruments. Society will discover its own creative potentials only when it seeks to know the human being as the real source of those potentials.
- The implication of this view is that even though it may be influenced, aided or opposed by external factors, society develops by its own motive power and in pursuit of its own goals. No external force and agency can develop a society. (Paul Hoffman, the Administrator of the Marshall Plan for European Recovery who later became the first head of the United Nations Development Program, said it succinctly: "Technical assistance cannot be exported. It

can only be imported." The aspiration of the collective expressed through the initiative of pioneering individuals is the determinant and driving force for a society's own development.

DEVELOPMENT AS SELF-CONCEPTION

Material and biological sciences focus on the interaction of physical conditions, materials and forces to generate results. The tendency to view social development in the same way has led to a host of mathematical equations seeking to define and predict the consequences of combining different external variables in different proportions and under different conditions. The underlying assumption of this approach is that social development is determined by external conditions.

The hypothesis on which our attempt at theory is based is that social development is determined by human beings, not external conditions. External conditions certainly can and do influence the process. People may even act and react in predictable ways to a given set of external conditions. But the results of any development equation cannot be reliably predicted on the basis of external factors.

Human development is determined by human responses based on choices made by people. To our knowledge, external forces alone have never unleashed a process of social development, but there are countless instances in which external agents have failed to do so. Human development is a function of human awareness, aspirations, attitudes and values.

Like all human creative processes, it is a process of self-conception. As the writer, artist, composer, political visionary and businessman conceive of unrealized possibilities and pour forth their creative energies to give expression to them, the social collective evolves a conception of what it wants to become and by expressing its creative energies through myriad forms of activity seeks to transform its conception into social reality.

The only major difference is that while the individual sometimes (but not always) is conscious of the conception he or she is trying to express, the society is usually (not always) unconscious of the idea and the urge that move it to create something more out of its own latent potential. Society is a subconscious living organism which strives to survive, grow and develop. Individual members of society express conscious intention in their words and acts, but these are only surface expressions of deeper subconscious drives that move the society-at-large.

The consciousness of a true collective organism is not merely the sum of its individual parts, but acquires its own identifiable character and personality. This is why the USA has been able to assimilate such large numbers of immigrants, yet retain its distinctive (but constantly changing) national character.

Immigrants are moved by the values of the collective to share in the national aspiration for greater individual freedom, practical organization and material progress. In a similar vein, the feverish collective behavior of the stock market, fashions and pop culture are subconscious social collectives that acquire their own distinct personalities.

ROLE OF THE INDIVIDUAL

Society has no direct means to give conscious expression to its subconscious collective aspirations and urges. That essential role is played by pioneering conscious individuals–visionary intellectuals, political leaders, entrepreneurs, artists and spiritual seekers who are inspired to express and achieve what the collective subconsciously aspires and is prepared for.

Where the aspiration and action of the leader do not reflect the will of the collective, it is ignored or rejected. Where it gives expression to a deeply felt collective urge, it is endorsed, imitated, supported, and systematically propagated.

This is most evident at times of war, social revolution or communal conflict. India's early freedom fighters consciously advocated the goal of freedom from British rule long before that goal had become a felt aspiration of the masses. The leaders spent decades urging a reluctant population to conceive of itself as a free nation and to aspire to achieve that dream. When finally the collective endorsed this conception, no foreign nation had the power to impose its will on the Indian people.

PROCESS OF VALUE CREATION

During the World Academy of Art & Science's meeting on development theory in Washington DC in May 1999, there was a broad consensus of participants that the formation of values was a critical aspect of the development process. In this chapter, we propose to re-examine the process of development as a process of value formation. If gross physical actions are the most visible and tangible form of human initiative, the creation of values is the most subtle and intangible. Yet human existence is powerfully determined by the nature of its values. Physical skills, vital attitudes, mental opinions and values represent a gradation of internal organizing principles that direct human energies and determine the course of individual and social develop-ment.

All human creative processes release and harness human energy and convert it into results. The process of skill formation involves acquiring mastery over our physical-nervous energies so that we can direct our physical movements in a precisely controlled manner. In the absence of skill, physical movements are clumsy, inefficient and unproductive, like the stumbling efforts of a child learning to walk. Human beings acquire social behaviors in a similar manner. Here, apart from the physical skills required for communication and interaction with other people, vital attitudes are centrally important. Each social behavior expresses not just a movement, but an attitude and intention of the person.

Acquiring social behaviors requires gaining control over our psychological energies and channeling them into acceptable forms of behavior. Change the attitude and the behavior changes. The developmental achievements of modern society are founded upon such intangible social attitudes as confidence in the government, trust in other people, tolerance and cooperation. Without such attitudes, our money would become valueless paper and our institutions would cease to function. The same process takes place at the mental level.

The mind's energy naturally flows as thought in many different directions without any structure to contain or organize it. The acquisition of knowledge involves construction of a mental structure of understanding that is analogous to the structure of skills and attitudes that govern expression of our physical and vital energy.

It forms an organizational framework for learning and application of what is learned. Human values are formed by a similar process and act in a similar manner. Although the word is commonly used with reference to ethical and cultural principles, values are of many types. They may be physical (cleanliness, punctuality), organizational (communication, coordination), psychological (courage, generosity), mental (objectivity, sincerity), or spiritual (harmony, love, self-giving). Values are central organizing principles or ideas that govern and determine human behavior.

Unlike the skill or attitude that may be specific to a particular physical activity or social context, values tend to be more universal in their application. They express in everything we do. Values can be described as the essence of the knowledge gained by humanity from past experiences distilled from its local circumstances and specific context to extract the fundamental wisdom of life derived from these experiences. Values give direction to our thought processes, sentiments, emotional energies, preferences and actions. Centuries of experience have been distilled by society into essential principles. Values such as hard work, sense of responsibility, integrity in human relations, tolerance and respect for others are not just noble ideas or ideals. They are pragmatic principles for accomplishment which society has learned and transmitted to successive generations as a psychological foundation for its further advancement.

The values of a society are a crucial aspect of its people's self-conception of what they want to become. Because values are intangible to our senses and their formation is the result of a very long process, we tend to overlook their central rôle in development. Social values constitute the cultural infrastructure on which all further social development is based. In this sense, values are the ultimate product of past development and the ultimate determinant of its future course.

DEVELOPMENT AND VALUE CREATION IN INDEPENDENT INDIA

In *Human Choice: the Genetic Code for Social Develop-ment,* we described the development process as one that releases, organizes and converts human energy into social capacity and material results. In summary, the process consists of pioneering individuals who consciously conceive and initiate new forms of activity which give expression to the subconscious aspirations and preparedness of the society. These pioneers are imitated by others so that the new activity gets replicated and diffused. Gradually, the general population comes to recognize, accept and support the new activity by formally organizing it through laws, policies, programs, systems, organizations and education.

Eventually, the activity may become so fully integrated with the society that the need for formal structures gives way to non-formal social institutions and still later becomes assimilated as cultural values of the society. Although we describe the process as a clean linear progression, its actual occurrence is more complex. Each stage of the process interacts with those that come earlier and later to effect a general movement in a certain direction. And while the underlying process remains the same, the external results and strategies employed to achieve those results may vary significantly from one place and time to another, even within the same society.

Both the stages and the complexity of the process can be observed by examining two remarkable development accomplishments of Independent India – the Green Revolution in Indian agriculture and the high tech revolution that is making India an international software powerhouse. The starting point for free India was a value base molded by centuries of social stagnation and foreign rule. During the British Raj, the predominant values espoused by the subject Indian population were respect for age and tradition, submission to authority, and acceptance of one's assigned place and role in society. Fear and insecurity were powerful social motives.

Ambition was frowned upon. Security was cherished. Industrial and commercial activities were severely restricted by the foreign rulers. Few had the means or opportunity to acquire education. Those that did invariably sought employment in the British administration or British firms, the twin seats of power and prestige in Indian society. After Indian Independence in 1947, the values of submissiveness and obedience persisted for several decades; even though they became increasingly inadequate concepts to meet the nation's needs or respond to its opportunities. In the 1950s and 1960s, educated Indian youth sought the security and prestige of government employment, when what was really needed was entrepreneurial initiative to build the national economy.

Having achieved Independence, the leaders of India's freedom fight turned to the challenge of developing the country, but found the same lack of awareness and responsiveness from the population that the earlier freedom fighters had encountered at the turn of the century. Waging a war on poverty without the active support and participation of the people proved even more challenging than waging a war on foreign rule without an army. Until the mid 1960s, India's economic progress was almost completely overshadowed by the explosive growth of its population, the combined effect of a release of national energies from the suppressed condition of foreign domination and the introduction of modern medical technology which drastically reduced mortality rates.

Beneath the surface, the spread of democratic voting

rights, implementation of legislation to eradicate caste privileges, and rising levels of education were breaking down traditional barriers, generating national pride and releasing fresh social energy, creating awareness of possibilities and preparing the society for the next stages of its collective effort.

These new attitudes could be observed primarily among the youth born after Independence, often taking on the appearance of assertiveness and crude self-seeking, rather than of noble values. This preparedness was called into action by the sudden impact of two successive years of severe drought in the mid 1960s, which threatened the country with famine on an unprecedented scale. The challenge of widespread famine—estimated by the UN to be threatening the lives of 10 million people—led to the launching of India's Green Revolution. With the support of large food imports, the country averted the immediate threat of famine.

Then in response to a concerted government action to implement a comprehensive, integrated development strategy, within a very short period of five years, millions of India's farmers adopted new cultivation practices, the nation increased its food grain production by 50% and achieved food self-sufficiency. Within ten years grain production had doubled. Within a quarter century it had quadrupled. The pride and confidence generated by this remarkable achievement helped spur a dramatic change in India's social values that was reflected in many walks of life. Areas in which agriculture had become prosperous began to industrialize. There was a marked increase in demand for education and for consumer products. Indian society became more active and dynamic.

In the 1970s the preference of educated youth shifted to employment in private companies. Then in the 1980s a generation born after Independence established itself in the nation's workforce, people who had never known a foreign master or experienced subjection or feared famine. New values began to emerge among the younger generation. Talented youth began starting businesses in increasing numbers. Many sought education and work experience overseas, then returned to India to establish companies of their own. The value of security gave way to an aspiration for accomplishment. The sense of knowing one's proper place gave way to an urge for higher levels of achievement, status and enjoyment. A fundamental change in social values underpinned a fundamental shift in the direction and expression of India's national energies from minimum survival to maximum development.

This shift has been by no means uniform, universal or entire. It has occurred at different rates and to different extents in different communities, classes and parts of the country, but the change in general direction became increasingly evident. The development process that led to India's Green Revolution differed in its external expression from that which has more recently led to India's extraordinary achievements in the global software industry. The very notion that India could achieve international fame in a high technology industry was inconceivable to the national consciousness 20 years ago. As recently as 1983, India was employing fewer than 10,000 software engineers generating about $10 million a year in software exports.

Sixteen years later, India's software export revenues are approaching $4 billion. Most major USA and many other large foreign computer firms have established companies or joint ventures in India to develop software for export. The country's two largest software training companies educate more than a quarter million programmers annually, roughly five times the total number of computer graduates produced by all US colleges and universities.

New software companies and training institutions are sprouting up in every urban area. State governments are competing with each other for dominance in high technology. And Microsoft's Bill Gates recently christened India as "the Silicon Valley of Asia". This phenomenal accomplishment was made possible by and has further contributed to a general shift in social values that is evidenced in the behavior of people at all levels and in all parts of the society, including youth, students, women, farmers, lower castes, minorities and entrepreneurs.

Viewed from the perspective of the traditional values that had characterized India during centuries of foreign occupation, this shift appears to some as a degradation of social values (a decline in respect for age, tradition and authority; a loss of deference, humility, and the spirit of idealistic self-sacrifice) in much the same way that the advent of democratic values in Europe seemed abhorrent to those who embraced the values of the feudal, aristocratic society that was disappearing.

Attention has focused on the vulgar self-seeking, greed, crass materialism and corruption associated with India's economic and social awakening – so much so, that the positive values that have been responsible for the country's recent accomplishments and form the infrastructure for its future progress are often overlooked. The essential knowledge India has derived from five decades of development experience has been distilled into a new set of social values based on national self-confidence, self-reliance, boldness, insistence on one's rights, greater social tolerance and social equality, and aspiration for higher accomplishment.

SAME PROCESS, DIFFERENT STRATEGIES

The challenge for development theorists is to discover in India's recent experiences fundamental principles and processes that are common to these two distinctly different instances of rapid social advancement, as well as to other instances of development in other countries, periods, and fields of activity. At first glance, the differences are far more apparent than the similarities. Green Revolution was the result of a conscious, planned initiative by government which passed legislation, established new organizations, widely disseminated information and skills, introduced programs and offered financial incentives to spur India's agricultural community to action.

In contrast, the software revolution was the result of initiatives by individual entrepreneurial pioneers which were not planned by government and were not part of a conscious national strategy. The role of government was largely confined to removing administrative and tax barriers that discouraged import of computer equipment and to investment in the essential telecommunications infrastructure required to support this industry. Yet on closer inspection, India's progress in agriculture and software conform to a common process. Both achievements were made possible by a general social readiness and awakening of the population resulting from rising levels of education, public awareness, social freedom and national confidence. Achievement of Independence and self-government prepared the ground for the Green Revolution.

The breakthrough in agriculture prepared the ground for industrialization. Advances in engineering and science education, drawing on an historical Indian endowment in mathematics, the exposure of large numbers of Indians seeking higher education in the USA to the latest information technology, and the emergence of a thriving entrepreneurial business culture in India, prepared the ground for the country's active participation in the Information Revolution. India's agricultural achievements were very largely the result of conscious initiatives taken by visionary political leaders with the support of the scientific community.

The early pioneers of India's Green Revolution were public leaders, not private individuals as in the case of software. But in both cases the acceptance and spread of the new activity crucially depended on the willingness of the population to respond to the opportunity. In the case of Green Revolution, India's planners faced the seemingly impossible task of persuading millions of illiterate, traditional farmers to adopt new agricultural technology based on new varieties of wheat and rice, which required heavy investments in hybrid seeds, fertilizers and pesticides. The organization of more than 100,000 demonstration plots of the new varieties on farmers' fields, which proved that the hybrids would not only grow but would also generate many times higher yields and profits, spurred extremely rapid diffusion of the new cultivation methods in progressive agricultural regions of the country.

In the case of software, the demonstration effect was informal and private, but equally dramatic. The spread of information about young Indian engineers who had found high paying jobs as programmers in the USA, and about Indian software export companies that were growing rapidly, generated widespread interest and spurred others to imitate these successful practices. Examples spread by word of mouth from family to family about a son or daughter who had been recruited on campus for a job overseas at ten or twenty times the equivalent Indian salaries. The business press reported the export achievements of every new software startup. State governments announced ambitious plans to promote high tech industry. Politicians vied with each other to appear most in tune with the high tech culture. In both cases the initiatives of pioneers released an explosion of energy and initiative from the general population. Within less than half a decade in the late 1960s, millions of uneducated traditional farmers rushed to embrace the new production technology for food grains.

Within a similar period in the mid-1990s, hundreds of thousands of educated youth throughout the country have been inspired to enlist in computer programming courses and seek employment in the burgeoning software industry. For the initiative of pioneers to diffuse through society requires the active support of formal organizational mechanisms.

Government had a role to play in organizing both India's agricultural and its software activities, but its role in the two instances differed markedly. In the mid 1960s, India lacked dynamic private initiative capable of responding rapidly to challenges and opportunities. An adult population born under foreign rule and slow to believe in its own greater potentials, moved hesitantly to embrace change. India also lacked the social organization needed to support rapid change. Markets were undeveloped and inefficient, so that surplus food production in one region of the country was not efficiently channeled to meet the needs of markets in food deficit regions.

Information flowed slowly. Agricultural education and

scientific research, almost exclusively government activities at the time, had to be restructured and upgraded to support the new production technologies. Financial institutions were undeveloped and most wealth was in the form of tangible assets such as land that could not be readily converted into new forms of investment. As a result, the government had to play a very major role in supporting and promoting the Green Revolution through public agencies. Food Corporation of India, Warehousing Corporation, National Seeds Corporation, Fertilizer Corporation, Agricultural Price Commission and countless other agencies were established to provide the social infrastructure for modernization of agriculture.

So prominent was the role of government, that it led many to the conclusion that the government's administrative efforts were responsible for the Green Revolution and that similar results could be achieved in other fields through administrative mandate. The fallacy in this thinking was a major reason for India's slow progress in other fields following the success of Green Revolution. The country had achieved, but it had not yet drawn the essential lesson from its achievement. The real key to the success of Green Revolution was the response of the rural population to the opportunity. India's leaders astutely recognized that unless the farmer was confident of not only growing more but also selling more grain at a profitable price, there would be no motivation to adopt the new technology.

In the absence of established national markets for food grain, bumper harvests in the past resulted in falling prices and little financial benefit to the farmer. To overcome this problem, the Government instituted a guaranteed floor price for food grains and established Food Corporation to market surpluses in food deficit regions. The importance of these formal institutions has diminished significantly over the past few decades as the new methods have become standard practice among farmers and as private firms, markets, and research organizations have grown in capacity to carry out with greater efficiency the work initially undertaken by government. Development through formal organization has gradually matured into an informal social institution in this field.

In contrast, the principal agencies of the software revolution have been private companies. The role of government in India's software revolution focused primarily on providing a conducive policy framework to encourage the spread of technology and on investment in upgrading the telecommunications infrastructure to support a global information industry. While government did broaden the availability of computer education in government colleges, the dramatic increase in availability of programmers was primarily the result of private initiative. Software export companies recruited and trained their own staff. Software education and training centers proliferated. Investment in the software industry also came almost exclusively from private sources—banks, public stock offerings, venture capital and some foreign investment—with little government support.

Despite these differences, development in both fields has followed a similar course. The initiative of pioneers led to widespread imitation and adoption. Society accepted the new activity and established formal organizations (in one case public, in the other private) to support the new activity on a wide scale.

The knowledge and skills needed for modern agriculture and computer programming have been incorporated in the educational curriculum at higher and lower levels. The social attitudes and expectations of the population have been powerfully influenced by the country's success. Progressive rural farming families teach their youth the values of modern agricultural production. Educated middle class urban families encourage their offspring to pursue careers in high technology.

DETERMINANTS OF DEVELOPMENT

We have described social development as the release and channeling of social energies through more complex social organization to enhance productive capacity and achieve greater results. This process depends upon mechanisms to direct and channel the collective energies of the society into new and more productive forms of activity. We can identify four distinctly different levels or types of mechanism that serve this function—social aspirations, government authority, social-cultural structure, and social know-how in the form of science, technology and productive skills.

Social Aspirations

Economically, development occurs when productivity rises, enabling people to produce more, earn more and consume more. To do so, they have to be motivated to learn new skills, adapt to new work processes, and adopt new technology, changes which in past ages have met with considerable resistance. The driving force behind the whole movement is psychological. At the deepest level the energies of society are directed by the collective's subconscious aspirations. Society's self-conception of what it wants to become releases an aspiration of the collective for accomplishment. That aspiration exerts a powerful influence on the activities of the society. India's twin revolutions were spurred by a growing aspiration of Indian society for security, prosperity and enjoyment. A similar aspiration spurs middle class Americans today to invest their savings in the stock market.

We have traced the evolution of social aspirations in India from pre-Independence to the present day. The earliest expression was an aspiration for political freedom and self-determination. After Independence this aspiration evolved into an urge for self-sufficiency, a willingness to try new things and take risks. More recently it has matured into a movement of rising expectations permeating all levels of Indian society. At the turn of the 20th Century, many Americans of humble birth saw or read about neighbors, friends or others of their class who rose rapidly out of poverty into prosperity. Their example raised the aspirations and expectations of a whole generation of Americans and the generations that followed it.

So powerful was this budding movement that it prompted Henry Ford to conceive of the then outlandish notion of building a car affordable by the ordinary man. In 1900 only 8000 cars were produced in the entire USA to meet the needs of a small wealthy class. By 1929, Ford Motors alone had built 15 million Model Ts to meet the aspirations of the masses. The revolution of rising expectations, a term first used to describe Asia's awakening in the early 1950s, is the single most powerful force yet unleashed for social development. It marks a stage in which individual members of society not only venture to dream or hope or work for higher levels of accomplishment, but in which those aspirations have coalesced into a conviction and expectation that they will achieve, possess and enjoy more than their parents or they themselves have in the past.

Expectations rise when physical security and essential material needs have been met, when fear of punishment or social ostracism is withdrawn, when rights are safeguarded democratically, when information and urbanization expose people mentally and physically to possibilities and achievements they did not previously know even existed, when technology facilitates higher productivity, and when education enlightens attitudes and elevates social awareness. Without rising aspirations and expectations, society would not make the effort and take the risks to acquire new forms of behavior to achieve greater results. The psychological motive is primary; the mechanical, technological and organizational processes are secondary.

Some forms of economic analysis tend to view these secondary levers as the driving force and thereby miss the essential determinant of the process. In the course of social development, society is moved by a range of different psychological motives—the quest for survival and self-preservation, the urge to possess land, the seeking for social status and power, and the pursuit of wealth. The revolution of rising expectations represents a new and more powerful motive force for development, for by its nature it is not limited, as all the others have been, to a specific class or section of society.

GOVERNMENT AUTHORITY

Like social aspirations, the authority of government has the capacity to direct the flow of social energies through the instrumentation of law, public policies, administrative procedures, controls, incentives and fear of punishment. Here too there is a graded hierarchy of stages through which government influences the development process. Monarchy is a highly centralized form of government organization with significant capacity to restrict freedom and prevent unwanted activities, but with very limited power to promote social development, because of its limited power to positively motivate and direct human initiative. Modern authoritarian states have augmented the power of government to compel and control by evolving complex organizational mechanisms to reach out into every field of social activity. Its members submit by necessity to the power of the state, but continuously seek for ways around the strictures and demands it places upon them.

As the 20th century experiments in Eastern Europe amply demonstrate, its power as an instrument for development is severely limited. Countries with authoritarian governments that have succeeded in releasing social initiative for economic development, such as China, Taiwan and South Korea, have done so by loosening social control over economic activities, while retaining it over political activities. Modern forms of democracy greatly enhance the development capabilities of society. They are not only capable of enforcing a rule of law which to a large extent the population willingly accepts as in its own interest. They also promote far greater development of individual aspirations, thought, capacity, skill and initiative. The accountability of a democratically elected government necessitates that it continuously institute measures perceived as beneficial to the electorate.

Working through decentralized self-governing structures, it empowers more and more centers of activity in the society, leading to greater creativity and innovation. The basic human rights it endorses elevate aspirations and release human energies for higher accomplishment. The impact of democracy on development was illustrated by Nobel laureate economist Amartya Sen when he observed that no democratic country with a free press and independent judiciary has suffered a famine in this century. India's Green Revolution is a powerful testament to the power of governmental authority, though in this and every other instance, government's role cannot substitute for social readiness and social initiative, it can only aid in preparing that readiness, releasing that initiative and organizing the new activities.

SOCIAL-CULTURAL AUTHORITY

Government exercises authority over its citizens through law, administration and enforcement. Society exercises a far more persuasive authority over its members through its ideas, attitudes, customs and values. Different societies may develop at very different rates and in different directions under very similar forms of government, due to differences in social and cultural authority.

Modern societies are far more free and tolerant than those of previous centuries, yet they continue to exert a very powerful force on their members; only, the character of that force has changed. From being predominantly negative in the form of prohibitions and strictures, now the force of social authority acts far more as a spur to initiative, than a bar. The pressure felt by middle and working class families to 'keep up with the Joneses' has become pervasive throughout the world.

The bold initiative of a poor farmer in rural India to dig a bore well and become prosperous could act as stimulus for the rapid development of ten surrounding villages because the competitive pressure of social authority compelled his neighbors to keep up with his level of accomplishment. The spread of education tends to enhance this tendency. Apart from the practical knowledge and skills it imparts, modern education also instills a greater sense of individual self-respect and social rights that impels the individual to seek and maintain status in society.

Know-how

Here we include the complete range of capacities that determine the ability of the people to physically direct their energies to achieve productive results. The most important of these are scientific knowledge, technology and productive skills. These may appear very different in nature and action from social aspirations, government and social authority, but the character of their influence on development is quite similar. They provide the direction for the efficient organization of mental, social and material energies. Each of them carries with it an inherent authority and imposes a certain discipline on the expression of social energies. This authority usually takes the form of an impersonal authority of standards, rules and systems, such as the rules for maintaining an orderly flow of air traffic.

Adopting a higher level of technology, whether that involved in the cultivation of hybrid wheat, space travel or electronic commerce requires adherence to more stringent procedures and greater organization, without which it does not work. The Internet is a recent example of a technology that promotes freer and easier commercial and personal transactions, but accomplishes it by imposing rigorous standards of discipline on users in the form of a common computer language for communication.

MOTIVES FOR DEVELOPMENT

Societies throughout the world are presently preoccupied with achieving the material results of social development. But it is interesting to note that the process itself does not appear to be driven exclusively or perhaps even primarily by material motives, although these are uppermost in the social consciousness at the present time. Even in instances where material needs and wants have approached saturation, the process shows no signs of abating in speed or intensity. On the contrary, the momentum that has led to such incredible achievements over the past century continues to accelerate. In our search for the fundamental motive that drives the process, we have to look beyond the material preoccupations by which it is currently characterized.

While it is difficult to document at the social level, at the individual level it is readily apparent that physical security and comfort are important but by no means the only or even the most powerful motives for human action. Once these needs are met, there is still the seeking for social prestige and influence, the impulse of curiosity, the thirst for understanding, the drive for accomplishment, the urge for invention and creativity, the attraction of complexity and rich variety of experience—and the irrepressible and inexhaustible quest for enjoyment that all of these activities engender.

The process of development, even the limited sphere of social development, is not driven exclusively by material motives or confined to material achievements. The goals societies and individuals seek are determined by their needs and their values. In the hierarchy of needs, physical survival, security, and comfort are primary. Vital, social and mental needs gain prominence when the basic physical needs are met. As society prospers, the vital urge for intensity, excitement, enjoyment, adventure, changing experience and self-expression become more important determinants. Beyond these lie the mental urge for curiosity, knowledge, creativity and imagination, and the aspiration for spiritual realization.

This concept of development holds very important implications for the future of humanity and the prospects for progress in the next century. Its suggests that there are no inherent limits either to the speed or to the extent of the development process, other than those imposed by the limitations of our thought, knowledge and aspirations. If we change our view, the character of this process can be transformed from the slow, trial and error subconscious process we have known in the past to a swift, sure leaping progress from height to greater height.

PHASES OF HUMAN CHOICE

Social development has always involved a tension between two poles of its existence, collective and individual. The collective strives to ensure its preservation, perpetuation and development, preparing and compelling its individual members to abide by its traditions, laws and values, and contribute their energy and effort to defend and support the community.

At the same time, individual members strive to ensure their survival, to preserve and, whenever possible, to elevate their material and social positions, personal comfort and enjoyment. For a very long period of recorded history, the collective compelled the submission and obedience of its members to support the development and free exercise of choice by a very limited number of individuals constituting its ruling elite.

This tendency reached its acme in the divine right of kings, a doctrine that effectively made the whole society subservient to the whims and fancies of a single individual as an embodiment of the collective will and collective good. All served so that one person could live fully.

Human progress over the past five centuries has moved very far away from this extreme pole of collective domination. The collective has discovered a new formula for its progress—all individuals should be encouraged to develop so that the collective may develop to the maximum. The translation of this new principle into practice has taken several centuries and is still only partially realized. But the direction is clearly reflected in the continuous move toward democracy, universal education, human rights, and access to social opportunities.

Society is discovering that providing the maximum human choice to its individual members is the most effective means of releasing human energy, creativity and initiative for the maximum development of the collective. The Protestant Reformation was a landmark for Western society in the emergence of individual choice in the field of religion. A parallel shift has been identified by historians as one of the root causes for the decline of feudalism in Western Europe. The aristocracy discovered that a free farmer working for himself generated higher production and more tax revenue than an indentured serf working for mere subsistence. Since then society has experimented boldly with new ways to increase the range and quality of individual choice within a collective social framework. In subsequent centuries the rise of democracy extended human choice to the political field and the market system has institutionalized economic choice for workers and consumers.

But the collective's decision to empower individual choice can best be viewed as the first rather than the last step in human development. For the decision of the collective to encourage individual human choice is no guarantee that individuals will accept and exercise that choice or, if they do so, that they will do so wisely.

The phase of human choice that has characterized this century as the "century of the common man" can also been characterized as one in which most individual members continue to define their opinions, attitudes, values, preferences and aspirations very largely in terms that the collective sanctions and approves. Society may have consented to creative individuals exercising free choice, but for most individuals there remains a strong motivation to conform to the views and expectations of the collective and to depend on the collective as the primary determinant. So strong is this urge for conformity that even in science, a person's social position and prestige are often more powerful determinants of how the scientific community responds than the objectivity or rationality of the views expressed.

We can conceive of a time in the future when society has evolved to what we may term a second phase of human choice. In this society, not only the collective, but most of its individual members as well would have the realization that the individual human being is the determinant of its own future. This would constitute a true society of individuals, arriving at their own ideals, beliefs and values, discovering and expressing more fully their own innate potentials, rather than continuously looking to the collective as a role model for direction and support. We can imagine that this phase would be marked by an enormously enhanced level of energy, fresh initiative, innovation, invention, creativity and free expression and a far more rapid general advancement of the society as a whole in whatever fields of activity it chooses to develop. It might be a society of pioneers.

Yet such a phase, if achieved, would not in any way lessen the tension between the individual and the collective. Rather it might intensify the conflict to the point of threatening social cohesion and stability, in much the same way as the social and economic liberation of women in Western society may have affected the social institution of marriage. It might even become a society of rebels or revolutionaries with little tolerance for the status quo or the views of the collective. For an ultimate reconciliation of individuality with collective existence, we must envision a further phase of development in which social stability is achieved through the conscious understanding and consent of its individual members rather than by the force of collective authority or external limits imposed on the power of individual self-assertion.

In this phase, the individual would advance beyond the discovery of his own uniqueness and inner capacity to discover the complementary truth that the individual is a portion and expression of the collective society and can achieve maximum fulfillment only by discovering and relating positively with the other aspects and expressions of self which also form part of the larger social organism. If this comes to pass, we would then have witnessed the transition of society through three phases of emergence from undifferentiated collective existence. The undifferentiated phase is one in which the individuality is undeveloped and individual choice is suppressed or restricted to a very small ruling elite. The collective imposes its values on the individual.

Gradually the collective comes to recognize the necessity and value of actively promoting the development and expression of individual human choice in its members as a means for its own greater development. The collective discovers the value of the individual human being and the power of free human choice. This is the phase which most societies are in different stages of transiting: individuality is nominally encouraged, yet the vast majorities of people depends psychologically on the collective as the primary determinant and power for their development and subconsciously act in conformity with its expectations.

In this phase, individual members of society discover the source of creative energy and unlimited human potential within themselves and draw on that source to achieve far higher levels of development in any fields they pursue. The individual discovers the value and power of individual human choice. Conflict between the collective and its members would still be possible and could even increase. A phase could come in which individual members discover that they are only individual expressions of the collective and that their existence is fulfilled in consciously lending their energies for the pursuit and fulfillment of the aspirations of the collective. The developed individual consciously affirms the values of the collective as his or her own. This achievement would mark a further phase in the social development of the collective. It might also prepare the possibility of a truly spiritual development for the human community founded on the twin truths of spiritual freedom and spiritual oneness.

PARALLELS BETWEEN SOCIAL AND BUSINESS DEVELOPMENT

During a workshop presentation at the November 1998 World Academy Conference on the Global Century held in Vancouver, Canada, businessman Walt Stinson drew some interesting parallels between the principles of development theory outlined in the *Human Choice* paper and principles of business development set forth in several books by Fred Harmon, Garry Jacobs and Robert Macfarlane. We believe that the parallels he observed arise from the fact that both societies and businesses develop according to the same process, one macro, the other micro. We wish to identify some points of correspondence here as a basis for further exploration during the Madras meeting:

1. In the case of both business and society, development can be defined as an upward directional movement from

lesser to greater levels of energy, efficiency, quality, productivity, complexity, comprehension, creativity, mastery, enjoyment and accomplishment.

2. Businesses, like societies, develop as a result of a self-conception that is sometimes conscious, often subconscious. Both the democratic union of the 13 original American colonies and India's Green Revolution were the result of the conscious self-conception of a few perceptive leaders, while the population-at-large remained only vaguely aware of the process it was participating in. In the case of business, the original self-conception is usually the creation of a founding entrepreneur, but over time many other people contribute to its formulation. A noted instance of conscious self-conception was Fred Smith's idea for establishing an overnight delivery business to compete with United Parcel Service and the US Postal Service, at a time when both were already multi-billion dollar operations. The company he founded in the early 1970s, Federal Express, became for a time the fastest growing company of all time and now has annual revenues exceeding $12 billion. Smith's conscious conception may have been partially shared by many of the company's managers and employees, but many others may have participated in the process as part of their routine employment with only a vague notion of the larger vision that inspired its leaders.

3. The development of a business, like the development of a society, is fueled by the aspiration of its people. In the case of business, the aspiration of the owners and leaders is a critical determinant of how far and how fast the business grows. In the case of the society, the role of leadership is played by entrepreneurial pioneers that initiate new activities and the psychological intensity of their pursuit is a critical determinant of success. But in either case, the greater the aspiration of all the people involved, the more powerful the impetus for accomplishment.

4. We stated in *Human Choice* that surplus energy is an essential condition for social development. Only in the presence of surplus capacity can new activities be supported. The same is true in business. Companies struggling for survival or to meet the minimum requirements of their customers lack the excess capacity needed to plan and initiate new activities or elevate their functioning to a higher level of organization.

5. New modes of activity are introduced in society by pioneering individual initiatives that are imitated and disseminated by others, diffuse through the society and are eventually accepted and integrated with the normal functioning of the society. New modes of activity are introduced in a company by pioneering individual initiatives that are imitated and disseminated by others, diffuse through the company, and are eventually accepted and integrated with the normal functioning of the company.

6. Authority is a fundamental principle of organization that is essential to the survival and development of both societies and companies. Government, social and cultural authority as expressed through social norms, systems, institutions, laws, customs, and values determine the effectiveness with which surplus energy is converted by society into productive power. Corporate authority is expressed more and more through the discipline of impersonal rules, systems, coordination of activities, policies, corporate culture and values that determine the effectiveness with which surplus energy is converted by a business into productive power, rather than by top down personal exercise of authority by a management hierarchy. But regardless of whether the form is personal or impersonal, this discipline is fundamental to the successful functioning of an organization.

7. Social know-how in the form of technology, practical knowledge and skills determines the conversion of productive power into material results in both society and business.

8. The productivity of social resources is not subject to any inherent limits. It depends on the attitudes, information, knowledge, organization and skills creatively applied – i.e. on powers of mind. The productivity of a company's resources is not subject to any inherent limits. It depends on the attitudes, information, knowledge, organization and skills creatively applied – i.e. on powers of mind.

9. In research for his upcoming book on business in 2010, Fred Harmon is exploring the relationship between the five essential components of a business—market, technology, people, capital and organization—and the five parallel components of social development—social needs, technology, people, resources and organization. As a microcosm and child of the society, companies develop by attuning themselves to the direction, trends and changing needs of the wider society of which they are a part in each of these five major areas. This relationship is especially apparent in larger national and multinational corporations whose development is often closely tied to parallel developments in the societies in which they function.

10. The utilization of social development potential depends on the society's level of awareness, aspiration, organization, values, knowledge and skills. The utilization of business development potential depends on the company's level of awareness, aspiration, organization, values, knowledge and skills.

11. Both companies and societies depend for their development on three levels of organized infrastructure—a physical organization of production, transportation, communication, etc.; a social organiza-tion of legal, financial, commercial, and educational systems and institutions; and a mental organization of information, technology and knowledge. All three are needed for the achievement of progressively more complex forms of economic activity.

12. For both businesses and societies, values represent that

highest form of organization for directing human energies in constructive and productive activities. The quality and height of the values set the limits on the magnitude of developmental achievements.

Social development principles:

1. We define social development in its broadest social terms as an upward directional movement of society from lesser to greater levels of energy, efficiency, quality, productivity, complexity, comprehension, creativity, choice, mastery, enjoyment and accomplishment. Development of individuals and societies results in increasing freedom of choice and increasing capacity to fulfill its choices by its own capacity and initiative.
2. Growth and development usually go together, but they are different phenomena subject to different laws. Growth involves a horizontal or quantitative expansion and multiplication of existing types and forms of activities. Development involves a vertical or qualitative enhancement of the level of organization.
3. Social development is driven by the subconscious aspirations/will of society for advancement. The social will seeks progressive fulfillment of a prioritized hierarchy of needs – security of borders, law and order, self-sufficiency in food and shelter, organization for peace and prosperity, expression of excess energy in entertainment, leisure and enjoyment, knowledge, and artistic creativity.
4. Development of society occurs only in fields where that collective will is sufficiently strong and seeking expression. Development strategies will be most effective when they focus on identifying areas where the social will is mature and provide better means for the awakened social energy to express itself. Only those initiatives that are in concordance with this subconscious urge will gain momentum and multiply.
5. Development of the collective is subconscious. It starts with physical experience which eventually leads to

conscious comprehension of the process. Conscious development based on conceptual knowledge of the social process accelerates development and minimizes errors and imbalances.

6. Society is the field of organized relationships and interactions between individuals. Only a small portion of human activity is organized for utilization by society, so only a small portion of development potential (of technology, knowledge, information, skills, systems) is tapped.
7. Every society possesses a huge reservoir of potential human energy that is absorbed and held static in its organized foundations—its cultural values, physical security, social beliefs and political structures. At times of transition, crises and opportunities, those energies are released and expressed in action. Policies, strategies and programs that tap this latent energy and channel it into constructive activities can stir an entire nation to action and rapid advancement.
8. The act is the basic unit of social organization. The evolution of more complex and productive activities woven together by people to form systems, organizations, institutions and cultural values constitute the fabric or web of social organization.
9. The essential nature of the development process is the progressive development of social organizations and institutions that harness and direct the society's energies for higher levels of accomplishment. Society develops by organizing all the knowledge, human energies and material resources at its disposal to fulfill its aspirations.
10. The process of formation of organization takes place simultaneously at several levels: the organization of peace and physical security in society, the organization of physical activities and infrastructure, the organization of productive processes through the application of skills and technology in agriculture, industry and services, the organization of social processes we call systems, laws, institutions and administrative agencies, the organization

of data as useful information, the organization of knowledge through education and science, and the organization of higher social and cultural values that channel human energy into higher forms of expression.

11. Each of these levels of organization admits of unlimited development. Each of these levels of organization depends upon and interacts with the others. Elevating the organization at any of these levels increases the utilization of resources and opportunities and accelerates development.

12. Development requires an enormous investment of energy to break existing patterns of social behavior and form new ones. Development takes place when surplus social energies accumulate beyond the level required for functioning at the present level. The social energy may be released in response to the opening up of a new opportunity or confrontation by a severe challenge. Where different cultures meet and blend, explosive energies for social evolution are released.

13. Expression of surplus energy through existing forms of activity may result in growth—a quantitative expansion of society at the existing level of organization. Channeling the surplus energy into more complex and effective forms of organized activity leads to development—a qualitative enhancement in the capabilities of the society. The fresh initiatives that lead to this qualitative enhancement usually occur first in the unorganized activities of society that are not constrained and encumbered by the inertia of the status quo.

14. The rate and extent of development is determined by prevalent social attitudes which control the flow of social energies. Where attitudes are not conducive, development strategies will not yield results. In this case the emphasis should be placed on strategies to bring about a change in social attitudes—such as public education, demonstration and encouragement of successful pioneers.

15. The social gradient between people at different levels of power and accomplishment in society represents a 'voltage differential' that stimulates less accomplished sections of the population to seek what the more accomplished have achieved. The urge to maintain this voltage gap compels those at the top to seek further accomplishments. At the same time, the overall development of society is determined by its ability to make accessible the privileges and benefits achieved by those at the top to the rest of its members.
16. Development proceeds rapidly in those areas where the society becomes aware of opportunities and challenges and has the will to respond to them. Increasing awareness accelerates the process.
17. Social progress is stimulated by pioneering individuals who first become conscious of new opportunities and initiate new behaviors and activities to take advantage of them. Pioneers are the lever or spearhead for collective advancement. Pioneers give conscious expression to the subconscious urges and readiness of the collective.
18. Development occurs when pioneering individual initiatives are imitated by others, multiplied and actively supported by the society. Society then actively organizes the new activity by establishing supportive laws, systems and institutions. At the next stage it integrates the new activity with other fields of activity and assimilates it into its educational system. The activity has become fully assimilated as part of the culture when it is passed on to the next generation as values through the family.
19. Development is a process, not a program. Develop-ment is an activity of the society as a whole. It can be stimulated, directed or assisted by government policies, laws and special programs, but it cannot be compelled or carried out by administrative or external agencies on behalf of the population. Develop-ment strategy should aim to release people's initiative, not to substitute for it.

20. All resources are the creation of the human mind. Something becomes a resource when human beings recognize a productive or more productive use for it. Since there are no inherent limits to human inventiveness and resourcefulness, the potential productivity of any resource is unlimited.
21. Human beings are the ultimate resource and ultimate determinant of the development process. It is a process of people becoming more aware of their own creative potentials and taking initiative to realize those potentials. Human awareness, aspiration and attitudes determine society's response to circumstances. Development occurs only at the points where humanity recognizes its power to determine results.
22. The development of social organization takes place within a larger evolutionary context in which the consciousness of humanity is evolving along a continuum from physical to vital to mental. This evolution expresses as a progressive shift in emphasis from material resources to technological and information resources; from the social importance of land to the importance of money and knowledge; from hereditary rights of the elite to fundamental rights for all human beings; from reliance on physical forms of authority to laws and shared values. As society advances along this continuum, development becomes more conscious and more rapid.
23. Infinity is a practical concept. Human potential is unlimited. Development potential is infinite.
24. The same principles and process govern development in different fields of social life - political, economic, technological, scientific, cultural, etc.
25. The same principles and process govern development at the level of the individual, the organization and the society.

DEVELOPMENT THEORY

Development theory is a conglomeration of theories about how desirable change in society is best to be achieved. Such theories draw on a variety of social scientific disciplines and approaches.

MODERNIZATION THEORY

Modernization Theory is a theory of development which states that the development can be achieved through following the processes of development that were used by the currently developed countries.

Scholars such as Walt Rostow and A.F.K. Organski developed stages of development through which every country develops.

Samuel Huntington determined development to be a linear process which every country must go through. Modernization Theory, in contrast to Classical Liberalism, viewed the state as a central actor in modernizing "backward" or "underdeveloped" societies. Talcott Parsons' functional sociology defined the qualities that distinguished "modern" and "traditional" societies. Education was viewed as key to creating modern individuals.

Technology played a key role in this development theory because it was believed that as technology was developed and introduced to lesser developed countries it would spur growth. One key factor in Modernization Theory is the belief that development requires the assistance of developed countries to aid developing countries to learn from their development.

In addition, it was believed that the lesser developed countries would develop and grow faster than developed countries.

Thus, this theory is built upon the theory that it is possible for equal development to be reached between the developed and lesser developed countries.

DEPENDENCY THEORY

While Modernization Theory understood development and underdevelopment as a result from internal conditions that differ between economies, dependency theory understood development and underdevelopment as relational. Informed by Marxist insights, they argued that development was a result of underdevelopment, and underdevelopment was a result of development. Their conclusion was that for underdeveloped nations to develop, they must break their ties with developed nations and pursue internal growth. One type of policy crafted from this insight was Import substitution industrialization.

WORLD SYSTEMS THEORY

In response to some of the criticisms of Dependency Theory came World Systems Theory, which the division of periphery and center was further divided into a trimodal system consisting of the core, semi-periphery and periphery. In this system, the semi-periphery lies between the core and periphery and is exploited by the core and exploits the periphery. This division aims to explain the industrialization within lesser developed countries.

World Systems Theory was initiated by Immanuel Wallerstein in, among other writings, *World Systems Analysis*, and focuses on inequality as a separate entity from growth in development and examines change in the global capitalist system. One distinguishing feature of this theory is a distrust for the state and a view in which the state is seen as a group of elites and that industrialization cannot be equated with development. Out of this theory stem anti-systemic movements which attempt to reverse the terms of the system's inequality through social democratic and labor movements.

STATE THEORY

In response to the distrust of the state in World Systems Theory, is State Theory. State Theory is based upon the view that the economy is intertwined with politics and therefore the take-off period in development is unique to each country. State Theory emphasized the effects of class relations and the strength and autonomy of the state on historical outcomes. Thus, development involves interactions between the state and social relations because class relations and the nature of the state impact the ability of the state to function. Development is dependent upon state stability and influence externally as well as internally. State Theorists believe that a developmentalist state is required for development by taking control of the development process within one state.

Development Economics Theories

A number of theories are concerned with how economies develop over time. Some of these theories include:

- *Comparative advantage:* Predicts all countries gain if they specialise and trade the goods in which they have a comparative advantage. This is true even if one nation has an absolute advantage over another country.
- *Rostovian take-off model:* A linear theory of develop-ment that argues that economic modernization occurs in five basic stages of varying length - traditional society, preconditions for take-off, take-off, drive to maturity, and high mass consumption.
- *Harrod-Domar model:* Explains an economy's growth rate in terms of the level of saving and productivity of capital.
- *Dual Sector model:* Explains the growth of a developing economy in terms of a labour transition between two sectors, a traditional agricultural sector and a modern industrial sector. (Also known as the Lewis model)

Social Development Challenge

- Equitable and sustainable development requires tailored responses to a country's social context and the needs and priorities of poor people.
- As the World Bank's Social Development Strategy emphasizes, overcoming poverty is about more than getting economic policies right. It is also about empowering people by creating more inclusive, cohesive, and more accountable societies.
- *Inclusive institutions* promote equal access to opportunities, enabling everyone to contribute to social and economic progress and share in its rewards.

- *Cohesive societies* enable women and men to work together to address common needs, overcome constraints and consider diverse interests.
- *Accountable institutions* are transparent and respond to the public interest in an effective, efficient and fair way.

Social Development Response

- The World Bank supports social development by listening to poor people and promoting their voices in the development process; understanding and addressing their needs, priorities and aspirations; and building formal and informal institutions.
- We work with government, communities, civil society, and the private sector to help foster a state that is accessible, responsive and accountable to citizens.
- Social Development's key message to the development community for the last twenty years has been the need to 'put people first' in development processes. Social development includes the poor and excluded in the development process, and translates the complex relationships between societies, states and communities into operations.
- Poor people's own voices tell us that poverty is more than low income—it is also about vulnerability, exclusion and isolation, unaccountable institutions, and powerlessness.
- Social Development at the World Bank managed an operational portfolio of $7.7 billion in FY07. Across the Bank, Social Development has a network of over 150 social scientists and economists.

Highlights of Social Development across the Bank

Social aspects of climate change:

- The international community now recognizes that climate change will affect poor people's resources, social organization and institutions, and livelihoods – the social dimensions of climate change. The Social Development

Department is leading work on the social dimensions of vulnerability and adaptation to climate change, and the links between climate change and human security, conflict and migration.

- The operational agenda will support community and national level efforts to adapt to climate change and reward carbon fixing land-use practices.

Social dimensions of infrastructure:

- In the Bank, Social Development specialists work closely with infrastructure teams and focus on improving people's access and promoting social inclusion; reducing political and social risks; enhancing governance and reducing corruption through voice and participation; sharing benefits through social safeguards; and improving the design of infrastructure operations in conflict affected and fragile states.
- Social Safeguards aim to promote inclusion of the most vulnerable people and protect involuntarily displaced and indigenous peoples. 263 Bank projects currently affect indigenous peoples, and involuntary resettlement is a component of 325 Bank projects.
- Social and political analysis focuses on diversity including gender; formal as well as informal institutions, such as tribal and caste structures; and participatory processes involving the poor and other stakeholders. It also addresses social and political risks.

Local governance, participation, civic engagement:

- In recent years, the Bank has begun to address corruption, accountability and governance, focusing mainly on traditional public sector reforms—*the supply-side of governance*. Social Development has developed approaches that emphasize civic engagement—*the demand-side of governance*. The demand and supply side approaches are outlined in the Bank's Governance and Anti-Corruption Implementation Plan, approved by the Board last week.

- Social Development's portfolio includes operations designed to bridge supply-side and demand-side accountability of local governments to improve service delivery to communities (for example, in South Asia, East Asia and East and Central Europe).
- Community Driven Development (CDD) approaches can empower communities to plan, design and implement initiatives to improve their livelihoods. They also lead to more effective local service delivery because they strengthen citizens' opportunities to hold local authorities to account. CDD lending increased from about $325 million in FY96 to about $2.1 billion currently (approx 10% of total Bank lending).

Conflict Operations in the Sustainable Development Network:

- The approach to conflict operations in the Bank has evolved from a focus on physical reconstruction to conflict and development more broadly. Social Development specialists support country teams and operational research on conflict. Such support may include an analysis of the socio-political context to understand how Bank operations may affect conflict dynamics, and to identify the opportunities operations can offer to promote more cohesive and peaceful societies. 35-40 Bank clients are conflict-affected, most among the poorest borrowers.

5

Paradigm Shift of Corporate Sector Participation in Social Development

A Statement of Intent Generating wealth in a manner that is socially and environmentally sustainable must be the common goal of domestic and international business. In this age of open world economy, brand reputation, repositioning of government activities and privatization, it is increasingly important to do business ethically, morally and with concern for the society. Business today is realizing that the world is not made up of strangers. There is bondage- human bondage. There are customers, employees, shareholders and the neighbours. The business class should render their support to the general people. If they will be uplifted socially and economically, the productivity of the corporate is also bound to increase. The corporate sector in India very often blames the government for poor governance and lack of farsightedness. The question that comes every time into mind is, does the corporate sector perform its duty to contribute to the overall growth of the country? Does it have right to blame the government for poor governance? Does it contribute to nation building?

In India, most of the corporate do not have a clear policy on social responsibility. While developed countries like England have separate ministries to look after the issue of corporate social responsibility, in India, the government does not have a clear policy on the issue. Out of very few companies who contribute to the social development, the basic intention was not to ensure the good of the nation, rather a business policy to stay away from the tax net. The corporate and the government should try to build up a relationship between the business and the society. The concept of corporate social responsibility (CSR) has so far failed to take deep root in India because the nomenclature is not properly defined. The CSR is in a nascent stage. Much needs to be done to bring changes in attitude towards CSR and bring awareness among the corporate about their social responsibilities.

The corporate should be made aware about the changing nature of business due to Globalisation, transformation of market environment and deepening of competition. The market economy has paved the way for enterprise-led development and a new cultural perspective is taking place in Indian business environment that has a strong bearing on social responsibilities. Social responsibility encompasses the sectors like health, education, employment, income and quality of life. It should be binding on the corporate sector to work on the above aspects, which are thought to be primary social indicators. They have enough money to serve the nation on the above segments of the society. They should not forget that if general health of the mass were good, they would have better bying capacity.

In 1970, Milton Friedman of New York Times rightly wrote: "the social responsibility of business is to increase profits." This view is often held and propounded by those who do not see much merit in companies being engaged in issues of Social Responsibility other than the making of profit. However, increasingly, the profit case, evident indicators that are tangible and the altruistic/ philanthropic/ ethical case, evident in the intangibles are getting blurred. In this context the purpose is to highlight the need for a paradigm shift in the importance of greater investment in intangibles to enhance corporate value. Significance of CSR for India The ideal corporate citizenship has ethical and philosophical dimension, particularly in India here wide gap exists between people in terms of income and living standards as well as social status.

A latest survey by the Tata Energy Research Institute (TERI) called 'Altered Images: the 2001 State of Corporate Responsibility in India Poll' Traces Back the History of CSR in India and suggests that there are four models of CSR. Ethical model The origin of the first ethical model of corporate responsibility lie in the pioneering efforts of 19 th century corporate philanthropists such as the Cadbury brothers in England and the Tata family in India. The pressure on Indian industrialists to demonstrate their commitment to social development increased during the independence movement, when Mahatma Gandhi developed the notion of 'trusteeship', whereby the owners of property would voluntarily manage their wealth on behalf of the people.

Gandhi's influence prompted various Indian companies to play active roles in nation building and promoting socio-economic development during the 20th century. The history of Indian corporate philanthropy has encompassed cash or kind donations, community investment in trusts and provision of essential services such as schools, libraries, hospitals, etc. Many firms, particularly 'family-run businesses', continue to support such philanthropic initiatives. Statist model A second model of CSR emerged in India after independence in 1947, when India adopted the socialist and mixed economy framework, with a large public sector and state-owned companies. The boundaries between the state and society were clearly defined for the state enterprises.

Elements of corporate responsibility, especially those relating to community and worker relationships, were enshrined in labour laws and management principles. This state sponsored corporate philosophy still operates in the numerous public sector companies that have survived the wave of privatization of the early 1990s. Liberal Model Indeed, the worldwide trend towards privatization and deregulation can be said to be underpinned by a third model of corporate responsibility – that companies are solely responsible to their owners. This approach was encapsulated by the American economist Milton Friedman, who in 1958 challenged the very notion of corporate responsibility for anything other than the economic bottom line.

Many in the corporate world and elsewhere would agree with this concept, arguing that it is sufficient for business to obey the law and generate wealth, which through taxation and private charitable choices can be directed to social ends. Stakeholder Model The rise of globalisation has brought with it a growing consensus that with increasing economic rights, business also has a growing range of social obligations. Citizen campaigns against irresponsible corporate behaviour along with consumer action and increasing shareholder pressure have given rise to the stakeholder model of corporate responsibility. This view is often associated with R. Edward Freeman, whose seminal analysis of the stakeholder approach to strategic management in 1984 brought stake holding into the mainstream of management literature.

According to Freeman, 'a stakeholder in an organisation is any group or individual who can affect or is affected by the achievement of the organisation's objectives.' Perception and practices of CSR in India A survey was conducted by ORG-MARG for TERI-Europe in several cities of India in 2001. The basic purpose of the survey was to capture perceptions and expectations (related to corporate responsibility) of the following three sets of stakeholders such as general public, workers (skilled, semiskilled and un-skilled) and corporate executives (head of corporate relation, labour relations, welfare dept. and manufacturing dept. in MNCs, large and medium sized Indian companies).

The poll gathered that people believe that companies should be actively engaged in social matters. A majority of the general public feels that companies should be held fully responsible for roles over which they have direct control. These include providing good products and cheaper prices, ensuring that operations are environment friendly, treating employees fairly without any discrimination based on gender, race or religion and applying labour standards globally. More than 60% of the general public felt that the companies should also be held responsible for bridging the gap between the rich and the poor, reducing human rights abuses, solving social problems and increasing economic stability. CSR as business success CSR is considered to be an important aspect of business success– through efficient resource management, environment protection, employment, eco-friendly atmosphere, etc.

Ashok Khosla, President of Development Alternatives, an Indian NGO, is of the view that sustainability includes sustainable consumption and sustainable production and is thus the responsibility of both procedures and consumers. The CSR is not a one size fits all. The NGOs, citizens and governments must look at sizes, types and locations of companies to explore how CSR can be brought to bear on companies.

The civil society is good for business and a tool for advancing corporate take-up of CSR. Therefore, the business should view civil society as being the CSR auditors for business and a friend to business, much like traditional auditors. There are lessons for business to learn from their interactions with civil society that cannot only reduce risk but improve overall competitive advantage.

The business of the 21st century will have no choice but to implement CSR. The sooner corporate houses realize this and aggressively pursue this process, the better off they will be. The laws need to be formulated to help in reinforcing CSR practices. Indian CSR has traditionally been a matter of classical paternalistic philanthropy, financially supporting schools, hospitals and culture institutions. However, far from being an add-on motivated by altruism and personal glory, the philanthropic drive has been driven by business necessity. With minimal state welfare and infrastructure provision in many areas, companies had to ensure that their workforce had adequate housing, healthcare and education and simultaneously the country grows at a fast pace.

The CSR should not be merely a statement of intent. It should be made compulsory for the corporate operating in

India. This will definitely help in upholding human rights. In this context, the following measures may be made mandatory to ensure participation of the corporate in social development:

- Incorporation of a section on social actions in annual reports of companies
- Appointment of an independent social accounting committee to measure, monitor, evaluate and report impact of CSR in annual reports
- Separate department to look after the CSR
- Periodic training programmes and awareness camps to train personnel on CSR
- Linkage between CSR and financial success should be established
- A certain percentage of profit should be earmarked for social development that should reflect in the annual balance sheets of companies.

THE NEW DEVELOPMENT PARADIGM AND PHILANTHROPY

New developmental strategies and actions are replacing conventional theories and approaches in the context of modern day quality oriented rights based social and economic development. The term 'philanthropy', evolved over time from mere 'charity' to social investing and organised development, derives its roots from two Greek words "philos - love and "anthropos man". With the paradigm shift in development thought and practice, philanthropy now is widely accepted as a viable informal social safety net. This has further been reinforced by concepts and actions of the three stakeholders i.e. public, corporate and nonprofit participation in development mainly focussing on rectifying low 'Human Development Indicators' (HDI).

Despite pervasive poverty and inequity, which is the root cause of social problems, there is an enormous potential for positive change particularly through synergistic trisector resource mix and partnerships. Another contributory factor for this optimism is the presence of a huge reservoir of philanthropic resources as we are one of the top giving nations, a fact duly corroborated by evidence based research on philanthropy in Pakistan. Between the state, the NGOs and the philanthropists we have the knowledge- base, the finance and the expertise to build social capital. It is this vision of a group of eminent citizens of the country, now on the Board of the Centre, which helped establish this support service organisation dedicated to the cause of philanthropy promotion.

Pakistan Centre for Philanthropy (PCP) emanated out of original research on philanthropy and is an outcome of recommendations of 'The International Indigenous Philanthropy Conference of 2000'; attended by His Highness the Aga Khan and President Musharraf, who supported the idea of fostering an enabling environment for civil society and endorsed the creation of PCP to promote structured and strategic approaches to enhancing philanthropy for social development. PCP is an independent nonprofit support organisation with a mission to promote the volume and effectiveness of philanthropy for social development in Pakistan. The Centre is licensed under section 42 of the Companies Ordinance 1984, with the Securities and Exchange Commission of Pakistan (SECP).

Instead of getting into direct service delivery mode or receiving grants, PCP seeks to promote altruistic efforts of national and international philanthropists (individual, corporate & diaspora) by establishing effective linkages between the grant-maker and nonprofit organisations (NPOs).

This requires bridging the information and credibility gap that exists between these two and is often a major impediment in the promotion of philanthropy. In line with the vision and mission and to achieve the objectives, PCP has designed innovative programmes:

i. Nonprofit Organisations Certification
ii. Philanthropy Support Services: mobilizing corporate philanthropy for education under Public Private Partnerships (3Ps) and an online web-based development market place Philanthropy Portal (2p) Give 2 Pakistan

iii. expanding the philanthropy knowledge map through evidence based Research and
iv. Communication and Advocacy to enhance societal understanding of philanthropy and development.

PUBLIC PRIVATE PARTNERSHIPS: THE 3 PS

The 3 Ps involve a partnership between a public sector agency, a private for profit entity and a non-profit organisation to achieve a collective outcome. The project translates our vision of mutually collaborative linkages between stakeholders into synergistic projects for development. We envision such partnerships making a measurable difference in the quality of life of Pakistan's disadvantaged communities through projects in any sphere of social development.

GOALS

Increase the volume and effectiveness of corporate philanthropy for increasing access to and enhancing the quality of education for disadvantaged children.

Through this project the Centre aims to: The 3Ps is a real partnership; with shared responsibilities and shared rewards for all participants. Skills and assets of each sector (public and private) come together in delivering education related service for civic benefit.

This means multiplying inputs to achieve sustainable development outcomes. Bureaucratic procedures are minimised by the use of tested template agreements to accelerate the process. At the same time partnerships are formed only where the community identifies a need and expresses willingness for the private sector to become an active social investor. This translates into a healthy corporate-community relationship and builds company goodwill. Most importantly, the arrangement ensures long-term success, by engaging the coalition of partners including the beneficiaries in planning, implementation and monitoring.

The Centre's Philanthropy Portal is a unique on-line

facility which aims to help grant-makers find and reach the most suitable destination for their charitable funds. This mechanism is based on an engine that sifts through a databank of credible, certified organisations (meticulously evaluated by PCP) and returns donation options based on preferences identified by grands-makers. A growing number of philanthropists are seeking ways of involving themselves in development projects in Pakistan. They ask: is there a support organization that functions as an interface between grant-makers and grant-recipients? The answer is yes... if you are a foundation, corporation, individual, or a group of like-minded charitable people the portal operates as a doorway to a menu of self- researched giving possibilities for you.

Our support services provide contributors a menu of options and grant management services so our clients can invest where their giving will change the most lives while also giving them the satisfaction of getting first hand information on the utilisation of their grant funds and the impact created. We are vigilant about grants. Therefore PCP only recommends organizations that have been through the rigorous certification process and have been critically evaluated against strict parameters in the areas of internal governance, programme delivery, financial transparency, documentation, disclosure, accountability and organizational effectiveness. PCP conducts detailed monitoring and evaluation field visits to give first hand feedback of the project and sends periodic reports to the grands maker on programme delivery and utilization of funds.

As an extension of the 'Give-to Pakistan' service, and to harness the vast potential of indigenous philanthropy in Pakistan, the 2P team began designing a Payroll Giving Programme (PGP) in 2006. PGP will encourage companies with huge employee bases to make a contribution from their salaries for humanitarian projects such as sponsoring a child's education, paying for treatment of a patient or contributing to reconstruction of the earthquake affected areas etc. Payroll programmes have been very successful in promoting philanthropy amongst individuals globally. The Programme has a large potential in Pakistan since businesses increasingly desire to appear socially responsible to their consumers.

The idea of establishing a certification programme for nonprofit organisations (NPOs) in Pakistan emerged during the course of stakeholder consultations for the Enabling Environment Initiative (EEI) in 2002 reinforced by subsequent researches. Various stakeholders including large corporate donors and diaspora philanthropists indicated that a mechanism was needed to identify credible partners from civil society for development initiatives. Government, international donor agencies and individual philanthropists also expressed the view that philanthropic activity would increase in volume as well as effectiveness if the existing information and credibility gap between donors (individuals, corporate sector, government and international agencies) and recipient NPOs are bridged. Consensus emerged that the existence of a reliable system of updated information about various nonprofit organisations would facilitate giving.

Certification

It was in this context that PCP set out to develop a system whereby reliable information about various organisational and programmatic aspects of NPOs is collected on a voluntary basis. The result was PCP's NPO certification regime, which seeks to evaluate NPOs on standardised parameters in critical areas of internal governance, financial management and programme delivery and widely disseminate information about organisations that qualify on these parameters.

Developed after considerable brainstorming, review of international best practice and consultations with stakeholders (including the NPOs), certification is essentially a 'seal of good practice' for certified organisations. Certification, thus, offers a useful service to key stakeholders in philanthropic giving. On the one hand, it promotes credible organisations from its platform through PCP's website and Gateway to Giving - Directory of Certified NPOs, the first of its kind in Pakistan.

On the other hand, it provides philanthropists with

credibility assurance about institutional partner NPOs thereby facilitating linkages between the certified NPOs and various donors (individual as well as institutional). Research and development go hand in hand. Despite its prime importance and being an extremely useful tool for informed policy decisions, research remains a neglected intellectual discipline in our country and too often strategic decisions are taken without adequate research on ground realities. Dearth of research in the realm of philanthropy in particular made action research the central agenda of PCP, reinforced by the fact that the Centre itself emanated out of original philanthropy research.

Philanthropy related evidence based research programme aims to enhance societal understanding of various dimensions of philanthropy and civil society. This programme on one hand endeavours to expand the empirical map on voluntary giving which largely remains untapped, while simultaneously the research findings help stakeholders, particularly policy makers, better plan and organise social investment for civic benefit in Pakistan. Sharing this evidence-based information through effective communication channels is also an integral part of PCP's mandate. Publication of these reports within a short span of five years reflects our commitment to authentic evidence based research.

The interest generated by the corporate survey led PCP to launch the first ever Pakistan Corporate Philanthropy Awards (PCPA) in January 2007. Prime Minister Shukat Aziz presented 12 awards to top giving companies. The corporate report has become a regular feature on PCP's research agenda and the Centre plans to undertake further research on "Effective Giving" which will document best corporate giving practices and a study on the nature and origin of "Family Foundations in Pakistan". In the pipeline are reports on "Earthquake Philanthropy", "Exploring Dimensions of the NGO Sector" and an "Indigenous Philanthropy Study". PCP recognises that all stakeholders need to be educated in the statistics and mechanics of philanthropy. For this purpose a multi- pronged media strategy was used to advance discussions and awareness on philanthropy including regular updates on the PCP website, global developments, e-mail alerts, news reports and the distribution of in-house publications at various forums. "Profiles in Philanthropy" have been produced to feature interviews with major philanthropists, showcasing good giving initiatives.

The Centre also completed a series of weekly 'philanthropy and NGO' discussions on Radio Pakistan hosting discussions on development and philanthropy. Following the October earthquake, PCP rapidly made arrangements with FM100 for an interview plan covering the efforts of self-help earthquake response initiatives and local NGOs; this was complemented with a month-long spot campaign on radio.

Organisation/ programme specific information, models, research and other findings are circulated through brochures, booklets, flyers, news articles, talk shows and reports. Through its links with the international/regional networks that own and share valued contemporary resources, the Centre has a tremendous information advantage. Thematic articles are also contributed to magazines and journals as international readership.

These include the Asia Pacific Philanthropy Consortium (APPC) Post, the International Journal of Civil Society Law, Alliance and the Accountability Forum. PCP is on the Governing Council of the 13 member Asia Pacific Philanthropy Consortium, and is also a regular participant at the Global Philanthropy Forum, USA. Through its website the Centre has been able to place programme information, events, various publications, certification application forms, evaluation parameters, process and all other relevant information for public use and benefit. The website also serves to link the corporate sector and NPOs.

Corporate Social Responsibility (CSR), can be described as, the continuous commitment by corporations towards the economic and social development of communities in which they operate. The concept of corporate social responsibility of large industrial groups has occupied a prominent place in the greater national discourse on economic issues since the pre-independence era in India. Gandhi described large business as 'trusts' of the 'wealth of the people' and thus emphasized on the larger social purpose that industrial wealth should serve in independent India. In the early days of the post- independence period, the Indian state under the heavy influence of Nehruvian socialism encouraged private industries to play an active role in the economic and social development of the backward sections of the society, while at the same time setup a mammoth public sector for serving larger societal interests.

As Nehru's gentle socialism gave way to the more radical policies of nationalization and extensive state regulation of the Indira Gandhi era, industrial groups desperate to avoid the draconian state policies and regulations in economic affairs resorted to large scale corporate welfare programs to demonstrate that private wealth also played a important role in poverty alleviation and the socio-economic development of the nation and was not anti-people. An impeding crisis in Indian economy led the Rajiv Gandhi and Narashima Rao governments to dismantle the 'license raj' and introduce much-needed economic reforms in the country, which marked the beginning of the economic liberalization and the free market economy in India.

The major impact of these economic reforms has been the increased presence of transnational corporations in the country and transformation of Indian businesses into large global enterprises. In this scenario, there is an increased focus on the social role of these private enterprises by both the proponents and opponents of liberalization in India. In this chapter we analyze the fundamental changes in paradigm of corporate social responsibility and the new innovative practices being applied for its implementation in the last decade in India, in the context of the liberalization of the Indian economy. Our central argument in the paper is that the rise of private enterprise in the free market setup has radically transformed the perception and understanding that corporations have of their large role in society and consequently, their has been a revolution in implementation of corporate social responsibility programs at the ground level.

THE NEW PARADIGM OF CORPORATE SOCIAL RESPONSIBILITY

The conceptualization of corporate social responsibility up till the 1990's was purely in terms of philanthropy or charity. Welfare programs or initiatives were introduced not as a duty or a responsibility but as a form of charity that was supposed to indicate the virtues of the company or the organization. Many industrial groups like the Tatas or Birlas setup charitable trusts that provided financial grants for various worthy causes. Although there were some cases where the corporation took up a more active role like the establishment of the Birla Institute of Technology, Pillani by the Birlas or setting up of primary schools by several major industrial groups for their workers 's children but even in these cases the approach was philanthropical.

The problem with the philanthropy -based model has several problems:

- The corporation does not commit its resources fully behind such a project and often confines itself to one-time or periodical financial grants.
- Since its an act of charity, the corporation does not feel the need for community participation in the designing or management of such initiatives and people par-ticiption, if any, is restricted to limited implementation aspects reducing the efficiency and effectiveness of corporate social responsibility measures at the ground level.
- The lack of involvement from the primary resource provider i.e. the corporation leads to low levels of accountability and transparency at the implementation level.

However the post-liberalization phase has seen a fundamental shift from this philanthropy-based model of corporate social responsibility to a stakeholder-participation based model.. The change is evident in the statements about corporate social responsibility being made by India's leading industrial groups like the Tatas, "over the years, the nature of the company's involvement with the community has undergone a change.

It has moved away from charity and dependence to empowerment and partnership" and the consistent transformation in their corporate social responsibility practices in the last decade. In the stakeholder model the community in which the corporation is present in is seen as a stakeholder in the company and therefore, the company has certain obligation and duties towards it like it has towards its other stakeholders (customers, employees, shareholders).

It is a recognition of the fact that companies perform in non-financial arenas such as human rights, business ethics, environmental policies, corporate contributions, community development, corporate governance, and workplace issues and company should be held accountable for its 'triple bottomline' that includes social, environmental, and financial performance and not just the financial aspect. The question that arises at this juncture is what the reasons for this shift are in the basic paradigm in corporate social responsibility in the post-liberalization era.

John Samuel and Anil Sari have argued that this transformation has been the result of three reasons:

- Recognition of the importance of 'reputation capital' for capturing and sustaining markets. Therefore corporate social responsibility is basically a new business strategy to reduce investment risks and maximize profits by taking all the key stakeholders into confidence.
- The growing importance attached to the 'eco-social' stability i.e. social and environmental stability and sustainability is necessary for the survival of a free-market economy in the long run.
- The importance being attached to accountability, transparency and social and environmental investment as the key aspects of corporate governance in the era of Globalisation.

Others like S. Sailaja have attributed the shift in conceptualization to a simpler 'benefit' argument that basically implies that the stakeholder model has been adapted as it makes CSR programs more effective and efficient, the need for which is recognized by corporation who see multiple benefits like increased sales and customer loyalty, enhanced brand value and reputation, increased ability to attract and retain quality employees, investors & business partners, better productivity of workforce, cooperation with local communities, efficient operations resulting in improved financial performance, increased stock value, reduced litigation & environmental costs, better and faster governmental approvals, rewards, tax benefits that come from good CSR practices.

While both these arguments are pertinent, we would venture to supplement them by drawing attention to two other important reasons for the basic shift in the corporate social responsibility model. Firstly, the post-liberalization phase saw the increased presence of large transnational corporations like IBM in India which have highly developed corporate social responsibility initiatives based on the stakeholder participation model that were introduced in India by them. The success and effectiveness of these programs had a 'rub- off' effect on Indian enterprises, which were also operating in the same market, in their approach to corporate social responsibility initiatives. Secondly as Indian industry started competing in the developed markets of Europe, America and the Far East it had to comply with entry level norms like certification for responsible corporate practices like ISO 14000, SA 8000, AA 100 as well as compliance codes formulated by OECD and UN Global Compact which meant that they had to adapt new corporate social responsibility standards. Whatever be the reason, this change in the conceptualization of corporate social responsibility to stakeholder participation model has led to drastic change in the planning, management and implementation of corporate social responsibility initiatives as we illustrate in our new section.

THE NEW INNOVATIONS IN IMPLEMENTING CORPORATE SOCIAL RESPONSIBILITY

With the shifting of the corporate social responsibility paradigm to a stakeholder centric approach, practices at the ground level have also undergone a radical transformation.

In every aspect of corporate social responsibility measures the last decade has seen corporations innovating to increase efficiency, effectiveness and accountability. The focus has been on initiatives that are people-centric with active community participation at all levels. Further, the corporations themselves have moved away from the charitable initiatives like giving financial grants or sponsorships to providing products and services in a manner that would make a real difference in the target communities.

The first perceptible change has been the introduction of a host of innovative programs and schemes in several areas like education, healthcare, rural development, environment protection, protection of artistic and cultural heritage and disaster management that are customized to meet the specific needs of the target group and corporations devote not only financial resources but expertise, man-power, products and services for the successful implemen-tation of these schemes:

- Lupin India Ltd, India's third largest manufacturer of pharmaceuticals has started a project for providing sustainable development in 154 villages across Rajasthan. The scheme instead of providing for piecemeal assistance that does not lead to effective alleviation of poverty or adequate development is designed as a holistic action plan that includes an Agricultural Income Generation Scheme, land cultivation and fruit plantation programs, fodder preservation schemes, sericulture and water-recycling programs, establishment of medical and educational centers, adult literacy programs and credit schemes.
- Cipla, another Indian pharma major has found a novel approach to fulfill its corporate social responsibility obligations by offering to sell a cocktail of three anti-

HIV drugs, Stavudine, Lamivudine and Nevirapine, to the Nobel Prize-winning voluntary agency Medicine Sans Frontieres (MSF) at a rate of $350, and at $600 per patient per year to other NGOs over the world. This offer has to lead to a significant decrease in the prices of these drugs worldwide increasing the accessibility of these drugs especially in the developing countries.

- Ranbaxy, one of India's major pharmaceutical firms operates seven mobile healthcare vans and two urban welfare centers that reach over a lakh people in various parts of northern and central India as part of its corporate social responsibility initiative.
- Tata Consultancy Services (TCS) has set up a fully-equipped computer training laboratory for children from the Society for the Welfare of the Physically Handicapped and Research Centre, in Pune for imparting basic computer knowledge. NIIT has launched a highly popular 'hole-in-the-wall' scheme where it places a computer on a public wall in urban and rural areas so that neighbourhood children can learn computer basics using the play-way method.
- Bharat Electronics Ltd built cyclone proof houses for the victims of the super cyclone in with the help of the victims themselves so that the houses are built according to their needs.
- Ion Exchange has founded a profitable venture for environmental protection through water treatment, afforestation and organic farming.

Along with innovation, corporations have worked hard at integrating corporate social responsibility into their core practices. There is now greater evaluation and stricter accountability and transparency norms for social initiatives along the lines of norm set for mainstream projects and ventures. Sudha Murtjy of the Infosys Foundation, the social initiative arm of the IT major Infosys, explains the great efforts that corporation are going into ensure that the projects they are involved with are actually genuine and serve a purpose, "We get a lot of projects, so we do a round of elimination....make a shortlist, as to which are the good ones, after a lot of verification. Then we supervise the implementation part by visiting the area. But we have to work very hard, during all holidays, weekends and 18 hours every day."

Several organizations like Gas Authority of India Ltd. (GAIL) have introduced benchmarking exercises for their CSR activities and industry bodies like Confederation of Indian Industries and FICCI have introduced cross-sectoral programs, for the first time, in CSR related areas.

PUBLIC SECTOR ENTERPRISES, CORPORATE SOCIAL RESPONSIBILITY AND LIBERALISATION

In our narrative so far, we have focused on the private sector and its greater societal obligations. India, also, has a large public sector with several huge corporations and companies operating in various sectors like petroleum, heavy industries, aviation, mining, steel, equipment manufacturing and shipping.

The Indian public sector has had a long tradition of corporate social responsibility and the initiatives of corporations like the Oil and Natural Gas Commission (ONGC), Steel Authority of India Ltd (SAIL) and Gas Authority of India Ltd. (GAIL) have critical in the development of several backward regions of the country. Indian Airlines and Bharat Heavy Electronics have been widely acclaimed for their disaster management efforts.

The era of liberalization has led to the privatization of several public sector units and others being forced to make switch from being monopolies to being free market players with intense private competition. These dynamic processes have raised several key questions related to the corporate social responsibility of the public sector:

- What should the social involvement levels of a company or corporation once it is privatized?
- Should public sector units continue to play the same social role as they did in the pre-independence era or is there a need to scale back their social responsibility initiatives?

These are questions that are central to the post-liberalization debate and need further analysis and research.

Meanwhile the opponents of privatization have used an 'corporate social responsibility' argument for their cause, they argue that considering the vital importance of the social role played by the public sector in India, there should not be any privatization of these vital industries.

Once again the lack of adequate research specifically empirical data restricts us from an objective examination of this issue. The new economic era in India i.e. the post-liberalization phase of the Indian economy was a catalyst for the radical transformation in the corporate social responsibility related practices in the country, the change was two fold: transformation of the conceptual understanding of corporate social responsibility and innovations at the implementation level.

At the conceptual level, there was a fundamental transformation from the charity- oriented approach to the stakeholder-oriented approach where the target group was seen as stakeholder in the community whose well-being was integral to the long term success of the company. However, the real revolution occurred at the implemen-tation stages where companies have started committing manpower, expertise in addition to financial resources in order to provide a host of services, programs and schemes that are flexible enough to accommodate the needs of the target community. The CSR initiatives have also see greater people participation at all stages and tighter accountability standards.

The issue of norms for corporate social responsibility seems to have been adequately dealt with by industry practices like benchmarking, CSR ratings and certification by different agencies. While the situation in the private sector seems satisfactory, there is fierce debate on the social role of the Indian public sector in the post-liberalization phase especially in the light of the twin processes of privatization and the dismantling of monopoly/quota regimes. There is a need for extensive research especially in form of empirical studies to address the questions related to this issue

PARADIGM SHIFT IN PLANNING CONTROLS

Ongoing policy reforms in the urban sector including economic liberalisation and democratic decentralisation demand the compatibility of the contemporary planning process in India which may involve certain radical changes. Planning is the foundation of the development superstructure comprising of land, housing, infrastructure and construction. It can either act as a barrier to the policy reforms or can become a catalyst of new generation changes. As per 2001 Census, there are 5161 cities and towns in India inhabiting a population of 285 million. Of these about 1500 master plans have been prepared, many of which are statutory. The Delhi Plan with the approval of Parliament in 1962 was the first comprehensive exercise and has been a model of modern town planning in India. Apropos the economic and urban reforms and with new forms of governance, a debate is in the offing on the fundamental premises of planning and its necessity.

POLICY REFORMS

During last decade the government of India initiated radical policy reforms in the form of 74th Constitutional Amendment Act (74th CAA) and economic liberalisation. The Union Ministry of Urban Development during recent years took up the Habitat themes of "Inclusive Cities", "Cities without Slums" and "City to City Cooperation". At the same time, the Govt. of India and the United Nations Centre for Human Settlements (UNCHS) launched "Good Urban Governance Campaign". It is seen as an integral process of urban improvement and better sense delivery. The hypothesis is that better infrastructure service, security of tenure, political empowerment and participation in civic decisions will lead the urban poor to higher levels of economic and social life. The UNCHS campaign for Good Urban Governance gives emphasis on inclusive cities, participatory, transparent and accountable management, community empowerment, poverty reduction, capacity building and security of tenure.

There is a clear paradigm shift in the approach, which envisages public-private partnership, a facilitating approach, institutional capacity building and legislative and procedural reforms. In the context of new National Housing and Habitat Policy, the Corporate, Private and Cooperative Sectors are to take the lead role in terms of land assembly, construction of houses and development of amenities within the projects. Emphasis is on creation of housing stock on ownership and rental basis. Corporate sector is to be encouraged to provide for hosing for staff and to facilitate their employees in acquiring their own houses. Cooperative Sector is to be given preference in allotment of land and house sites to encourage housing development. State Governments have taken up schemes in collaboration with the private sector for slum redevelopment on cross-subsidization basis.

The policy reform also encourage the preparation of district and metropolitan development plans, which integrate investments and their spatial implications, and need a suitable plan making mechanism and techniques. This requires serious consideration so that the planning framework responds to the climate of new economic policies and democratic decentralisation. In order to enable the implementation of the new strategy, it would be necessary to restructure town planning departments, development authorities and the local bodies and to equip them to the new policy changes. The challenge is to evolve a decentralised, localised planning structure with public-private partnership approaches. In spite of basic policy reform, the planning generally continues to be performed in the conventional manner – top down approach, centralised, comprehensive and controlling in nature. Except few States, the planning functions are yet to devolved to the local bodies, as enshrined in the 74th CAA.

The state town planning departments sitting in the headquarters continue with the old practice of preparing the master plans of various cities and towns. These plans generally depend upon the conventional theme of "government does all". They are based on policies like large scale acquisition, mass public sector housing and infrastructure development to be provided by the govern-ment sector. They tend to control the development, rather than promoting it. The private sector often complains that planning controls prevent and inhibit enterprise. The negative answers to most of the applications and inordinate delays occurring through planning process have become a normal phenomenon. Planning process is performed by the government authorities under all kinds of bureaucratic restrictions. This results in long delays, arbitrary decisions and discretionary interpretation of the plans and regulatory framework. Government controlled planning often leads to dull uniformity squeezing out the variations which fail to respond to different income groups, perception, tastes and life styles.

The bureaucrats and planners sitting in judgement do not necessarily have the superior knowledge required. The ability to visualise future growth or to have superior knowledge or judgement is not a prerogative of a group of official planners than another group which may be lacking the official position. Development activities are usually suspended or frozen due to non-finalisation of the plans. Regulation and organisational problems are attributed generally to the insufficiency of staff in the planning department. Due to limited, expensive and time-consuming process of development, the whole development becomes more expensive. Planning may create a false market and in huge alterations in property values by determination of locational suitability of road network, infrastructure and land use.

As such, there is widespread politics of influence and it is a fact that fortunes can be made or lost due to official decisions. As a result, besides illicit payments, the pressure groups, local leaders and politicians temper the planning decisions. A major pitfall of planning had been the adoption of the borrowed concept of single use zoning against the popular mixed use syndrome. The restrictions on land use, zoning regulations and compartmentalisation of activities hinder the opportunities of self-employment. Small enterprises, which are traditionally operated from the living places, are required to be shifted to discriminate commercial/industrial areas, which become beyond the affordability of general masses.

Shifting of offices, industries and other commercial activities due to prevention by land use zoning results in great loss of jobs and discourage growth. Bulk of the working force in Indian cities constitutes the 'informal sector' or the 'unorganised sector' of employment. A consequence of strict zoning had been alarming loss of intensively lively urban urban atmosphere and variety which prevailed in the traditional cities. The proposals attempting to 'rationalise' and 'compartmentalise' land use are contradictory to develop residence work-place relationship. Invariably the master plans taking cognizance of the census data on population growth and urban concentration recommend that the migration to the city should be curbed. This stems from thinking that rural migrants by swarming to the city ruin the city life and creates housing and services problems by utilising the infrastructure without paying the taxes.

This is a perverse and colonial view of urbanisation, which looks upon cities as the exclusive preserve of the rulers and the rich with the paraphernalia of the service sector. Large scale land acquisition for urban growth had been a favourite pipe dream of the planners in India. Modelled on Delhi's strategy, predominantly the state and urban bodies take upon themselves the role of the developers, city builders and housing suppliers. The exclusion of the private, informal and unorganised sector from the development and housing process, in spite of severe restrictions, could not be sustained. At present about half of the housing stock in Delhi is comprised of informal, organic or unauthorised units and the fact remains that the government bodies, local authorities or organised sector all over have proved to be inadequate to meet the demands.

The land policies, plans, byelaws, zoning regulations fail to accommodate most of the sub- standard, self-help and community housing development (hence unauthorized), comprising nearly half of the total dwelling units built every year. Often the city development plans prove to be the impediments to organic, indigenous and community approach to employment and housing largely catering to the poor section of the society.

The avowed objective of planning often stand defeated in the face of changing hazards to the community, viz, critical shortages of basic services, particularly water and power, traffic congestion, massive encroachments, noise pollution, haphazard signboards and hoarding, and other forms of nuisance. It is a sheer wastage of manpower and resources of the local bodies largely preoccupied with checking of deviation in individual buildings up to nearest centimeters, when there is no machinery and resources available to check the major sources of nuisance and pollution causing critical threat to social health, convenience and safety.

The studies indicate that to obtain planning permission for a group housing project, it would take 4 to 8 weeks in Singapore whereas in India, it may take few years and would involve dealing with at least 20 to 30 organisations/ government bodies. The effect of delays and time loss is spectacular. This not only hinders city and economic development but inverts the creation of jobs. The propensity of planning officials to reject a development plan on technicality, instead of passing it subject to appropriate changes, results in loss of time and energy. The growth of local wealth and tax base is suspended and the jobs are lost (except the job of the officials). There is a built-in bias against growth, expansion and extension and most of the official planners are afraid to take a positive view, largely because they want to avoid allegations of corruption and favourism. The 'status quo' attitude imposes inflexibility which does not respond to the changing needs of a developing and dynamic society.

The provision of administrative discretion has bequeathed a system in which the planning officers can intervene with all kinds of prejudices, which are not compulsory and mandatory. Often there is a built-in bias against growth, expansion and extension and most of the official planners are afraid to take a positive view, largely because they want to avoid allegations of corruption and favourism. The 'status quo' attitude imposes inflexibility which does not respond to the changing needs of a developing and dynamic society. The provision of administrative discretion has bequeathed a system in which the planning officers can intervene with all kinds of prejudices, which are not compulsory and mandatory.

The complex, many a time contradictory and over detailed rules, regulation and byelaws fail to protect the endowed objectives of public health, safety and convenience, but are used as the tools for denial of the proposals and schemes, sometimes to expropriate illegal favours and thus breed corruption. The existing institutions are incapable of controlling the process of urbanization, providing basic needs for the majority of the people or halting environmental deterioration. The masses are disadvantaged by complexity of laws, impenetrate bureaucracies, onerous system of taxes, fees and licences, regulations, which are a barrier to self-help and their access to resources. Making human settlement institutions more effective and more responsive to people's needs and aspirations should be a major goal.

Changes in Planning Process

In view of above challenges, there is a need for a paradigm shift in the planning approach and process, the key areas being the following: In order to translate new policies and paradigm into practice, the planners have to prepare themselves for a new role and much wider responsibilities.

As a bridge between the civil society and the politico-economic structure, the planners have to perform the role of the catalysts of change. At the organisational level, the local bodies and town planning departments have to gear up for a major shift in their roles. Traditional town planning has to be replaced by strategic and Action planning and Building Bye-laws and Development Controls to be replaced by a comprehensive regulatory framework with an orientation to support and promote the planned develop-ment by the community/private initiatives.

This requires a rigorous capacity building - at individual, corporate and organisational levels. They have to reaffirm their commitment towards the profession, society and city. As the agents of change there is a need to integrate a broader cross- section of professionals and develop an aptitude of flexibility.

With the ongoing globalisation, economic liberalisation and devolution of power to local bodies, gone are the days of armchair professionals. Their insulation from the general masses and the political system may be catastrophic in the changing environment, where participatory decision making is becoming institutionalised. Among the professionals, who require expertise exercised with integrity, skills are necessary to strike a balance between the political process and service delivery together.

In the context of decentralisation of power from Central/ State Governments to local levels, there is a clear need to strengthen the Urban Local Bodies and endowing them with the finances, commensurate with their assigned responsibility. The experience indicates that the first and foremost priority should be to strengthen the local bodies and improve their performance, which have the primary responsibility to provide urban services.

This would involve the following key initiatives:

- The introduction of short and medium-term, Integrated Action Planning, to complement comprehensive long term objectives - simplification of plans and procedures
- Assets Inventory and Management for optimum utilisation and the increase of the revenue base
- A new urban land policy, to match with the National Housing and Habitat Policy, whereby the local authorities act as the facilitators and harness the resources of private sector/community

- Upgrading technology and environment focus for Infrastructure services and transportation
- Exploring new options and public-private partnership for development and financing of infrastructure, land development, housing, conservation, environmental improvement and slum/JJ rehabilitation.
- Adoption of Multi-year Investment Planning to match priorities of state budgets/5 Year Plans with urban projects
- A new approach towards Development Controls, to mobilise private sector in provision of services and community facilities, and adoption of concepts like white zoning, Accommodation Reservation, Transfer of Development Rights (TDR), Excess condemnation, etc.
- Networking with international and national urban prgrammes, e.g. Citynet, Healthy Cities, UMP, etc.
- Mandatory performance management system and MIS - networking with NGOs, CBOs and private sector for planning, management and maintenance.

A leveraging strategy should be adopted so as to encourage private sector to participate in infrastructure/city development for which there is an urgent need of intersectoral cooperation. It is necessary to explore the areas where the government can cooperate in partnership. With the private sector participation, encouraging cooperation, partnership and competition is a critical area of concern.

There are numerous success stories of innovative partnerships in various areas of development, as given below:

- Reforms in Municipal Administration - Andhra Pradesh,
- District Planning Committees - Kerala
- Efficiency Enhancement - Ludhiana
- Devolution of Powers - Allahabad
- Fiscal empowerment - Bangalore, Chennai, Guwahati, Indore, Jaipur, Mumbai,
- Ludhiana, Mysore, Patna, Vijayawada
- Accrual Based Municipal Accounting system - Tamilnadu

- Partnership in Urban Services - Nasik, Panvel, Pune, Jaisingpur, Baroda,
- Chennai, Tiripur, Hyderabad, Visakhapatnam, Indore, Delhi-NOIDA, etc.
- Geographic information system - Mirzapur
- Asset Management - Mirzapur
- Property tax - Mirzapur, Nagpur, Patna
- Poverty alleviation, slum rehabilitation and micro-credit - Ahmedabad, Mysore, Pune
- Municipal Bonds - Ahmedabad, Bangalore, etc.
- Innovative building bye-laws - Greater NOIDA.

A major effort should be made to reverse system of top-down planning and management. Planning should relate to local social, cultural and environmental conditions and facilitating popular participation in habitat development. It should encourage new forms of popular participation through stimulation of direct action groups, public-private joint ventures, and non-governmental organisations dedicated to community action. This requires an increased flow of information to the people and to nongovernmental organisations, and improves the feedback of information from the people to institutions. Capacity building of institutions and training of community leaders would improve and assure grass-roots participation in government support programmes. New ways will be needed to share and coordinate responsibilities among local, regional and state authorities and also between planning, housing, transport, energy supply, etc. Authority for decision making should be decentralized to increase community control over actions affecting them.

PLANNING CONTROLS VS. PROMOTION SUPPORTS

During recent years significant changes have taken place in land use zoning, planning norms and parameters, subdivision regulations etc. These include Master Plan of Delhi 2001 (Development Code), Simplified Development Promotion

Regulations of Urban Affairs and Employment (1996), General Development Control Regulations for Navi Mumbai, CIDCO (1994), and also the regulations of Singapore Redevelopment Authority, Chennai Metropolitan Development Authority and Greater NOIDA. The innovative concepts of zoning such as given below should be included in the Planning and Development Controls:

- Planning Unit Development Zoning (PUD)
- Transfer of Development Rights (TDR)
- Performance Zoning
- Evolutionary Zoning
- Floating Zoning
- Conditional Zoning
- Incentive Zoning
- Accommodation Reservation
- White Zoning
- Excess Condemnation
- Squatter holding zoning

Also various kinds of planning permissions charges/taxes required to be paid thereof may form part the subordinate legislation.

These may include –vacant land tax, Development Charges, impact fees, betterment levy, conversion charges, Purchasable Development Rights, misuse charges, parking levy/charges, additional FAR charges etc. In the context of changing scenario and increasing role of private sector there is a need to evolve a new set of regulatory framework, which are simple, transparent, responsive, flexible and clear.

Keeping in view the availability of large number of qualified professionals, prevalent corruption and harassment, it is time to review the need of Building Bye-laws which can be replaced by zoning/planning controls so that the infrastructure services, environment, aesthetics, parking and other public concerns like safety and health are safeguarded rather than internal features of buildings.

This will facilitate development which is environmentally appropriate and would meet the social needs of the public at large. In order to avoid sustained litigation between the developers and local bodies, these should have a strong legal backing. In place of emphasis on individual buildings, the focus should be on environment, infrastructure services, and area based schemes. The zoning and urban controls have to address to emerging issues of environment, services, urban design, renewal and conservation. These should ensure welfare of the handicapped/disabled and weaker sections of the society. As a basic principle, the regulation of building activity should make it redundant for an official to enter a private building. This means that the controls and bye-laws should do away with the regulations for internal features, like room size, ventilation, sanitary fittings, etc.

Building bye-laws should be extremely simple and limited to the external elements of buildings, such as bulk, envelope, height, setbacks, parking etc. Registered Architects may be given powers to sanction the building plans, subject to conformity with the zoning/development controls. This would reduce the burden of the local bodies and eliminate corruption to a great extent. In this way, a graded approach for regulation of planning/building permissions activity can be evolved. This would comprise of no approval stage, prototype sanction, sanction by registered architects, instant sanction, Block Sanction, Planning Permission and Urban Design Approval. For example, no sanction may be required for plots upto 50 sqm. and for plots up to 500 sqm. sanction by registered architects should be sufficient.

For multistoreyed buildings, group housing, layouts, redevelopment schemes, etc., sanction of local authority in respect of Zoning Regulations, planning permission, urban design approval and approval of Fire Department should be necessary. The requirement of obtaining various permission and building sanction may be reduced to grant of planning permission which may be necessary for any scheme above 4 ha., where the role of qualified town planner and Land Scape Architect becomes mandatory.

FLOOR AREA RATIO (FAR)

The FAR is the most crucial aspect of Planning Regulations and has a direct bearing with the property value. There are large variations in FAR in the country, which are usually arbitrary and fail to capture the value addition due FAR for city development and municipal services. In the urban context, planning regulations can use FAR as a major resource for the local bodies, who have a responsibility to provide infrastructure services and confer development rights. It would be most pertinent to provide a basic FAR of 100 (FSI of 1.0) in the regulations together with an upper ceiling for which the planning/local body may be empowered to charge Purchasable Development Right Levy for FAR in excess of a basic FAR (say 1.0). Thus, Planning Regulations can act as a gold mine for the local bodies, which are always short of the funds for development of infrastructure. This will also help in the localisation of the planning and regulatory functions conferred under the 74th Constitutional Amendment Act, 1992.

LOW INCOME HOUSING

The present development control framework is not conducive to promote low- income housing through cooperative/private sector. The difficulty arises in balancing FAR and density and there is generally gross under-utilisation of FAR for EWS/ LIG housing. As such, it is recommended to regulate development controls only through FAR so that use of limited urban land can be maximized. It is also proposed to review the standards like minimum width of roads, parks, standards of community facilities and open space etc. which are realistic and affordable. In this regard, IS-8888 should be reviewed and incorporated in the Local Codes/Planning Regulations.

Most of the co-operative societies cater to middle and high income groups, and there is hardly any provision for community services, personnel and informal sector working as domestic servants of the residents. It is proposed that a bonus FAR of 10 to 15 per cent may be allowed which will be utilized for construction of tenements upto maximum 25 sqm. plinth area. These tenements should revert to development authority or the local body for community services personnel/ EWS. This will generate a large housing stock without any investment of the local/government bodies.

REHABILITATION OF SQUATTERS/SLUM DWELLERS

By using FAR as a resource and by promoting formation of cooperative societies of slum and squatter clusters, the private sector and slum residents can be activated in resettlement and self-help upgradation programmes. For this, an incentive FAR (up to 50 percent) may be allowed and 10 percent of FAR may be permitted for commercial activity, by sale of which in the market, the whole scheme can become self-financing. Also, relaxation in set-backs and density should be available for such schemes. In this way, planning regulations can act as a tool of providing access to housing and services to economically weaker sections and slum dwellers.

RENEWAL AND RECONSTRUCTION

The inner city areas, urban villages, and regularized unauthorised colonies need renewal, upgradation and reconstruction. The concept of incentive zoning will promote redevelopment of such areas if they are offered incentives of FAR, ground coverage and mixed land use and will discourage unauthorized construction. The regulations should be framed keeping in view the requirements of circulation, parking, services and community facilities and for freehold properties up to 2000 sq.m. there may be no need to surrender land for community facilities and road widening and for larger areas benefit of FAR should be available for land required for facilities and road widening.

After 30-40 years, most of the public housing also usually becomes ripe for renewal. To facilitate urban renewal of housing complexes more than 20 years old, the submission of original building plans may not be insisted upon and power of attorney transfers may be acceptable. Such system will facilitate better use of dilapidated derelict old buildings and housing, which have become redundant with fast changing life-style and economic prosperity. The concept of white zoning adopted in Singapore has proved to be effective tool of urban turnaround of dilapidated, old areas. Under this, the developers/owners join together and work out a viable renewal or redevelopment scheme.

This is examined by Singapore Redevelopment Authority and sanction is given for mixed use or proposed activities as may be justified from services, transport and economic viability points of view. The Redevelopment Authority provides budgetary and infrastructure support to the developer, who transforms the area into something beautiful and functional. The narrow streets have been widened, where the owners do not loose FAR due to its widening, and modern infrastructure services could be extended in erstwhile substandard areas.

LEGAL AND REGULATORY FRAMEWORK

The maze of archaic legislation, which governs habitat sector and municipal resources, hardly inspires the people and the investor confidence. Rather than encouraging fiscal discipline and prudent management of debt, it places severe limits on municipal resource raising, a thorough revision of the regulatory framework is thus a need of the hour. An important issue that needs to be considered is the setting up of a regulatory authority for decisions related to fixing tariffs, quality of service etc. This was felt needed in the U.K. after privatisation of power, water and urban services so that other monopolistic trends of private sector operators and fall in quality of service do not take place. The Australian initiative of the utilities commission to take care of such issues of public interest in the delivery of urban services such as power, telecommunication, roads, etc. is worth mentioning.

In India this could be done through State Level Regulatory Bodies or at the level of important cities, which are financially strong and could decide upon the nature of tariff and other service related matters. Another important legislative instrument is the regulation of Public Private Partnership in city infrastructure provision through BOO, BOOT, etc. financing and managing mechanism on the lines of the federal law brought out by the Philippine govern-ment. The sustainability of infrastructure project depends on the success of policy planners in implementing a strong techno-Financial and techno-Legal regime based on viably rates of return for private sector participation. The techno-financial and techno- legal regime should support each other so that a conducive and sustainable environment is maintained for constant investments in the sector.

AN AGENDA FOR PLANNING REFORMS

In the above context and to compliment with the ongoing policies of economic reforms and democratic decentralisation, there is a need to embark upon several basic changes in the planning approach. The focus is to remove the barriers created by planning, with service delivery on ground with speed and efficiency. The key areas where such changes are necessary are given below:

Decentralised Governance:

- From Statutory/comprehensive planning to Integrated Action Planning, with focus on implementation and flexibility
- Localisation and Decentralisation of Planning
- Community Partnership and constituency planning interfacing administrative and political constituencies.
- Corporatisation of planning organisations.
- Strategic Planning with a view to mobilise private sector.
- Integrating physical planning with Institutional, Financial and Infrastructure Plans.
- Government as Facilitator and Catalyst in planning for self-rule, self-build and self-reliance.
- Political apparatus for people centred planning.

Market Economies and Privatisation:

- Efficiency, equity and employment/economic potentials as the criteria of planning.
- Emphasis on quality and innovative demand driven planning.
- Incentives for infrastructure and housing investments.
- Release access to land, housing, services, finance and information by public- private partnership.
- Focus at the grass roots and a pro-poor perspective.
- Planning to promote micro-enterprise and micro-banking.
- Mixed land use as a tool of planning for poverty reduction strategy.
- New methods of land assembly and development.
- Regularise land tenure
- Simplify and expedite land registration
- Review and simplify property taxation
- Emphasise cost recovery and 'user pays'
- Develop enabling strategies.
- Upgradation of infrastructure in slums and lower income population areas.
- Identify and incentivise private and community sector institutions.
- Target subsidies to the poor.
- Empowering the community.
- Encourage self-build housing and small businesses.
- Eliminate monopoly practices including government monopoly.

Make urban development self-financing and self-sustaining by developing the concepts of Excess Condemnation, TDR, Accommodation Reservation, land pooling and readjustment, development and conversion charges, betterment levy, additional FAR charges, BOT, franchising, contracting out, etc.

Environmental Concerns:

- Developing local environment Standards.
- Environment Impact Analysis

- Circular Metabolism for infrastructure systems
- Blue network planning.
- Waste Management and Recycling
- Services upgradation
- Cyclic Renewal
- Urban form and housing appropriate for environment and ecological compatibility.
- Energy saving, adoption of non-conventional sources of energy.
- Rainwater harvesting
- Industrial zoning, typology and locational decision.
- Public transport policy, plans and technology as major ingredients of environmental protection.
- Health concerns of planning, housing, services and slum/inner city renewal.
- Microclimate, pollution, dust and noise minimisation.
- Conservation of heritage.

Planning Promotion Supports in Place of Controls:

- Reduce the number of approvals required for private sector participation.
- Time limit for approvals
- Devolve and delegate powers to approve.
- One window system
- Replace lowest tendering system by alternative/Project Management Contract Systems
- Replace building approval under Building bye-laws by Planning Permissions.
- Resort to Free Development Zoning and White Zoning in City Plans.
- Invoke concepts of Transferable Development Rights (TDR) and Accommodation Reservation (AR).

Information Technology:

- Develop GIS and computer aided design for planning.
- Human Resource Management and Capacity Building.

- Assets Management.
- Need for Systems Approach.
- Computerise land/property records and digitise plans, layouts.
- Community/CBO/NGO Networking.
- Online planning and property information.
- Flexible zoning & dynamic networking
- Computerised system of approvals/planning permission.
- Intelligent services, buildings and transport.
- Development of I.T. infrastructure and Parks.
- Environment monitoring

MIS Legal and Management Reforms:

- Review all planning/building legislations and scrap outdated ones.
- Remove unnecessary controls
- Simplify procedures.
- Reduce regulatory complexity and deregulate wherever possible.
- Establish Regulatory Authority for urban development and privatisation.
- Minimize legal complexity, maximize enforcement and empower the community.
- Effective horizontalisation among actors, resources and people.

The above planning reforms will go a long way in the urban transformation and planning in concert with new economic policies and democratic decentralisation.

It is imperative that the planners and urban managers reconsider their approaches, ways and procedures and their impact on the economy, infrastructure and housing. The planners will have to redefine their roles so that they provide necessary supports to the growing importance of market philosophy, while safeguarding the social interests of the poor sections of the society.

RURAL DEVELOPMENT AS CAREER

Our national development agenda has its focus on rural development. Most of India dwells in rural areas and therefore the national development agenda rightly seeks justice for those who often live in poverty, in the state of hunger and malnutrition and deprived of clean environment, sanitation and medical facilities. Rural scenarios are generally represented by agriculture, which involves all the land-related activities, such as cropping, forestry, agro forestry, plant protection, horticulture, animal husbandry, poultry, rural-based agro-industries, and the likes.

The state agricultural universities, the Indian Agricultural Research (ICAR) institutes and the rural development institutions belonging to public and private sector work in accordance with the national development stream – the rural development. Agriculture is the soul of rural India and hence agricultural development represents the true spirit of national development.

A university is composed of four pillars:

i. Its infrastructure,
ii. Students,
iii. Teachers/ researchers/ extension workers, and
iv. Stakeholders, especially farmers. Students form the largest base of the University and, haplessly, this strong base has been and is being addressed inadequately. If tapped properly we can transform students' energy into a kind of synergy that would be phenomenal towards changing the overall Indian rural scenario.

OLDEST AND THE YOUNGEST

India is the oldest civilization and yet today it has the largest proportion (40 percent or so) of the youth in the world. This population gives a youth flare to India. This segment of the population should be regarded as a boon rather than a bane. We must have enough enthusiasm, affection and affinity for this proportion of humanity. A fairly large proportion of this young population in the country is that of students who are supposed to be the future of a shining country. Reports from all corners of the world are pouring that India is shining and that China and India are the future leaders of the world. Much of India's shining would be contributed by the current strength of our youth, particularly the students.

The most important factor which could trigger the very positive role of students in rural development in India is how we as a university plan to shape their future. Students are getting exposure to a world view. They are being overdosed under the umbrella of information age. They are also dreaming about rendering their valuable services to the affluent countries of the North in order to enjoy better economic returns and all possible amenities ensuring high standards of life. Under such circumstances, challenges before the agricultural universities like that of ours appear to be difficult to be met. Youth energy is critical to development, but at the same time its proper management is equally difficult.

NEED OF A PARADIGM SHIFT

Rural development processes are still not very mature and upright. Despite unusually high number of agricultural universities and institutes in our country, we have not been able to make our students' mindset rural-oriented. Our youth are desperate to acquire lucrative jobs in big corporate houses or in foreign countries. Rural areas remain on the periphery of their thinking. A thought of work in and for rural areas, unfortunately, is like a nightmare for an average student in agricultural universities.

We need to ignite their thinking and reshape their attitudes so that they find rural areas as a better place for them to render their valuable services for which agricultural universities were established. This requires a paradigm shift in our basic thinking. Universities are signing protocols with foreign universities of the West and with big corporate houses, but we are neglecting our rural bodies playing vital role for the country. We are formulating exchange programmes with world renowned scientists but we are hesitating to visit our farmers and social workers in rural areas. Such an environment is fueling different types of interests in the minds of our students that keep rural areas and rural development away from their vision and future mandate.

Rural development processes must have primacy of youth involvement. This should begin with special orientation inherent in our course curricula.

Most of the subjects taught to the students at agricultural universities are not only relevant to rural areas and farming communities but also emanate from a vision of rural development evolved together by our by a galaxy of educationists, planners and statesmen. The courses are natural allies of the rural development processes. But the pedagogic mechanism is unable to stimulate amongst the students any strong emotional affinity towards Indian culture, heritage and rural elements of national develop-ment paradigm. Students, unfortunately, keep on thinking about acquiring physical amenities and fat salaries through services in urban and industrial environments and/ or in western or European countries.

Our public system should make sincere efforts for creating employment opportunities in rural areas. There is large number of agro-based industries which should especially be established in rural areas. These industries might range from cottage industries to the ones manufacturing finishing products of high value and low volume, such as perfumery, vegetable seed production, dairy product processing, etc. University graduates and trained post graduates if employed in these rural-based agro-industries after building up a proper infrastructure, a revolution in rural economy would no more remain a dream.

Indian agricultural universities have a track record of producing excellent students who are providing excellent services to different sectors all over the country as well as in foreign countries. There is no doubt that they would revolutionise the Indian rural areas once a paradigm shift with rural-centric thinking is realized in practical manner.

PHILOSOPHY THAT HELPS TO MEND OUR ENVIRONMENT

Every nation, every civilization, every era and every age cherishes some kind of philosophy which is evolved with trial and error over millennia. This philosophy imbibes in the generations of a civilization. We need to evolve a right kind of philosophy that should help our country and the world at large to heal them, to go vibrant, to sustain blossoming values, to make transcendental progress and that should constantly nourish the roots of our survival and sustainability.

India's culture is basically an *aranya* (forest) culture. Our vision has been nature-centric, not blindly an anthropocentric. As we know today, forests impart an essential ecological integrity that ensures sustainability of our systems - habitats, agriculture, livelihoods, and of every kind. The first principle of ecology states that everything is linked with everything else. We also know that in order to be sustainable every system must have an ecological integrity of its own. In the wake of global warming leading to ghastly climate changes, we need to revive and develop ecological philosophy. This ecological philosophy (the meaningful fusion of ecology and philosophy) has come into being with the outstanding efforts of Professor Henryk Skolimowski. His efforts have brought the ecological movement on the roads.

Tapping the elements from Skolimowskian philosophy, the eco-philosophy is about the appropriate, symbiotic and coherent relationship with our nature, austerity, frugality (grace without waste), utilization of natural resources, spirituality, integrity, reverential attitude towards nature and natural resources for their conservation and it is about life-enhancing karma.

Students are extra-sensitive to the issues that might irreparably affect our environment and socioeconomic development. The issues of global warming and climate changes are of that sort. The world is desperate to get out of the messy situation our global environment is in and the peculiar nature of the eco-crises the globe is in the vicious circle of.

Students need be exposed to ecological philosophy which would help them becoming sensitive towards the environment and social ecosystems they are part of. This would help us restore our dying planet and mend our environment to meet the climate change challenges of our times. Eco-philosophy would help the students in every walk of life. In whatever job they get absorbed in they would be involves in right thinking and right behaviour and do everything in the interest of nature, in the interest of symbiotic and synergetic relations and for the enhancement of life.

LIBERAL EDUCATION

The GB Pant University of Agriculture and Technology has a grand experience of the Liberal Education Programme. Conventional course curriculum is the soul of an academia, but it is not just enough for the students to impart a dimension of holistic development. The conventional programmes contribute to generate experts, but we need more than that. We need an educational supplement that could contribute to holistic development of the students. Liberal Education programme attempts to provide a holistic and more creative dimension to students' personality development.

The Liberal Education, while inculcating amongst students social, cultural, humane, spiritual, ethical and aesthetic values, also aims at equipping the young generation with the knowledge relating to the social value systems, environments, habitats, earth and cosmos they are the part and parcel of. The students get opportunity to learn various provincial and international languages, art, cultures, music, yogas, etc. This is basically a Certificate Course, absolutely voluntary and having no bearing on the overall grade point average of students. This is run by the University in need of holistic human development to articulate in intellectual and emotional involvement of the young generation in promoting a culture of peace, tranquility and values in the course of developing a more inhabitable, sane and sustainable world, which is an imperative of our times.

ADDING VALUE TO RURAL DEVELOPMENT VIA STUDENTS' PARTICIPATION

Student life is full of energy, dreams and enthusiasm. Creative thoughts always keep imbibing in students. They can be molded in any direction their predecessors want. They can be instrumental in changing the whole rural scenario should their full potential be unleashed and effective participation be realized. Agricultural university's course curriculum has practical applications of the agricultural education. Practical Crop Production, extension programmes, field laboratories, etc. are the many rural development-oriented programmes that are imparted to students. Students exposed to these programmes and inculcating deeper values of life, naturally, would readily be the part and parcel of the rural development processes. Their participation would also add substantial value to rural development.

The face of rural India is changing. With the government increasing budget of rural development and other ministries extending their shares of schemes and also with the large-scale intervention of Public Sector Undertakings as a part of their social obligation in the field of rural development, the job opportunities at various levels are also increasing. While the rural development is still a mission for development agencies, it has become a profession for young graduates which gives them dual satisfaction of earning livelihood as well as undertaking social service.

One can join a government agency, a non-government organisation or even freelance. This chapter gives an insight to those aspirants who have social science background and want to make social service a career. Rural development as a career has gained much importance as this area is very vast and employment opportunities in this area would increase in the years to come. The all-round development of rural area ranges from infrastructure development to upliftment of rural poor and the downtrodden, health, education, economic self reliance and empowerment of women.

The concept of rural development has changed in the

last decade. It traversed from charity to making rural folk self-reliant and capable on the lines of Mahatma Gandhi's thoughts. This was the major breakthrough in the domain or rural development that came to be known as 'paradigm-shift'. The paradigm shift was not merely a change in the philosophy of rural development but in its functional aspects as well – there is now a thrust on quality and not quantity, development and empowerment replaced charity and welfare, dependecia (acute from the dependence) was overthrown by self-help.

The new concept is "instead of handling out fish, impart the training of fishing" i.e. Make people self-reliant through their capacity building; make them healthy by educating them about health precautions. Making them aware of their rights and duties would be their real help. The task of rural development was gradually adopted as a profession in our country, various educational institutes came forward to offer professional course in rural development in order to prepare a cadre of skilled and committed rural development professionals, adoption of such tasks by corporate sector as a part of their social responsibility has further strengthened the roots of this profession. Various corporate companies like Tata, Reliance, Mafatlal, Arvind Mills and ITC etc. Have specially setup their rural development units that require competent professionals.

As we all know the government is doing its best for rural development and has increased the budget of rural development manifold in last few years. The union government at present is the largest funding agency that finance voluntary organisations and non government organisation (NGOs) involved in rural development. It has a monitoring system that supervises the proper utilisation of funds. Other government ministries like ministry of health, human resource development, ministry of social justice and empowerment are also having a large chunk of their budgetary allocation earmarked for undertaking schemes and programmes in rural areas.

Apart from government, Indian and foreign donor agencies have their stakes in popularizing and strengthening this profession in India by sponsoring small to large-scale projects of rural development. Rural development as a profession is gradually gaining popularity with more and more young and competent professionals joining it as their livelihood and also because of the increasing number of educational institutions offering related professional courses.

The course of rural development is unique in itself. On one hand it provides an understanding of human issues while on the other hand, it enables the students to operate the mechanical devices like computer. If students know the art of motivating rural people and getting their participation; they also know the managerial skills of managing a projects, if they have an understanding of human psychology, behavioural science, they are also well versed in natural resources. This balance of theoretical sessions and practical is the uniqueness of this course.

The course of rural development emphasises principles like 'grass roots learning, 'hands on culture', learning by doing' and 'land to lab'. That is why apart from learning within the four walls of classroom, the students also learn under the open sky - in agricultural fields, in villages, in forests, in the operational areas of the voluntary organizations, etc.

Course syllabus of rural development encompasses classroom sessions, presentation, symposia, organisational visits, rural camps and dissertation (summer projects). The dissertation is the one of the most highlighted areas of the source because during this period students practice the theories thought in the class room, deeply understand the chosen development issue in the operational area of different voluntary organisations. This two months' project (period may vary from institute to institute) serves as the exercise board for the students.

In this way, the course prepares a cadre of such professionals who have the understanding of the dimensions of rural development and skills as well to manage those dimensions optimally. Employment opportunities in this field are immense because of the newly created interest of the corporate sector in it, government's increasing attention towards rural development and missionary spirit of the voluntary organisations who have pioneered and led the task of the rural development in our country.

In the changes scenario (in which rural development is no more philanthropy but a profession), corporate sector, government's development units and voluntary organisation rely on professionals for the professional accomplishment of their tasks. The horizon of the profession is gradually expending and so is increasing the competition the quality and competition in it.

Recognition of the Course

All the institutions offering course in rural development have either an affiliation to the local university or approval from all India council of technical education, Delhi thereby making the course as good as other management courses. There is still a need to bring about an altitudinal change towards this profession that can transform Gandhi's vision of India's rural development into reality. The aspirants are advised to check from the website of AICTE fro recognition of particular institute.

Course Structure

Two years divided into four semesters. Separate examinations are held in each semester. Passing each semester individually is compulsory.

Probable Employers

Government development agencies/ departments/ state resource centers:

- Voluntary Organisations.
- Social Development Units of corporate sector.
- National/International donor agencies
- Self-Employment (running one's own voluntary organisation or doing research and project formulation as a freelancer)

There are diversified employment opportunities in this sector that can be obtained as per one's capability and orientation. Employment opportunities can be in the following forms:

- Trainer
- Researcher
- Consultant
- Project coordinator (leading to superior posts like project director)

Apart from the above mentioned institutions, almost all universities run professional courses in rural development in the form of MA (Sociology), MSW PG Diploma in Rural Development etc. The aspirants are thus advised to first choose their area of interest from various aspects of rural development and then admission to the concerned institution. Most of the institutes now admit candidates through entrance examination. The admission notices appear in the newspapers between February and March while the admission process is completed by the May-June. The examination usually includes written, viva-voce and or group discussion.

EVALUATION FOR DEVELOPMENT

The First Biennial Conference of the International Development Evaluation Association (IDEAS) was held in New Delhi in April 2005. It was attended by civil society leaders, parliamentarians, and evaluation practitioners, managers of development and evaluation, and users of evaluation from developing and developed countries around the world. The conference highlighted the implications of the changing context of development for the evaluation community and identified new processes shaping development evaluation. In recent years, human rights and sustainability have become increasingly central to development. Beyond economic growth, the paradigm of development is shifting to focus on whether interventions result in equity and equality for citizens and communities.

In the new landscape, development encompasses human development and well-being through expanded capabilities, greater freedoms, wider choices, security, and the protection of human rights. This demands concomitant changes in evaluation processes. Evaluation will play a crucial role in improving governance and encouraging policy reforms that support the new, more equitable dynamics of development. New forms of partnerships will be needed to advance evaluation beyond the traditional paradigm of aid effectiveness. IDEAS act as a key liaison between the national, regional and international evaluation communities. India provided a vivid backdrop to this Conference. One of the ten fastest growing economies in the world, India also faces critical development challenges; it still struggles with widespread poverty, inequality, and child malnutrition—issues shared with other developing countries.

EVALUATING THE MULTIPLE DIMENSIONS OF DEVELOPMENT

Major shifts are occurring in the global landscape of development, with a trend toward sustainable development. However, the evaluation community has been slow to adapt its frameworks to encompass related factors such as globalisation, security, human rights, equity, gender, partnership, and policy coherence. The evaluation of Policy Coherence for Development would shift the focus of analysis toward global public policies and include the evaluation of international multi-country development programs that have largely escaped scrutiny; regional, national, and global policies; and the impact of regulatory regimes on developing countries. Involving developing countries in the evaluation process will require a major commitment to evaluation capacity development from donors, with both funding and governance arrangements that give substantive control of the agenda to developing countries.

Evaluating the Impact of Developed Country Policies on Developing Countries

The Millennium Development Goals constitute the first concerted move to set clear indicators for evaluating international development efforts. Mutual accountability is vital; however, developing countries often lack the capacity to evaluate development policies. Participatory evaluation must be encouraged to gain the perspectives of developing countries receiving aid. Human rights and development: Implications for evaluation. In the last few years, human rights have become increasingly central to development action. Kofi Annan talks about "freedom from wants and fears." The implications of operating in a human rights framework and evaluating development outcomes in human rights terms are many and far-reaching.

The challenge for development evaluation within the human rights framework is that the emphasis must move from rights as entitlements only to obligations for all the actors—states, civil society, and citizens. Evaluations should focus on the most vulnerable groups and determine whether interventions bring equity and equality.

Evaluating the Environmental Sustainability Dimensions of Development

Over the last 50 years, human-induced changes in ecosystems have resulted in a substantial and largely irreversible loss in the diversity of life on the planet. However, a shift to focus on the environmental sustaina-bility of development programs is beginning to occur. The significance of organizational performance and accounta-bility is increasingly recognized and ecosystem approaches to assessment are being adopted. It is critical to develop ways to evaluate the environmental impacts and sustainability of campaigns. Security and conflict: Implications for evaluation Development is increasingly recognized as a key element of conflict prevention and peace building.

Evaluating programs through the lens of development and conflict will require a political-economy analysis and understanding of the root causes of conflict situations. Data collection and analysis must be observer-based and objective. However, security issues have hampered the collection of data and consultation with local populations. The coordination of information, analysis, and data can also be challenging in post-conflict situations. New conceptual frameworks, approaches, tools, and institutional and partnership arrangements are needed since standard models are insufficient.

Developing Evaluation

The future of development evaluation hinges on global, national, and sub-national trends highlighting new evaluation policy directions, functions, forms and constituencies. Aid evaluation must be reformed to become more responsive to the emerging dynamics of sustainable development.

Global Trends in Development Evaluation

There is a growing trend of increased emphasis on robust impact evaluations of development interventions. Impact evaluations are a key component of evidence-based policy or program design—a critical challenge, though, is the unfavourable cost-benefit equation for key actors. Most developing countries have weak capacity and little incentive for development evaluation, and subsidies are needed to reduce the cost of evaluations for these countries.

Country-driven and Country-owned Capacities in Development Evaluation

The prerogative for evaluation, previously centered on government bureaucracies, is increasingly being challenged by civil society voices advocating participation, human rights, and equity; by private sector as it is increasingly sensitized to corporate social responsibility; and by Parliaments demanding government accountability. One of the challenges is to develop nationally owned systems that serve the needs of multiple partners. There is a growing will to do so, as part of harmonization and of the streamlining of development cooperation—however, sufficient financing is essential.

Local and Citizen Dynamics in the Evaluation of Development

In recent years, there has been a conceptual shift in support of citizen participation in the development and evaluation of interventions designed for their benefit. However, a number of challenges must be overcome. Entry points for citizen involvement are difficult when programs are still being developed and implemented without their involvement.

Aid Evaluation and its Future

The shift from aid evaluation to development evaluation will require new priorities and approaches that encompass management for development results, human develop-ment, human rights, public accountability, country-based evaluation, and national ownership. National ownership of the development agenda must be seen as key. Aid evaluation should aim to create national capacity to autonomously evaluate results, and the scope of evaluation should be widened to observe policy issues and develop-ment effectiveness.

Governance of Evaluation

In the new development context, it is important to examine the institutional arrangements, participants, and stakeholders that promote accountability in development through the use of evaluation, and to correct asymmetries in the conduct and governance of evaluation.

Government and State Accountability

With the new global compact for sustainable develop-ment, the governance of development evaluation requires considerable reshaping, with increased accountability to citizens. Governments have commitments to donors and financial institutions, and to citizens. Parliaments can be an effective instrument of accountability and oversight.

Corporate Social Responsibility

The advent of new partnerships between development

agencies, governments, civil society, and the private sector constitute an enormous paradigm shift. Foreign direct investments are now three times higher than aid. However, along with private sector development is the concept of corporate social responsibility, that beyond financial and economic objectives, corporations can also achieve social and environmental objectives. Corporate social responsibility principles are being increasingly adopted by international institutions.

Civil Society and Accountability

Civil society organizations have become integral to the development landscape. However, accountability is particularly challenging for them because they are required to "account" to governments and donors, funding agencies, constituents, as well as partner civil society organizations. It is important to build civil society's capacity to participate in the planning, implementation, and monitoring of programs. Evaluation must be undertaken as a partnership, rather than being driven by donors; ideally, it would be led by aid recipients.

Moving Forward

The emergence of new development trends is creating new evaluation needs. The Delhi conference linked knowledge and practice and brought together national and regional evaluation communities, practitioners, decision makers and beneficiaries from developed and developing countries. It was an important forum for exploring the various ways IDEAS could help evaluation contribute to development:

- Bridge building Convening forums
- Facilitating new partnerships for change
- Developing new communities of practice
- Addressing north-south asymmetries
- Capacity building Promoting innovation and learning
- Creating knowledge
- Giving voice to evaluators.

BUSINESS PARTNERSHIPS IN INDIA-A NEW PARADIGM

We are living in a time when no organisation can succeed itself. The development of results-focussed nonprofit and business creates a growing opportunity for these organisations to work together and create new possibilities that further their respective missions. Nonprofits know they must become more businesslike. Businesses know they must become more socially responsible. As we look around us in a new century, we realise that business and nonprofits in today's interconnected world will neither thrive nor survive within the walls of their own organisations. They need to look beyond the walls and find partners who can help achieve greater results and build the vital communities to meet the challenges ahead.

Increasingly enough, the need for cross-sector partnering between businesses and nonprofits for social development efforts in rural and urban areas is greatly realized in almost all the developed and developing countries to respond to the development demands of humanity. To quote James Austin, "the problems facing our cities seem to defy solution. But the only certainty is that these increasingly complex challenges exceed the capabilities of any single sector—public, private, or nonprofit—to solve them alone."

Around the world, in particular developed countries, many businesses have been actively involving themselves in corporate giving either directly or though nonprofit sectors for community development initiatives. The importance of corporate partnership for community service was not only widely accepted but also very expressively demonstrated by many businesses by way of 'corporate giving', thanks to the management philosophy of Oliver Sheldon in 1923 who attempted to blend social ethics with the practicability of scientific management.

In point of fact, his principles of the 'ethics' or 'ought ness' of industrial management and the human elements of corporate responsibility were widely accepted by the corporate sector in the 20th century and are now very much considered to be the need of the hour in every country in the present changing global cultures. Today, community service as a part of the business culture is very much practiced by many corporate in the developed and developing countries. James Campell, President of Norwest Bank, Minnesota, USA said "There's something magical here, a feeling of responsibility, of giving back to the community and making everyone's life better. It (service) is an ingrained expectation".

Indeed there is a growing recognition among corporations of the value of nonprofit-business collaboration for taking up community service programmes for developing healthy societies. But building cross sector relationships of business and nonprofits do not just happen. They are built. Such cross sector partnering will surely be a collaboration paradigm of the 21st century. Peter F. Drucker, the living legend in the field of management has stated "Today's business/nonprofit partnerships are leading the biggest change in philanthropy since the rise of the foundations 100 years ago-the shift from philanthropy to investment. We are now talking about a true partnership to build community and produce people who are needed by healthy businesses and a healthy society."

While many corporate sectors in India are directly or indirectly involved in building social infrastructure of a community namely education, health care, housing, economic development, culture, sports, civic measures, environment development and improvement of other human environments, the questions raised are? Are these corporate initiatives ensuring full participation of the poor, the marginalised and the disabled in the economic and developmental process? Are their rights and duties in a civil society enforced? Are their corporate partnership initiatives geared towards meeting the major social development issues namely?

- Eradication of poverty
- Expansion of productive employment and reduction of unemployment and

- Fostering social integration? How do nonprofit business collaborations respond to these vital issues?

CORPORATE PARTNERSHIPS- INDIAN SCENARIO

There are many motivations that lead corporate sector to support cross sector collaboration. To quote from Larry Perlman "a corporation in this world today carries with it a responsibility broader than just running the business every day. Business will not endure in a society that's not functional, so in a sense it's the most effective form of long-range strategic planning".

In the Indian scenario, the religious tradition of philanthropy carried through ages has influenced corporate giving for community development. Historical evidences reveal that since 1893 there have been many large corporate groups in India which have had been organising social development activities and providing corporate care for community directly through their own foundations/trusts and also some corporate groups practicing 'cheque book charity' or giving funds to the 'CEO's wife's charity' for community care activities or donating material resources to various development organisations from time to time.

Getting Involved

Why do corporate sectors collaborate? To what extent are business sectors connected to the social purpose of the collaboration? What is the purpose of the collaboration? Where does the relationship fall on the collaboration continuum and where does each partner want it to be-philanthropic, transactional or integrative. Do both partners have written collaboration purpose statements? What are the missions, strategies and values of each partner what specific benefits will accrue to each partner from the collaboration? What resources of each partner are of value to the other? What is the level of organisational commitment to the partnership and how is this commitment demonstrated?

There are many internal and external reasons, which have prompted corporate sectors in India to be socially responsible to society. The internal reasons being employee morale and customer and shareholder satisfaction, and the external reasons include satisfying local communities, publicity and tax benefits and enlightened self-interest etc. Interestingly enough, it was TATA family in India which was on the forefront in corporate giving in 1893, which was by followed many other enlightened corporate houses. The doyen of the Indian industry, Jamshedji Tata set up an endowment scheme for higher education and his heirs Ratan Tata and Dorab Tata carried the tradition of the Tata culture of corporate social responsibility.

Following the clarion call given by Gandhiji, the father of our nation to the business communities in India during the freedom struggle movement, many corporate sectors came forward to contribute to social development sector through institution building roles. It is found that leading Indian companies namely Mahindra and Mahindra groups, the Birla, the Bajaj, Lupin etc have since then been involved in social development mission which have not only benefited the communities to economic stability and improved quality of life of the people but also added more credibility to the corporate image.

Data gathered indicate that there are 135 Indian companies, which are involved in charity missions or social development work. These Corporates undertake programmes on various issues concerning children, women, health, disability, education, environment, disaster, communication, youth, rural development, water, multiple services and other human development activities. Further, it is noticed that there are 12 categories of Indian Corporates namely:

1. Advertising and Communication
2. Manufacturing
3. Telecommunication
4. Airlines
5. Bank
6. Chemicals and Pharmaceuticals
7. Consulting and financial

8. FMCGS
9. Government Companies
10. Big Industrial Groups
11. Information Technology
12. Others involved in Promoting

Interestingly enough, the Confederation of Indian Industry is also involved in social development activities namely population and health, education and literacy and community development.

It is quite revealing that multinational and national corporate sectors like Citibank, Coca Cola India, Dupont South Asia Ltd, Balmer Lawrie, Bharat Petroleum, Indian Oil Corporation, Shell Foundation, Bank of America, Business standard, Proctor and Gamble, Hindustan Lever, ITC, Lalbhais, AMM Foundation, Bajaj Auto, Sarabhai, Videocon Group, Wockhardt Dr.Reddy's Laboratories, Excel Industries etc have been taking up partnership programmes in India mostly through their direct service delivery networks. But nonetheless, there are many more corporate houses in India that have to be socially responsible and involve in social development efforts in both rural and urban areas. Interestingly enough, most of the Public sector undertakings have been actively involved in corporate giving/philanthropy or running direct and/or indirect programmes though various support activities in the fields of education, health, rural development, housing etc.

The survey conducted by the Indian Research Market Bureau (2000) has revealed that the concept of 'corporate partnership' was not understood nor the importance of corporate giving was realised by many companies in India. It was reported that of the 600 companies surveyed, there was no indication of any upward trend as to the increasing role of the corporate sector in social development activities. Furthermore, nearly 70 per cent of the companies surveyed were undertaking social development activities by way of donations or directly or indirectly organising community services programmes through their own foundations/trusts.

More than 80 per cent of such programmes were of a long-term nature. Sadly enough, cross- sector partnering between these companies and nonprofits was not very much evidenced. Even those few corporates, which are taking up community assistance programmes in alliance with nonprofits, they are not of long term in nature nor multi-year partnering. Surprisingly enough, there are many companies in India which are actively and indiscriminately involved in event sponsorships namely a cultural/music event, fashion show, beauty contest, sports etc, which mostly benefit their business rather than benefiting the community. These companies rarely get involved in cross sector partnering with nonprofit organisations in social development activities.

COLLABORATION CONTINUUM

The forms of business collaboration with nonprofits are mostly 'philanthropic' and not 'transactional'-when organisations carry out their resources exchanges through specific activities, such as cause-related marketing, event sponsorships, licensing and paid service arrangements, nor 'integrative'-when collaborative relationship is developed and the partners' missions, people and activities begin to experience more collective action and organisational integration.

In Indian scenario, relatively not a substantial number of Nonprofits and companies have advanced to this degree of integration. Though many nonprofits in India are expectantly looking for business collaboration for social development activities in rural and urban areas, corporate partnerships have a long way to go before arriving at this integrative stage.

CROSS-SECTOR COLLABORATION-THE NEED OF THE HOUR

If more companies in India were to involve in cross-sector collaboration with nonprofits for promoting the quality of life of children and women in particular through development efforts in and around the place where the companies/ industries are located, much of the community needs could be fulfilled. Corporate giving to nonprofit organisations in India should become a part of every company's strategy for it yields benefits to the company in four important areas: strategy management, human resource management, culture building, and business generation.

To quote an example, Citicorp, a global financial services corporation has incorporated community service an integral part of its new worldwide corporate strategy and one of six key indicators to measure the company's performance. 'Citicorp's management has described the rationale for this strategic engagement in this way: "We do this because it is the right thing to do and can offer profitable business opportunities. We also do this because we want a positive image with customers, potential customers, regulators, legislators, and community groups all of which supports our global image as a trusted brand name. We are talking here about how we run our business, not just about contributions, volunteerism and PR. It has moved from 'nice to do' to 'need to do' as part of our business strategy'.

Corporate sectors in India have to work in alliance with nonprofits on a long-term basis in the effectively delivering the community services such as:

1. Strengthening primary education especially in rural areas
2. Primary health care initiatives
3. Micro-enterprise lending programmes for the poor
4. Provision of drinking water
5. Environmental awareness and sustainable development programmes
6. Promoting children's rights
7. Preventive health education for adults on alcoholism and drug abuse, HIV/AIDS
8. Promoting peace and communal harmony in the community.

As the world communities are beginning to form a 'global society', nonprofits and businesses have their social responsibility. Peter Drucker has stated 'Too few in our society truly understand the concept of partnership or the nature of the social sector. With government and business, the social sector is one of the three pillars on which modern society is based, and by far the most diverse.

But no one sector can do its jobs alone; business cannot thrive in a sick society. All three must work together. We must establish the independence and the interdependence of each sector. The Drucker Foundation has viewed 'A healthy society requires three vital sectors: a public sector of effective governments; a private sector of effective businesses; and a social sector of effective community organisations'.

THE FUTURE OF CORPORATE SOCIAL RESPONSIBILITY

In the mid-1990s, the Board and Senior Management at VanCity Credit Union saw how integrating corporate social responsibility (CSR) into the business operations was a natural and logical direction for a democratic, member-focused credit union. At the time, CSR was identified as one of three strategic business goals, and products and services were developed that included social and environmental components. Since then, VanCity has come a long way. We've learned that in order to become a true CSR leader, we need to go much further than just developing products and services with a CSR edge - we need to work towards embedding CSR into all facets of the our operations.

It's become part of our long-term strategic direction. Part of becoming a leader in CSR understands the longer-term trends in social and environmental issues and how they may impact stakeholder demands, potential partnerships, and consumer attitudes in the years to come. VanCity commissioned this study as part of an overall scan to understand CSR trends.

VanCity engaged CSR Consultant and former VanCity Board Member Coro Strandberg of Strandberg Consulting to explore and summarize the trends that CSR leaders saw developing in the long-term, to "take a look around the corner". Strandberg interviewed nearly 50 "CSR thought leaders" in North American and internationally, to explore the evolution and trends expected in the next five to 10 years.

These trends include those on social change, governance and accountability, innovation, and standardization of CSR. While there are a number of valuable lessons from the report, a key learning is that measuring the impact of our social and environmental actions is a work in progress and can always be improved. We hope the themes identified in this report can be used not only by other corporations, but also governments, NGOs and other stakeholders that are looking at their own long-term CSR planning. Corporate social responsibility (CSR) has been around in various guises for a quarter century or perhaps longer, depending on one's view of history. It has evolved to the status of a profession and is being debated on the world stage, advanced by Globalisation and technology.

There are (CSR) consultancies and think tanks in most developed and developing countries around the world. Social (e.g.9-11, HIV Aids), environmental (e.g. climate change) and economic (e.g. Enron) shocks are elevating issues of corporate responsibility to the international arena. Companies which aspire to be, or are, leaders in corporate social responsibility are challenged by rising public expectations, increasing innovation, continuous quality improvement and heightened social and environmental problems. They are forced to chart their CSR course within a very complex and dynamic environment. To assist this exercise it can be useful to reflect on the longer term trends in CSR - the future of corporate social, environmental and ethical responsibility 5 - 10 years from now, beyond the immediate operating environment.

How will the social/environmental /economic dimensions of corporate sustainability evolve 5 - 10 years out? What will be the stakeholder demands on companies in the future? What forms of collaboration and partner- ship will emerge? What will be the new CSR issues confronting corporations? What will be the regulatory environment and government's role in

CSR? In effect, what will be the new CSR operating environment for companies? The following is an attempt to capture some of this thinking of over 45 CSR "thought leaders"- those people who spend their livelihoods in the CSR field whether as an advisor to corporations, governments and NGOs, a business executive, social investor researcher, NGO or consumer advocate or CSR academic.

These CSR thought leaders have been asked to project how they think CSR will evolve in the future. Their ideas are summarized below into the themes most commonly expressed which they believe will emerge over the next decade as drivers and influencers of CSR. It is hoped that companies, governments, NGOs and other stakeholders will find this information of benefit as they work to improve social, economic and environmental conditions around the world.

METHODOLOGY

The views of forty-seven people were gathered, primarily through interviews though in select cases through written material during August, 2002. They were identified as CSR thought leaders by their reputation and through peer referral. Fourteen were from the UK, 18 from Canada, 8 the US, and one each were from the Netherlands, Hong Kong, Belgium, Switzerland, Australia and Italy.

The majority were CSR "advisors"(16), the rest were in Finance and Investment (7), Business - with some overlap with Finance (7), Academic (6), Stakeholder (6), Polling, Media and Commentators (3) and Government (2). Modest attempt was made to solicit input from various sectors, though this was constrained by the time frame of the research. The interviewees were asked open-ended questions designed to elicit their views on the future of CSR, though no strict questioning formula was adopted.

Their responses were summarized into eight key themes that emerged from the range of ideas presented. No definition of CSR was proposed for the purpose of the study, though by and large CSR was understood to mean the integration of social and environmental values through- out a company's operations and the engagement of stakeholders in this exercise. For many participants the term CSR is interchangeable with Sustainable Development (SD).

KEY THEMES

Slow Progress on CSR, But Moving into Mainstream Business There were different levels of optimism about the future of CSR, ranging from disillusionment that CSR will never be more than a cover for corporate activity to the most hopeful view that CSR is part of a paradigm shift from industrial capitalism to sustainability capitalism. This paradigm shift, it is predicted, will witness businesses finding a way to deliver on substantial social change, even - in some quarters - working to curtail the power business itself wields in society.

CSR pessimists predict:

- Increasing inconsistencies between corporate actions and stated CSR commitments; companies will become astute at shielding their actual performance
- CSR will be a technical fix
- Really substantive issues won't be addressed by CSR; we will come to the point where we say there have been great improvements, but what's really changing?
- Most businesses will hold back waiting for the business case to develop - however, they may never be satisfied by the evidence of business case and may use this as an excuse for inaction
- The business case will not be clear enough for companies to take up en masse, unless it is legislated or there are other incentives
- CSR will not be on the public's radar screen and there won't be any clarity around what CSR is and why it is important
- CSR will become too prescriptive and get labeled as

needless red tape increasing the cost of business

- Companies that once embraced CSR will lose interest and pursue other objectives
- Those engaged in CSR shift to minimal CSR activities, never moving beyond baseline CSR
- Pressures on business to cater to shareholders at expense of all other stakeholders will continue if not increase; the imbalance of power will not change unless the membership on company boards changes to include stakeholder interests or until government legislation is brought to bear.

CSR optimists believe that the pessimists are only looking at the gap of where we are and where we need to be, without acknowledging that mindset change takes time and recognizing that the slow incorporation of these ideas is underway in business. They believe that the disillusionment is a function of the hope for too much too quickly. CSR optimists believe that:

- In the future a significant number of companies will be convinced it's in their strategic interest to incorporate CSR substantively into their operations
- There is a crisis in industrial capitalism, which lacks in trust and social responsibility, and within this we will see a rethinking of the role companies should play in society.
- CSR is at a crossroads, in a time of real discontinuity, enormously in flux.

We are in the very early stages of transition with cracks in the foundation of business such as Enron, World com, WTO protests, sustainable forestry campaigning, 9 - 11. These are little tremors before the big earthquake - we will see bigger and deeper cracks; there will be more shocks similar to 9-11 environmentally and socially - this will drive CSR in substantial and unpredictable ways in the future:

- High profile stumbles will continue to drive CSR
- The crisis in global markets is broadening the discussion of accountability and transparency - in this climate there is more openness to CSR ideas. CSR will be seen as good corporate governance

- There will be pressure through competition for better CSR performance - this will impact on suppliers, etc.
- A small group of companies will be moving ahead quickly
- There will be differentiation between different models and levels of CSR as a result of continuous improvement and quality assurance
- CSR will advance, but it will advance inconsistently across sectors, depending on a company's economic performance, economic downturns, competitiveness of the market, etc.
- Underlying structural drivers will impact large scale companies, such as the value of knowledge workers and other intangible assets, driving companies to take different issues into account
- We see only a few companies committed to CSR because we are at the beginning of a long path on this journey; the shift toward sustainable capitalism is a long term trend and in 5 - 10 years only a few companies will be moving in this direction
- Increasingly businesses will see CSR as resulting in increased competitiveness and profitability
- The cynical corporations are dinosaurs and will be swept aside, though not in 10 years; change will be there, but it won't be dramatic
- CSR is part of a search for a new social contract between business and society.

This new social contract will not necessarily be through the creation of a set of rules, but about a new set of norms arrived at through experimentation. In spite of the difference in views of social impact and degree of corporate commitment, the majority of the optimists and the pessimists agreed that 5 - 10 years from now CSR will nonetheless become increasingly mainstreamed within business, even if not within the public consciousness. CSR tools, resources, language - all will become more aligned with business norms and systems. CSR standards - to greater or lesser effect - will be part of business basics and not an add-on. Most of this speculation points to continued, albeit slow progress toward increasing integration of CSR values into the corporate sector with varying levels of commitment and impact within the 5 - 10 year time frame.

A CSR Continuum - CSR-lite to deep-CSR Consistent with their views on the progress of CSR and the ability of CSR to bring about social and environmental improvements, CSR thought leaders felt there will be different degrees of commitment to and styles of applying CSR within industry in the future, much like today. Collectively they described a continuum of CSR, from CSR "lite" to deep-CSR:

CSR Lite:

- These companies will have a superficial or marginal commitment to meaningful social or environmental improvement
- They will be primarily concerned about responsiveness to complaints, not CSR - the business model will not be changed
- They may be using generalized standards such as the Global Reporting Initiative and as such think they have a handle on CSR when in fact they don't
- Included in this group will be those companies which have been legislated into compliance with CSR objectives, whether their transgressions have been on the environment, corrupt business practices, etc. They do not show any commitment to social or environmental progress.

CSR Compliant:

- Companies will take on voluntary environmental and social obligations to maintain their license to operate
- They will keep abreast of emerging standards and norms of CSR and ensure they are compliant with those standards CSR Strategic
- Companies will become strategic about different aspects of CSR
- They will become compliant with standards and then will create niches in specific areas of CSR more strategic to their companies. They will develop business strategies within one or two aspects of CSR around which they can

develop a competitive advantage and have significant impact

- Companies in certain sectors will believe their key to survival is providing products and services acceptable to broad public interests or they will go out of business CSR Integrated
- Further along the continuum will be those companies that fully integrate CSR throughout their business model, not as a strategic advantage, but in the belief of the need to take social and environmental impacts and opportunities into account
- They will have comprehensive CSR policies covering all areas of their operations and will be operationalizing their CSR principles through rigorous performance standards, objectives, reward mechanisms, etc.
- CSR or sustainable development will inform decision-making and business strategy throughout the company Deep CSR
- A group of companies will adopt or be founded on business models whose mission is to improve social or environmental conditions
- Some leading companies will realize that the low-hanging benefits of CSR have been achieved and the early- stage CSR measures have been mined and exhausted.

These companies will move to addressing the real tradeoffs between different elements of the triple bottom line in sustainable consumption, resource extraction, just transitions, intergenerational equity, etc. The first two themes above point to the current debate in the CSR field over how strongly meaningful CSR will be embraced by the corporate world. Overall, the range of CSR performance - from the cynics to the believers - is expected to exist in the future as it does today, though there will be more and more uptake of CSR by companies and more progression to deep CSR by new market entrants and continuous improvement corporations. Efforts will continue to move beyond bland endorsements of CSR to considerations of how it affects corporate business practice.

Is it predicted this move will help overcome the confusion about where and when CSR principles should override shareholder interests. Additionally, it was pointed out, there will continue to be greater progress on the environmental aspects of CSR relative to the social aspects, given the extent of government regulation, availability of tools and systems and more established business case for environmental management.

More Significant Roles for Stakeholders

One of the top trends around which there is consistent agreement is the increasing importance of stakeholder engagement in the future of CSR. Not only will stakeholders be engaged in increasingly significant ways, they will gain in influence, and will continue to innovate and bring forward new and challenging values. Stakeholders here include consumers, employees, shareholders, suppliers, NGOs, governments and business partners - all those that have a "stake" in a company's operations.

Process: Shift to Stakeholder Dialogue, Co-Production and Governance CSR companies in the future will be increasingly moving from identifying and managing stakeholders and their social issues to active engagement of stakeholders in issues of mutual concern. Many are calling this stakeholder dialogue, as distinct from one-way communication or two-way consultation. Stakeholder dialogue in future will be a process of multiple stakeholder participation focusing on learning and innovation.

Indeed, some thought leaders see the future CSR Company engaging its stakeholders in co-production, a process of developing product and service innovations through joint problem solving tables with stakeholders. Companies will bring together all stakeholders involved in a product's use, creating collaborative design teams with the end result a more useful product with enhanced environmental and social properties.

Others believe that should these relationships develop,

they will be limited in number in this 5 - 10 year timeframe. A few see the emergence of new governance models, predicting an increased role for stakeholders in governance, such as stakeholder councils and other forms of engagement. Many suggest that increased stakeholder engagement will require the development of problem-solving and decision-making tools to facilitate the consensus-building process.

Techniques will be developed to help people understand they wear different hats as employees, investors, citizens in communities, and therefore need to compromise certain benefits to get other benefits important to them.

Others believe that compromise is a suboptimal outcome and decision-making technologies will be developed to optimize triple-bottom-line solutions. The development of these approaches was felt to be particularly important to those who thought that with an increasingly interconnected world there will be a need to acknowledge that more and more different people value different things. The key will be finding the outcomes acceptable to most parties. Regardless of approach or rationale, many pointed to the likely development of tools and processes to help stakeholders and companies address the trade-offs which need to be addressed in future as CSR increasingly confronts the social and environmental challenges ahead. It was also suggested that these advances in stakeholder engagement will be experienced primarily by civil society stakeholders as consumer and employee opinions are and will remain actively solicited. Consistent with the development of tools and processes, increasingly stakeholder consultation will become a core competency of all staff, who will be expected to have productive relationships with stakeholders.

For the few that were less certain significant stakeholder engagement models would develop there was agreement that companies will continue to make progress in the engagement of communities in the local decision-making process at the site level through decentralized decision-making of large corporations. To avoid decision paralysis, in which companies become paralyzed thinking they cannot make decisions without consulting, in the future these companies will make decisions when they know something is "right" and consult on controversial or challenging issues. A few thought leaders believed that some NGOs and CSR idealists will not be able to accept compromise, while others wondered if stakeholders will lose their ability to challenge corporate activity as a result of their close involvement with business. Actors: Same Players, More Influence All agreed about the significant influence increasingly sophisticated and organized stakeholders will have in the market.

Now and in the future, stakeholders are viewing their access to timely, comprehensive and accurate information about companies as a right. They expect to be treated fairly and honourably. With the benefit of internet technologies stakeholders will know more and be able to communicate their views to a wider audience to influence decisions before they are taken. The following is a summary of the trends expected within each stakeholder group. Ethical Consumers (Slightly) More Powerful For the most part, thought leaders believe there will be a CSR consumer in future - though it will be a small but potentially powerful market segment. This "vigilante" consumer will be high income with increasing influence in the marketplace. Some expect that increased social and environmental catastrophes will heighten consumer awareness and information of these issues thereby growing the ethical consumer market. However few believe future increases in CSR consumption will be dramatic.

Most recognized that the polls on consumer CSR behaviour only measure intentions, demonstrating a gap between what consumers say they will do in the market and their actual behaviour. Some feel this gap will be bridged in the future through increasing consumer information on CSR issues. Some of their additional thoughts include:

- Ethical consumers will continue to make CSR purchases, but not for all their products.
- CSR consumption will not be an even trend of growth; it

will fluctuate with the economy and corporate crises; it is a volatile market.

- CSR will be a tie-breaker at the shelf - not only will it be a retail competitive advantage in the future, it will be a negative motivator if a company is a known abuser.
- Consumers will be looking for trusted actors to sort information for them. Companies that provide a tailored service that guarantee products are aligned with the values of a customer will create market share.
- Consumers will be increasingly informed and aware that profits are often made through child labour, bribery and corruption, environmental exploitation, etc. Though previously they were only interested in paying the lowest price, increasingly they will be prepared to pay a premium. They will increasingly believe that it matters how corporations earn their profits.
- Consumers will become more organized in the future; the feeling of being powerless will multiply; collective consumer organizations will start to promote ethical purchasing issues to their constituencies; this trend will be driven in part by government downsizing and deregulation; consumers will start to organize to protect their interests.

On the whole, it is believed ethical consumers will comprise about 5 - 10% of the market, depending on the issue and sector, while mainstream consumerism will remain price-sensitive. However, people will increasingly start to take action as they see the tangible impacts environmental and social degradation is having on their quality of life, not to mention their investments and the future of their grandchildren. NGOs Increasingly Sophisticated, Coordinated, Challenged and Divided There was considerable agreement that in 5 - 10 years NGOs will be more sophisticated, better coordinated amongst each other and working on common campaigns. They will be targeting global companies through coalitions united in their opposition.

More watchdog groups will emerge and they will be

working cross-sectorally and internationally on global issues of concern. Additionally, many commented, NGOs will increasingly come under the microscope themselves as their brands, their footprints and their influence grow worldwide. Significant gaps in their scientific and technological knowledge will emerge and they will be challenged to have more accountability, much as they are asking of their corporate targets. In the future, NGOs will be subjecting themselves to scrutiny, audits and verification. Five to ten years from now there will be an increase in business-NGO partnerships and the culture gap will disappear for some. In this environment, NGOs will become increasingly sophisticated about using their brands to affect corporate change. Meanwhile, as a result of this increased participation in multi-stakeholder dialogues, stakeholder fatigue will develop for many NGOs who are strapped for cash and capacity.

Some CSR companies will be contributing in an arms-length way to enhancing this capacity to facilitate meaningful NGO participation. In other instances, NGOs will be engaged primarily within sectors at the principle-setting stage in areas of moral controversy and companies will be expected to implement on their own. A view was expressed that while there will be a trend to sophistication within some sectors on some issues, the numbers of NGOs sophisticated enough to form partnerships and participate in company dialogues will be few and far between over the 5 - 10 year period. Some also predicted that there will be increasing divisiveness in the NGO sector, with more cracks in their solidarity as some move to collaborate with business while others prefer to campaign from the outside. Some go further to say that on the whole fewer antagonistic relationships between business and civil society are expected to exist in the future. An interesting prediction is the possibility that NGOs will be using the justice system to resolve their issues, through class action suits and other legislative means. Courts may become more activist in this scenario, awarding huge damages to some causes.

Finally, in some regions such as Canada NGOs may continue their focus on regulatory over market interventions and may be slower to develop these trends within the 5 - 10 year timeframe. Employees a Growing CSR Force Most predictions point to increasing numbers of employees concerned about the social values of their employer. Expectations are that the best and the brightest - those companies most desire - will increasingly use their clout in the labour market to affect increased CSR performance of corporations. A small but growing proportion of those who expect they can get good salaries will ask more searching questions of companies they join. Certainly companies with a bad CSR track record will have difficulty recruiting compared to their more advanced CSR counterparts. Younger entrants to the work force, particularly, are expected to seek work with companies aligned to their values.

More generally it is expected that employees will increasingly demand that their work and the organizations they work for be aligned with their personal values. Non-responsive employers will find their staff, particularly their most talented staff, leaving for other more compatible settings. In a mobile workforce employees won't put up with companies that don't reflect their values. Another expected trend 5 - 10 years from now is the increased hiring of NGO activists and social scientists within corporations.

Increasing Investor Clout on CSR

There is some skepticism about the impact socially responsible investment (SRI) will have on the future of CSR, though this was primarily directed at the SRI mutual fund industry and socially screened portfolios. It was felt that these would not comprise a significant force in the future. Screening out stocks that negatively impact the environment, labour conditions, human rights or that positively impact communities for example, will increasingly be seen as the weaker investment tool for encouraging CSR. However, there was widespread agreement that shareholder action and institutional investors will have a significant impact in the future CSR marketplace.

Indeed, there is a view that capital markets will be central to establishing the incentives that drive corporations towards CSR in the future.

The doubling and tripling of shareholder resolutions both in number and in voted support witnessed today are only expected to continue into the future with greater and greater effect. It is anticipated that increasingly institutional investors will take a stewardship approach to their investments and will become more and more attuned to longer term performance issues over a short term quick fix "returns today" approach. In 5 - 10 years corporations, most agree, will have improved their environmental and social disclosure in response to SRI investor demands to help investors analyze their CSR performance. With this information, it is predicted that investors will be asking different questions of corporations, looking at different aspects of company behaviour, seeking different indicators that all is well.

For example, there will be a growth in investors looking at corporate responsibility as a contributor to a company's intangible assets and future earnings potential - whether that is its ability to retain people, engender trust in customers, build a good reputation or manage its risks. By 2010 CSR will be both a differentiator when a company deals with analysts and investors and one of the key questions which will be asked of certain companies in certain industries. A company's approach to risk management will be seen by investment analysts as one indication of the extent to which social and environmental issues have been incorporated into business management processes; increasingly "sustainability" or the long term view will become the lens through which risk is viewed. In response to these investor demands, CSR companies will increasingly link sustainable development with shareholder value, both building it into the business and building new business around it to create shareholder value.

An even bolder view of this trend is that 10 years from now prioritizing shareholder value as the primary role of business will be seen to be odd. In this scenario this priority is replaced by a focus on giving people products and services they value as the primary corporate goal. Related to this anticipated trend is one predicted in which investors are called upon to display their own social responsibility, a moral code parallel to CSR? "Investor Social Responsibility" will emerge as a challenge to the investor community, and a set of investor social responsibility principles will be developed. This trend will see the adoption of CSR by mainstream financial service organizations across all of their asset management portfolios. Through this, capital markets will push to hold companies increasingly accountable on CSR matters, driving adoption of standards across hundreds of companies simultaneously.

Proponents of this view believe that in the longer term the CSR field will establish a set of principles to determine when social or environmental obligations should override shareholder interests. They believe investors themselves will drive this outcome. One final investor trend predicted is an increasing concern over a company's climate change exposure. The anticipated international coordination and cooperation between institutional investors on SRI issues is expected to have a significant impact on the progress on this and other social and environmental issues.

The Ripple Effect Up, Down and across the Supply Chain

For those who addressed the issue of suppliers all agree that large companies will be driving CSR up and down their supply chain, thereby putting CSR on the radar screen of small business. This will come about due to the growing insistence that responsible companies look at the impact not only of their own operations, but that of their business partners. Another possible driver of this trend will be courts determining vicarious liability where business partners are responsible for each other's behaviour in joint ventures.

These trends will pressure companies to become more responsible for product and service stewardship over the life of the product or service. The social and environmental responsibility of financial institutions, for example, for their investment and lending decisions will become of increasing concern to stakeholders. Some predict that increased NGO campaigning will make companies vulnerable to attacks brought to bear at their weakest links which can often show up in their out-sourced operations - and are difficult to anticipate. In this environment, not only will small business be addressing its CSR footprint, but larger CSR companies are expected to find ways and means to build the capacity of small business to not only operationalize CSR but to use this as a means of fostering innovation within the supply chain.

ENVIRONMENT, SOCIAL EXCLUSION, GOVERNANCE, ACCOUNTABILITY AND ETHICS KEY THEMES

Top CSR Issues Concerns about the environment - particularly climate change and secondarily water quality and supply/ access - social exclusion - particularly poverty and access to necessities - and governance and accountability, including issues of transparency and integrity, were the top issues raised by CSR thought leaders. These are predicted to be the key CSR issues of the future. While these will be the key issues, the current CSR issues are not expected to change.

Increased measurement and monitoring will push the standards and norms higher for all CSR issues, with the result that some companies might specialize and segment within particular CSR areas relevant to their business. Additional issues that will grow in importance include core labour standards, sweatshop and living wage issues, human rights, bioethics (humane treatment of animals, genetic technologies, etc.), privacy, "anti-big" concerns, product quality and quality standards and toxicity. One view is that there will be new CSR challenges in diversity with aging populations and cultural and religious differences.

People will be thinking about diversity differently in the future and this will be reflected in the CSR debate. Another view is that increased attention will be placed on issues of democracy both in the economy and in the political arena - locally, nationally and globally. These issues will also be reflected in the CSR agenda. There was much interest in how corporate accountability and transparency will evolve over the next decade, and related issues of corporate governance and integrity. Most commented that demands for greater responsibility, accountability and transparency will only increase as a result of the perception that the private sector has amassed great power and influence and yet has not delivered on its promises to improve social and environmental conditions through voluntary initiatives. Some believe that transparency will shift from annual reporting to hourly if not instantaneous reporting.

Corporations will be demonstrating they have a high level of integrity at the top of the corporation. Some predict that a fourth dimension of TBL will emerge, that of personal and collective ethics. There will be demands on company boards to demonstrate their competency with CSR issues. Tools and techniques will be developed to facilitate corporate CSR governance. Globalisation will continue to be linked to CSR as will other broad north-south issues regarding trade, debt, third world poverty, etc. The legitimacy of global capitalism is expected to be under continuous challenge during this period. Some expect CSR to be part of the antidote to the excesses of Globalisation.

CSR Management Systems Standardize and Differentiate

There is widespread consensus that basic CSR systems will become more standardized and routine within 10 years. The codes of conduct debate will have been resolved. There will be convergence in codes and standards. Consensus regarding core CSR indicators will develop - a core CSR metrics "starter pack"- leaving companies to tailor standards to the specific business. Standard-setting bodies will have formed partnerships and brought about consolidation in the current myriad standards that exist. CSR concepts will become more tested and easier to adopt. There will be more clarification of what is meant by 'real' CSR to distinguish it from 'cosmetic' CSR. Leading edge CSR today will be baseline 5 - 10 years from now and the bar will be continuously lifted. CSR will continue to evolve with the evolution of social and environmental issues.

Standards and systems will continue to be affected by these developments in a very "organic" process.

The future will also see not only increased adoption of these standards, but increased experimentation within companies, sectors, at the site level and in regions. While there will be baseline standards, there is not expected to be a single standard, allowing companies to follow those which are most suited to their operations. Standardized materials will be used as a baseline from which to branch out. This will result in competing companies following different approaches to enhance their CSR competitiveness. There will be not only increased standardization, but there will be more robust standards, particularly measurement tools to demonstrate the progress stakeholders are seeking. The debate will move from discussions linked to auditing, regulation and the business case to practice - there will be open discussion around the problems and difficulties managing CSR and a focus on CSR continuous improvement.

There will be more concentration on management learning and implementation tools. Most but not all are convinced there will be standardized guidelines for social auditing or TBL reporting. These reports are expected to be reintegrated into annual reports - stand-alone reports will become a thing of the past. Instead, there could well be a series of audience-specific reports. In any case, there will be considerably more TBL reporting in the future than is seen today. Additionally there will be more use of stakeholder input in the use of these reports in future. With these reports SRI analysis will become more like conventional analysis where there is a core set of data in the public domain - TBL reports - and companies are asked a set of supplementary questions on their CSR performance. The new focus will be measuring and reporting on CSR impact - the degree to which a corporation's CSR performance has actually improved conditions in society or the environment.

More companies will have moved from simply reporting statistics to using them to improve or measure improvement, where the real value will be, and increasingly they will be reporting out on their progress in this area. Generally there will be more measurement that combines output, internal improvement, external impact and issues of concern to stakeholders. Companies will be showing how they have used the data and information on which they report and how they have used stakeholder input to improve their operations. Through this they will be enhancing their accountability to stakeholders.

As a result of this increased impact reporting, there will be more focus on outcome comparisons between companies. Efforts will continue to develop and adopt new metrics to measure intangible assets that are affected by CSR policies and contribute most directly to a company's TBL performance and long term shareholder value. Examples include reputation, brand, innovation, CSR risks from exposures, knowledge workers and social capital (i.e. measurement of the interaction between a company and its broader community). Growing disparity between corporate actions and standards practiced domestically versus those practiced internationally could emerge as a significant trend.

No predictions were made for the resolution of this trend, though stakeholders including governments in the international arena will no doubt have some influence. Some believe there will be a logo-mark to brand CSR companies - a harmonization of labels and standards to make it easier for consumers to determine which the ethical purchase is. Not all agreed with this development; some thought there would be a variety of social labels in use or that social labels would be more advanced in some regions than others, Europe for example. Others felt that there could well be CSR branding of management systems (e.g. ISO series), but this is unlikely to happen for a company's performance. CSR companies will move from creating specialized CSR departments analyzing stakeholder campaigns, assessing regulations to ensure compliance, etc. to the establishment of standards and measures integrated through- out the company which are assessed and reported on.

While there will be a continuing role for CSR specialists

they will serve as internal CSR consultants, supporting innovation, defining policies, leveraging knowledge, acting as whistle-blowers, etc. Full CSR integration across the company will become the norm, with tools and approaches implemented to ensure effective CSR performance and continuous improvement. There will be line accountability for delivery of CSR policies; accountability for performance will be tested periodically in this model. There will also be an increase in board CSR committees or subgroups focused on CSR policy. Tools will be developed to enhance CSR corporate governance. In the future companies will stop looking at CSR as a way of responding to external pressures and will start managing it, using the systems, tools and standards available to them, to increase CSR reputation and results, reduce risks and improve relationships.

Real measurement and real progress will be key to keep stakeholders at bay. Currently NGOs are more or less supporting the standards model, but will become increasingly discontent if progress does not result.

Governments Require Mandatory Disclosure, Voluntary Compliance

There were differing opinions on the degree to which governments will be intervening in the future to encourage more CSR behaviour from the private sector. Most anticipate governments will at a minimum be encouraging CSR performance through information provision, support for networking, and other voluntary measures.

Many believe there will at least be mandatory disclosure, in which companies are required to report on their social and environmental policies and performance, possibly with third party verification encouraged if not required. It will then be up to the individual corporation as to how strongly it wishes to follow a CSR path - in other words, voluntary compliance.

Most expect that governments will be working to support accountability and transparency in company operations, particularly through reporting. Others go further believing that some jurisdictions will embrace CSR as a competitive advantage for their economy, supporting CSR clusters domestically (integrated CSR knowledge, R & D and business networks, etc.) and working to build markets around the world based on social and environmental criteria. In this scenario competitive CSR products and services have a market advantage, as will those national economies.

A stronger case is made for increasing environmental regulation in the future as the most likely scenario - but it is also thought likely that governments will be moving to increased regulation on a range of CSR issues if the private sector does not progress within a voluntary CSR framework. Some governments will be using other voluntary and incentive-based tools such as preferential CSR procurement, export guarantees, investment subsidies, tax credits, CSR criteria for foreign aid and foreign direct investment, pension disclosure, etc. There will be increased experimentation with government interventions of this type in support of CSR. Within a decade trade negotiations are predicted to take more social and environmental considerations into account, international institutions such as the World Bank will be advancing CSR and more governments will be addressing the worst violators working in conflict zones or involved in illicit behaviour.

Within this period governments internationally might have moved to define corporate complicity in the realm of oppressive regimes. How Globalisation evolves will affect regional and domestic developments in any scenario. For example, it may result that CSR measures will be leveled up or down depending on their impact on competition; government CSR interventions will be either globally adopted or stripped away. It is generally expected that Europe will proceed ahead of other countries on regulation and that any regulation that does come into force will be geared to large not small business.

Much less certainty exists as to the degree to which North America will follow the regulatory path beyond disclosure.

There is a strong view that market leaders will increasingly call for regulation in an attempt to institutionalize the market levers that give them a competitive advantage. Alternatively, companies may be leading to shape rules and avoid intervention. In either case, there is extreme likelihood that corporate CSR leaders will be either neutral or supportive of future regulation, an environment that is increasingly conducive to government involvement.

Innovation and Learning Drive CSR

Many commented on the learning environment for CSR. It is widely believed that business schools will be teaching CSR skills as a core component of the curriculum and CSR business networks will be thriving, promoting continuous improvement. There will be in-house training programs to bring up the skills of employees across the company focused on how CSR is defined, how it is applied and how it impacts the business process. For companies going through a deeper CSR integration process there will be a focus on internal transformation beginning with personal and professional development of key personnel. There will be more academic research into CSR and CSR fundamentals. There will continue to be research on the business case, which itself will continue to evolve.

CSR in this environment will become a stimulant for creativity and innovation. New products and services which integrate CSR and stakeholder values will be developed and become market makers. Some companies will have discovered that by creating new environmentally and socially sustainable markets they can benefit from increased business opportunities.

Companies Expected to Achieve or Lever Greater Social Change

The big debate in CSR in 5 - 10 years is expected to be over its impact on social change. Within the next decade CSR will be criticized for not adequately addressing the big issues of environmental sustainability and the widening gap between the rich and poor; it will not have materially impacted the quality of life. Continued government downsizing and trade agreements in various jurisdictions will increasingly privatize social and environmental concerns. It is believed that committed CSR companies will be working to address these issues and improve their impact and social change outcomes. A few scenarios were proposed within this context.

Many are pinning their hopes on an emergent sector whose entire mission and agenda is sustainability, both social and ecological. Sometimes called the third sector or the civil economy, these companies have core CSR values and an ethos committed to integrated social and environmental responsibility. They include natural foods, natural pharmaceuticals, renewable energy, water, clothing, building and construction, community banking, social investment, travel and educational services, etc. Cooperatives, credit unions and non-profit enterprises are found in this sector.

This sector is expected to grow and evolve over the next 5 - 10 years and will impact the marketplace, society and the environment. They will be a competitive force in the economy, albeit in niche markets. They will be leaders in CSR innovation and will help raise the bar for CSR performance across sectors. One perspective is that the CSR leadership demonstrated by this sector comes not simply from their social and ecological missions, but from the fact they are insulated from short term market demands and often have stakeholder models of ownership. Non-profit enterprises, co-operatives and employee share ownership are examples of this model as are companies that shift from hierarchical governance to network governance, and owner-managed, founder run and family managed companies.

By nature these businesses are less profit maximizing than their larger publicly traded counterparts. There are some economies in the world - Italy's Emilia Romagnia being one - which are promoting this sector as a means of economic and social development. In these regions systems and structures are established to encourage the flourishing of polyarchy -

the distribution of power to non-profit firms, co-operatives and social enterprises. Directly accountable to where they live, these organizations are deemed to be much more in touch with local social and environmental conditions and their 'footprints'. New research into the benefits of social capital and trust within the marketplace is highlighting the important role these organizations play in improving economic performance of individual firms and entire regions. One cloud was identified on the horizon of this emergent "social economy", which is that this sector may not be able to succeed on its own without capitalization and public policy reform.

It lacks the capacity and economies of scale to have sufficient impact on the market economy and thereby will remain marginal to the economy, society and the environment. Another anticipated development is a growing insistence that responsible companies look not only at the impact of their own operations and those of their business partners, but address macro issues relevant to a company's sector - climate change, increased inequality, child labour, disparate access to necessities, resolving conflicts and violence, etc. It is expected that in this scenario, companies will be working in multi-stakeholder partnerships on macro social and environmental issues within their sphere of influence in addition to addressing their own internal CSR issues.

Within these cross-sectoral collaborations business will recognize it can't have its own single view and stake- holders will conclude that some problems are beyond the power of corporations to affect alone. CSR companies will be engaged in greater partnerships with civil society and government where there is joint accountability for progress. Another anticipated route for CSR companies to follow in their effort to affect social and ecological improvements is that of public policy advocacy. Some believe that as stakeholder pressure comes to bear on companies to address fundamental social problems, they will become more involved in influencing public policy. Real social change is thought to require broader financial and governing systems change and corporate CSR leaders are expected to become powerful advocates for progressive public policy on CSR.

CSR thought leaders are not a homogeneous group. Nor do they predict one evolutionary tract for CSR over the next decade. It is interesting to speculate how the conclusions might have been shaped differently if more business or other cultural views were included in the research and if the social, economic and political changes in non-Western societies were taken into account. However, of those interviewed for this study most agree more or less with the view that CSR progress will be slow over the next ten years, but will become increasingly mainstreamed by business. Increasing social and environmental crises will continue to drive this paradigm shift or modest business reform, depending on one's view of this trend. The continuum seen today - of companies' differing commitment to significant CSR - will be evident in the future.

More strategic, integrated and 'deep' CSR adherents will emerge over the decade. One of the most significant trends will be the increasing influence of stakeholders, whether through more engaging stakeholder dialogue or through stakeholder campaigns. Stakeholders will become more strategic and more coordinated, increasingly working together on issues of common concern. Consumers and employees will become more demanding as and when they perceive the connections between corporate behaviour and their quality of life. Suppliers will increasingly be pulled into CSR practice as companies through coercion or choice integrate CSR throughout their supply chains. Suppliers and other stakeholders will increasingly become part of the product design process as companies endeavour to reduce their negative and enhance their positive impacts. CSR issues are expected to remain the same, though the performance bar will continuously be raised.

The environment, poverty and social exclusion and governance, ethics, transparency and accountability are expected to be the dominant future CSR issues. The myriad CSR standards operating today will themselves become standardized and available as "starter kits" to new CSR companies. Companies will be adopting the core standards and tailoring the rest to their unique environments. The focus in future will be on continuous CSR improvement and most especially the impact CSR operations have on social and environmental conditions. The future CSR Company will require every policy, practice, operation, activity, member of staff, every decision to be measured against CSR criteria. Many companies will be redefining business purpose to optimize profits, that is, making profits responsibly and developing business principles consistent with this.

Most governments will be requiring mandatory disclosure of corporate social and environmental perfor-mance, and encouraging different CSR approaches to flourish through voluntary compliance on CSR standards and codes. Business schools will increasingly jump on the CSR bandwagon, integrating CSR curriculum within their business programs. CSR will be promoted as a means of fostering creativity and innovation and some companies will be reaping the benefits of this. Companies will be increasingly called upon to help address the growing social and environmental challenges emerging globally and locally. They will be bringing their resources and influence to bear on those problems through cross-sectoral initiatives. CSR companies will be promoting protection of human rights and generating economic, social and environmental benefits.

While this trend will still be in its infancy within 10 years, a more advanced trend will be catching attention. Increasing numbers of primarily small business whose mission is to enhance social and ecological conditions will be having an impact and will be part of the force that drives advances in CSR. Through this period, stakeholders will be watching to see if corporate actions are keeping pace with the standards, expectations and rhetoric of social responsibility. The future of CSR lies in the hands of the public and civil society organizations and their changing expectations, and the vision and leadership of the private sector.

6

Contemporary Views and Concept

In academic debates and business environments hundreds of concepts and definitions have been proposed referring to a more humane, more ethical, more transparent way of doing business. This point in time is an important if not critical moment in the development process of new generation business frameworks facilitating sustainable growth. A continuation of the creativity period - "let 100 flowers blossom" - will lead to unclear situations: by the time real progress is at hand a clear and unbiased definition and concept will be needed to lay a strong foundation for the following steps in the development process of corporate sustainability and especially in its implementation.

PROBLEMS WITH CURRENT DEFINITIONS

According to Göbbels, Votaw and Sethi considered social responsibility a brilliant term: "it means something, but not always the same thing to everybody". Too often, CSR is regarded as the panacea which will solve the global poverty gap, social exclusion and environmental degradation. Employers' associations emphasize the voluntary commitment of CSR. Local governments and some Non-Governmental Organizations (NGOs) believe public-private partnerships can, for instance rejuvenate neighbourhoods. Also various management disciplines have recognised that CSR fit their purposes, such as quality management, marketing, communication, finance, HRM, and reporting. Each of them present views on CSR that align with their specific situation and challenges.

The current concepts and definitions are therefore often biased towards specific interests. Banerjee states that corporate social responsibility is "too broad in its scope to be relevant to organizations" and Henderson, "there is no solid and well-developed consensus which provides a basis for action". The lack of an "all-embracing definition of CSR" (WBCSD, 2000: 3) and subsequent diversity and overlap in terminology, definitions and conceptual models hampers academic debate and ongoing research. On the other hand, an 'all-embracing' notion of CSR has to be broadly defined and is therefore too vague to be useful in academic debate or in corporate implementation.

A set of differentiated approaches, matching the various ideal type contexts in which companies operate, could be the alternative. Jacques Schraven, the chairman of VNO-NCW, the Dutch Employers Association, once stated 1 that "there is no standard recipe: corporate sustainability is a custommade process". Each company should choose - from the many opportunities - which concept and definition is the best option, matching the company's aims and intentions and aligned with the company's strategy, as a response to the circumstances in which it operates.

A HISTORICAL PERSPECTIVE

Past eras have shown acts of charity, fairness and stewardship, such as the medieval chivalry and Scholastic view on pricing, the aristocracy's noblesse oblige, the early 20th century paternalistic industrialists and the contemporary ways of corporate (and private) sponsoring of arts, sports, neighbourhood developments, etcetera. In academic literature, various authors 2 have referred to a sequence of three approaches, each including and transcending one other, showing past responses to the question to which an organization has a responsibility.

According to the shareholder approach, regarded by Quazi and O'Brien as the classical view on CSR, "the social responsibility of business is to increase its profits".

The shareholder, in pursuit of profit maximization, is the focal point of the company and socially responsible activities don't belong to the domain of organizations but are a major task of governments. This approach can also be interpreted as business enterprises being concerned with CSR "only to the extent that it contributes to the aim of business, which is the creation of long-term value for the owners of the business".

The stakeholder approach indicates that organizations are not only accountable to its shareholders but should also balance a multiplicity of stakeholders' interests that can affect or are affected by the achievement of an organization's objectives.

According to the societal approach, regarded as the broader view on CSR (and not necessarily the contemporary view), companies are responsible to society as a whole, of which they are an integral part. They operate by public consent (license to operate) in order to "serve constructively the needs of society - to the satisfaction of society".

The philanthropic approaches might be the roots of CS, but the different approaches to corporate responsibility clearly show that CSR is a new and distinct phenomenon.

Its societal approach especially appears to be a (strategic) response to changing circumstances and new corporate challenges that had not previously occurred. It requires organizations to fundamentally rethink their position and act in terms of the complex societal context of which they are a part. This is anew perspective.

VALUE SYSTEMS

Abraham Maslow declared the five basic needs of human individuals, implying that individuals would strive for the next need as soon as the former had been fulfilled. His contemporary Clair Graves concluded that there are many ways of achieving these needs. Individual persons, as well as companies and societies, undergo a natural sequence of orientations.

These orientations brighten or dim as life conditions (consisting of historical Times, geographical Place, existential Problems and societal Circumstances) change. The orientations impact their worldview, their value system, belief structure, organizing principles and mode of adjustment.

If, for instance, societal circumstances change, inviting corporations to respond and consequently reconsider their role within society, it implies that corporations have to realign all their business institutions (such as mission, vision, policy deployment, decision-making, reporting, corporate affairs, etcetera) to this new orientation. Graves, and his successors Beck and Cowan, have made clear that entities will eventually try to meet the challenges their situation - featuring specific life conditions - provide or risk the danger of oblivion or even extinction.

The quest to create an adequate response to specific life conditions results in a wide variety of survival strategies, each founded on a specific set of values and related institutions. These value systems reflect their specific vision on reality (worldview), their awareness, understanding, and their definition of truth. This is why in Seattle, Genoa, Prague representatives of the Global Civil Society clashed with politicians and industrialists; their value systems do not align, there are conflicting truths and worldviews and opposite strategies as to how to deal with (their interpretation of) the situation.

THE PRINCIPLES BEHIND EVOLUTIONARY DEVELOPMENT

Ken Wilber having studied evolutionary developments in great depth supports Graves when stating: "Evolution proceeds irreversibly in the direction of increasing differentiation/integration, increasing organization and increasing complexity". This "growth occurs in stages, and stages are ranked in both a logical and chronological order. The more holistic patterns appear later in development because they have to wait the emergence of the parts that they will then integrate or unify. This ranking refers to normal hierarchies (or holarchies) converting "heaps into wholes, disjointed fragments into networks of mutual interconnection".

As the natural orientations emerged, they clearly show an increase of integratedness and complexity, each stage including and transcending the previous ones. Wilber drafted twenty "patterns of existence" or "tendencies of evolution" which I shall briefly summarize: reality is not composed of things or processes; it is not composed of wholes nor does it have any parts. Rather it is composed of whole/parts, or holons.

This is true of the physical sphere (atoms), as well as of the biological (cells) and psychological (concepts and ideas) sphere, or simply said, apply to matter, body, mind and spirit. Atoms or processes are first and foremost holons, long before any 'particular characteristics' are singled out by us.

Holons display four fundamental capacities: self-preservation, self-adaptation, self-transcendence and self-dissolution. Its *agency* - its self-asserting, self-preserving tendencies - expresses its *wholeness*, its relative autonomy; whereas its *communion* - its participatory, bonding, joining tendencies - expresses its *partness*, its relationship to something larger. Both capacities are crucial: any slight imbalance will either destroy the holon or make it turn into a pathological agency (alienation and repression) or a pathological communion (fusion and dissociation).

Self-transcendence (or self-transformation) is the system's capacity to reach beyond the given, pushing evolution further, creating new forms of agency and communion. Holons can also break down and do so along the same vertical sequence in which they were built up. These four capacities or 'forces' are in constant tension: the more intensely a holon preserves its own individuality, preserves it wholeness, the less it serves its communions or its partness in larger and wider wholes and vice versa. This tension can be manifested, for instance in the conflict between rights (agency) and responsibilities (communions), individuality and membership and autonomy and heteronomy.

If holons stop functioning, all the higher holons in the sequence are also destroyed, because those higher wholes depend upon the lower as constituent parts. In the same way organizations and employees are mutually dependent, as a strike clearly shows. Naturally, organizations support their employees (vertical relationship), creating value as an (horizontal) agency, in constant exchange with its stakeholders (horizontal communion). Holons emerge holarchically, in a natural hierarchy, as a series of increasing whole/parts. Holons transcend and include their predecessor(s), forming a hierarchical system.

What happens if the system itself goes corrupt, turns into a pathological hierarchy? Given the characteristics of holons and hierarchies, a disruption or pathology in one field can reverberate throughout an entire system. The negative consequences of Globalisation are good examples of outcomes of a pathological system. With multinationals over-emphasizing their self-preservation (agency), and thus ignoring their participatory role within the community at large, the "threefold global crisis of deepening poverty, social disintegration, and environmental degradation" gave rise to major critique on the business environment. It inspired a few individual entrepreneurs to immediately transform their businesses.

The majority, however, tries to ignore it and continue to disregard their responsibility for its impact on the physical and social environment. As can be expected from theoretical exercises, countervailing power is emerging in the growth, both in number and impact, of the (global) civil society. Non-Governmental Organisations (NGOs) especially, are building up impact, influencing business and politics towards acting more responsibly and operating in a more sustainable way.

LESSONS TO BE LEARNED

In addition to the previously mentioned principles of charity and stewardship, often regarded as the roots of CSR, I would like to define two other principles, based on the 'natural tendencies of evolution'. These are the Principle of Self-determination (or agency, self-preservation) and the Principle of Communion.

In combination, the two principles allow each entity, individual or group to act according to its awareness, capabilities and best understanding of its situation, provided it does not conflict with current regulations or interfere with the freedom of others to act in obtaining a similar objective. "Freedom stops when it interferes with the freedom of others".

The right to be, the right to define its role within a given situation - the manifestation of agency or autonomy - is balanced by the moral obligation to be accountable for its impact on the environment. It is communion that stops freedom when it interferes with the freedom of others. Being an entity within something larger obliges to adapt to the environment, adjust it self to changing circumstances and be accountable for one's impact on others. These principles apply to water molecules as well as human beings and their organizations. When the chosen role and corresponding awareness appear not to be adequate responses to current circumstances, the system, other related entities in this situation, will influence the subject and try to correct and, as an ultimate response, bring the existence of the subject into jeopardy.

An increasing number of experiences can demonstrate this principle. So far we have seen that evolution provides a sense of direction, inspiring both in individuals and corporations goals for transformation. Challenged by changing circumstances and provoked by new opportunities, individuals, organizations and societies develop adequate solutions that might be new sublimations, creating synergy and adding value at a higher level of complexity. Since instability increases at higher complexity levels, entities can shift to lower levels should circumstances turn unfavourable or should competences fail to meet the required specifications.

A PRACTICAL CONTRIBUTION TO CORPORATE SUSTAINABILITY

Why will companies adopt CS practices? It simply stated: they either feel obliged to do it; are made to do it or they want to do it. In this chapter we briefly investigate trends within companies and within society that support the development of CS.

Corporate Challenges

Many companies have mastered their business operations and at the same time created "separate kingdoms". This manifests for instance in employees being more loyal to the business unit than the company, business metrics supporting unit management even at the expense of the performance of the mother company, transfer pricing and information asymmetry between HQ and its divisions. Another contemporary corporate challenge is managing issues in the supply chain. This is even more complex. In quality management terms these phenomena relate to making shifts or progress in the sequence of quality orientations.

Quality management can be oriented at a product level, at process level, at the organization as a systemic entity, at the supply chain and at the society as a whole. Each level includes and transcends the previous ones and each orientation represents a higher level of complexity. The former ones - product and process quality - can be managed with rather technical and statistical instruments. Creating an organization that functions as a whole instead of separate departments or with managing issues in the supply chain, management needs a shift of approach: the employees and their suppliers have become more important. For instance, be successful, management has to develop a climate of trust, respect and dedication and allow others to have their fair share of mutual activities (together win). We can conclude that organizations which continue to improve their quality ultimately have to adopt a more social management style, in other words, move towards (higher levels of) corporate sustainability.

Changing Concepts of Business

System theorists recommend, as "a cure to any diseased system, rooting out any holon that have usurped their position in the overall system by abusing their power..." and ignoring their duties and responsibilities, I would add. To root out cancer cells, medics developed surgical techniques and chemical cocktails. By fully abandoning business we would remove ourselves from the creation of wealth and necessary supplies, making the cure much worse than the disease. Mankind needs more subtle approaches to, for instance, increase the individual and collective level of awareness and understanding, support favourable behaviour and restore the imbalance of global institutions Business forms an important triangular relationship with the State and the Civil Society. Each has a specific mechanism that coordinates their behaviour and fulfils a role within society.

Generally, the State is responsible for creating and maintaining legislation (control), Business creates wealth through competition and cooperation (market), and Civil Society structures and shapes society via collective action and participation. Both market and control mechanisms have shown major fallacies with respect to organizing societal behaviour. Since civil society has gained importance, both business and government have respond to the collective actions of civilians, churches and especially NGOs. Corrective actions such as jeopardizing companies' reputations, challenge companies to apply more sustainable approaches in their business.

Once, there were circumstances which resulted in clear-cut roles and responsibilities for both companies and governments, both relatively independent, and an impact on civil society that could be neglected. As complexity grew business and government became mutually dependent entities. Since their coordinating mechanisms were incapable of adequately arranging various contemporary societal topics, the importance of civil society increased. Various representatives stressed 'new' values and approaches which politics and business no longer could ignore. Business has to learn how to operate within interfering coordination mechanisms, with blurred boundaries and surrounding layers of varying degrees of responsibility, overlapping one other.

Nowadays, governments increasingly leave societal issues within the authority of corporations. For instance, Schiphol Airport is supposed to limit noise and pollution, and at the same time accommodate the increasing demand for flights. NGOs and other stakeholders expect participation and involvement and request new levels of transparency. According to various sources in academic literature common values and norms play a major role in shaping society. Once it was the government elite that stated the societal values, later business leaders added theirs.

Along with the process of democratization, representatives of the civil society have increasingly been introducing 'common' values and norms and acting upon them to make government and business respond to these values. We see moving panels, changing circumstances and new existential problems arousing various members in society to act and transform into value systems and corresponding institutional arrangements. Accepting their new position in society, companies develop new values, new strategies and policies and new institutional arrangements that support their functioning in areas that were once left to others, redefining their roles and relationships with others.

CORPORATE SUSTAINABILITY

I will introduce three proposals to define CSR and Corporate Sustainability. I will also deal with the relationship between the two notions. Corporate Societal Accountability (CSA) The first one is suggested by Math. Göbbels. He concludes that the inconsistency and sometimes ambiguity of CSR is also due to language problems. Andriof & McIntosh's introduced the term 'corporate societal responsibility' in order "to avoid the limited interpretation of the term 'social responsibility', when translated into Continental European cultures and languages, as applying to social welfare issues only. The term 'societal responsibility' covers all dimensions of a company's impact on, relationships with and responsibilities to society as a whole".

He continued investigating the linguistic approach and concluded in line with Brooks and Klatt et al. that the word 'responsibility' should be replaced by 'accountability', for it causes similar problems as 'social'. This would imply a preference to use corporate societal accountability (CSA) as the contemporary term for CSR. Although I fully agree with its reasoning and suggestion, I expect it will be difficult for policy makers and executives to get used to another new generic notion. A hierarchical relationship between CSR, CS and Corporate Responsibility The second proposal was suggested to me by Lassi Linnanen and Virgilio Panapanaan from Helsinki University of Technology.

They consider Corporate Sustainability (CS) as the ultimate goal; meeting the needs of the present without compromising the ability of future generations to meet their own needs. In spite of the traditional bias of CS towards environmental policies, the various contributions at the Corporate Sustainability Conference 2002 at the Erasmus University Rotterdam in June clearly showed sufficient interest in integrating social and societal aspects into CS. The Erasmus University's Business Society Management has also placed CS as the ultimate goal, with CSR as an intermediate stage where companies try to balance the Triple Bottom Line.

Moreover, the theme of the EU Communication was CSR: a business contribution to Sustainable Development. The Finnish proposal implies a distinct disaggregation of dimensions - distinguishing sustainability from responsibility (CR) - to draw a more consistent picture. The three aspects of sustainability (economic, environmental, and social) can be translated into a CR approach that companies have to be concerned with. The simple illustration below depicts the relationship of CS, CR and CSR, plus, the economic and environmental dimensions. This is also to show how CSR as a new tool fits into the current CR or CS framework to complete the picture of corporate sustainability.

Although I fully agree with this new domain of CSR and consequently smaller interpretation of the social dimension of the organization, I doubt if the clock can be reversed. This smaller interpretation matches the term CSR, but in practice CSR is defined as a synonym to corporate sustainability. In general, corporate sustainability - and, unfortunately, also the contemporary understanding of CSR - refers to company activities - voluntary by definition - demonstrating the inclusion of social and environmental concerns in business operations and in interactions with stakeholders.

This is the broad - some would say 'vague' – definition of corporate sustainability. I will now differentiate this definition into five interpretations, CS ambition levels of corporate sustainability. Each definition relates to a specific context, as defined in Spiral Dynamics.

Also the motives for choosing a particular ambition are provided for:

- Compliance-driven CS (Blue): CS at this level consists of providing welfare to society, within the limits of regulations from the rightful authorities. In addition, organizations might respond to charity and stewardship considerations. The motivation for CS is that CS is perceived as a duty and obligation, or correct behaviour.
- Profit-driven CS (Orange): CS at this level consists of the integration of social, ethical and ecological aspects into business operations and decision-making, provided it contributes to the financial bottom line. The motivation for CS is a business case: CS is promoted if profitable, for example because of an improved reputation in various markets (customers/employees/ shareholders).
- Caring CS (Green): CS consists of balancing economic, social and ecological concerns, which are all three important in themselves. CS initiatives go beyond legal

compliance and beyond profit considerations. The motivation for CS is that human potential, social responsibility and care for the planet are as such important.

- Synergistic CS (Yellow): CS consists of a search for well-balanced, functional solutions creating value in the economic, social and ecological realms of corporate performance, in a synergistic, win-together approach with all relevant stakeholders. The motivation for CS is that sustainability is important in itself, especially because it is recognised as being the inevitable direction progress takes.
- Holistic CS (Turquoise): CS is fully integrated and embedded in every aspect of the organization, aimed at contributing to the quality and continuation of life of every being and entity, now and in the future. The motivation for CS is that sustainability is the only alternative since all beings and phenomena are mutually interdependent. Each person or organization therefore has a universal responsibility towards all other beings. The above defined principle of self-determina-tion allows each and everyone to respond to outside challenges in accordance to its own awareness and abilities. Any organization has the right to choose a position.

However not all these positions are equally adequate responses to perceived challenges offered in the environment. The principle of self-determination is balanced by the principle of communion: entities are part of a larger whole and thus ought to adapt it self to changes in its environment and respond to corrective actions from its stakeholders. The right to be and the capacity to create added value equals the duty to be responsible for its impact and to adjust itself to changes in its environment. Without conforming to this principle, organizations ultimately risk extinction. A differentiated set of CS definitions implies that there is no such thing as the features of corporate sustainability. Transparency, public disclosure, stakeholder engagement, societal approach to business, human capital, etcetera are all situational solutions that can be structured into coherent institutional frameworks supporting a specific ambition of CS.

Some positions include all these aspects, others, those more traditionally oriented, almost none. The coherent institutional frameworks supporting specific levels of CS can be difficult thresholds preventing companies from adopting higher levels of corporate sustainability. This might explain why, according to worldwide research by Ernst & Young among 114 companies from the Global 1000, 73% confirmed that corporate sustainability is on the board's agenda; 94% responded that a CS strategy might result in a better financial performance, but only 11 % is actually implementing it.

In Multiple Levels of Corporate Sustainability, Marcel van Marrewijk and Marco Werre show that specific interventions can only be adequately addressed within a specific context and situation. A higher ambition level and specific CS interventions require a supporting institutional framework and value system. The authors developed a matrix distinguishing six types of organizations at different developmental stages, their corresponding institutional frameworks, demonstrating different performance levels of corporate sustainability.

The overwhelming magnitude of recent corporate scandals has evoked a wave of soul searching among practitioners and academics. Driven by a quest to understand this remarkable decline in ethical conduct, an abundance of new research is being conducted. While most agree that social responsibility is a strong business imperative, there is little agreement about what it constitutes or how it should be incorporated. The problem lies in the disconnected silos of knowledge being concurrently developed and replicated in various business disciplines. Add to this evolving social standards and cultural differences superimposed on a global business landscape, and it is easy to see why the problem may appear intractable. As a first step, one must explore the evolution of the corporate social responsibility concept.

This historical trace identifies similarities and differences in themes and constructs among research streams. We hope that this will provide researchers with opportunities to enrich the discourse on corporate social responsibility. Another outcome of this evolutionary trace is the insight into the multidimensional nature of the CSR construct. We discuss ensuing problems and offer potential solutions. Our goal is to emphasize the importance of a multidisciplinary research agenda that utilizes multiple methods and multiple criteria.

EVOLUTION OF CORPORATE SOCIAL RESPONSIBILITY CONCEPT

The following discussion traces the evolution of the corporate social responsibility concept with regard to three questions. What is corporate social responsibility? Why should firms pursue social responsibility objectives? How does it affect firm performance?

Bowen, often regarded as a pioneering advocate of corporate social responsibility, suggested that CSR refers to "... the obligations of businessmen to pursue those policies, to make those decisions, or to follow those lines of action which are desirable in terms of the objectives and values of our society." Further attempts to elaborate the construct focused attention on firm obligations that extended beyond the economic and legal domains to include employee and community welfare, and the political and educational needs of society, thus giving rise to the modern concept of corporate citizenship.

This broadening of responsibilities was articulated by the Committee for Economic Development, which saw CSR as the service of a wider range of human values to improve the quality of life. They also suggested that the future of business was dependent on the quality of managerial response to changing societal expectations. According to researchers at the time, CSR was distinguished by its long (as opposed to short) term managerial focus and discretionary rather than mandated actions. CSR was comprised of two phases, first to not "spoil" society and second, to improve and provide solutions to societal problems through voluntary assumption of obligations and commitment.

Carroll summarized the discussion by offering the following definition: "Social responsibility of business encompasses the economic, legal, ethical, and discretionary expectations that society has of organizations at a given point in time." Note that economic and legal obligations refer to (clear-cut) mandated responsibilities while ethical and discretionary obligations refer to (not so clear-cut) societal expectations. This was followed by an attempt to broaden the CSR concept to one of corporate social performance that included three components: principles, processes, and policies.

The most significant contribution for our purposes came from Wood who elaborated and connected these three interrelated themes. First, she explained why industries, firms, and managers should endeavor to engage in socially responsible behavior (principles of legitimacy, public responsibility, and managerial discretion). This was followed by an explanation of how socially responsible objectives might be formulated and achieved (processes of environmental assessment, stakeholder management, and issues management). Finally, a description of what outcomes or results (i.e., social impacts, programs, and policies) should be expected with respect to the CSR domains was provided. In an effort to validate its usefulness to skeptics, management researchers circumscribed the scope of CSR by developing stakeholder theory.

Stakeholder theory armed its protagonists with strategic arguments to favor those stakeholders that might affect long term success and survival.

In a similar attempt to delineate the scope of corporate social and environmental responsibility and clarify its potential value, marketing researchers developed the constructs of corporate citizenship, environpreneurial marketing, and corporate environmentalism. This delimited view of CSR has much appeal since it provides a basis for firm strategy and aids accountability. More recently, an alternate perspective argues that the stakeholder approach be translated into a model of corporate sustainability, that demands managerial attention to economic, environmental, and social issues.

This view is supported by a sustainable theory of the firm, and calls to support the creation of sustainable value. Quite early in the CSR discussion, Davis attempted to justify socially responsible decision making by asserting the long term benefits of socially responsible decisions. Later, Johnson asserted that social responsibility was necessary since firms needed to balance multiple interests (e.g., stockholders, employees, suppliers, dealers, and local communities) to ensure the achievement of multiple goals and long-run profit maximization. Manne suggested that trying to gauge actual motives for business expenditures would be too difficult, since many business expenditures have multiple motives.

In summary, these views held CSR as instrumental to the accomplishment of firm objectives such as profit maximization, long term success, and or survival. Another perspective (a.k.a. Iron Law of Responsibility) was offered by Davis who suggested that unless businesses behaved responsibly, they would lose the power and legitimacy granted by society. As this concept gained support, researchers began to argue for a normative approach to CSR. They contended that firms were moral agents due to their contractual obligations to satisfy societal expectations and should therefore assume moral responsibilities.

In the mean time, the instrumental view continued to muster support through empirical inquiry. The debate over whether social responsibility arises due to normative or instrumental reasons has raged hard over the last decade. Currently, the key word is sustainability. At one end, this lays the foundations for a new theory of the firm by asserting that firms provide stakeholders with a *raison d'etre*. At the other, it provides a logical argument for simultaneously pursuing sustainable development and shareholder value for the creation of sustainable value. Early themes in CSR conceptualization emphasized that corporate volunteerism was critical to the discharge of social responsibilities.

Additionally, it was proposed that managers should accept that it would not be possible to gauge the economic impacts of socially responsible actions in most cases. This view clearly saw CSR as being at best subservient to the economic interests of the firm. Taking this a step further, Manne and Wallich argued that in order for business expenditures to qualify as socially responsible, they must provide lower returns than an alternative investment. The dominant logic was that firms should accept the costs for discharging social responsibilities that might negatively impact or at best not affect the bottom line. This premise was later replaced by the lexicographic view of social responsibility, which suggested that firms paid attention to social responsibility issues only after they had met their profitability goals. Subsequently adapted as a theory of slack resources, this view is still offered as an explanation for variations in firm social performance.

For a long time, social responsibility was viewed as a cost to the firm rather than a source of revenues. However, the emerging paradigm that views CSR and shareholder wealth as complementary goals is motivated by a different school of thought. This new business imperative owes its origin to Drucker, who was the first to suggest that not only were social responsibility and profitability compatible, but also that social opportunities could be converted into business opportunities. He went on to propose that businesses should turn social problems into economic opportunities and benefits, and ultimately into wealth. Theoretical and empirical support for this view came initially from the literature on environmentalism, that is, research on how firms mange their relationships with the natural environment.

For instance, Porter and van der Linde argued how stringent regulations could be turned into opportunities to improve firm efficiencies, while Hart explained competitive advantages accruing to environmentally responsible firms by adapting the resource based view of the firm. Research has shown that pollution prevention type (as opposed to end-of-pipe) technologies improved environmental and financial performance, while incorporating environmental issues into the strategic planning process provided superior financial performance. The movement has gathered momentum in recent years and has evolved into the sustainable growth business model, which extends beyond environmental responsibility to encompass community and employee welfare, corporate philanthropy, and supplier / distributor partnerships.

This is evidenced by a new corporate sustainability index designed to meet the needs of social investors. The DJSI identifies and monitors the performance of "innovative and future oriented firms" that achieve competitive advantage from environmental and social growth opportunities. In a similar vein, our thesis propagates and extends our understanding of how firms may satisfy stakeholders and simultaneously meet social and economic objectives. In summary, we find that CSR is a multidimensional construct deserving of multidisciplinary attention. While such attention has been forthcoming lately, there is a problem in that parallel and overlapping themes and constructs are being simultaneously developed in various business disciplines. This has resulted in lack of clarity and differences in meanings assigned to constructs. It is necessary to clarify, integrate and coordinate CSR research for its proper advancement.

MULTIDIMENSIONALITY OF THE CSR CONCEPT

In this section, we discuss the multidimensional nature of the CSR concept and offer potential solutions for addressing this problem.

Multidimensionality is problematic for researchers as it necessitates the study of several domains and disciplines and must be considerate of multiple perspectives. In addition, it requires more comprehensive research design - a problem for most researchers already constrained by time and cost limitations.

CSR multidimensionality arises from six different factors: Diversity in the set of processes deemed to constitute a set of socially responsible firm behaviors: For instance, Wood points out that it is not a single process, rather a set of processes by which a firm's social performance can be judged. In her opinion, in order to evaluate a company's social performance, "researchers would examine the degree to which principles of social responsibility motivate actions taken on behalf of the company, the degree to which the firm makes use of socially responsive processes, the existence and nature of policies and programs designed to manage the firm's societal relationships, and the social impacts".

Multiple stakeholders with differing, often conflicting interests: There is often conflict between competing stakeholder claims. Recent analyses of firms engaging in socially responsible behavior have shown interest in showcasing firms deemed responsible by one set of stakeholders and largely irresponsible by another. For instance, the Body Shop is often cited as the paragon of environmental friendliness. However, there are many who question the inherent worth of cosmetic products to society.

Differences in corporate missions or values that motivate firms to engage in socially responsible activities: Differences in corporate missions and cultures with respect to CSR may be attributed to external environmental forces such as public opinion or regulatory pressures or internal drivers such as top management commitment or the need for competitive advantage. Such differences in antecedent influences lead to wide variations in performance, making it harder for researchers to partial out the effects of socially responsible initiatives.

Variances in performance attributed to socially responsible behavior: A number of studies have shown significant differences in firm performance with regard to socially responsible initiatives.

Not all socially responsible behavior has the same effect on firm performance and such initiatives are often moderated by a variety of firm (e.g., size, employee skills, and brand reputation) and environmental characteristics (e.g., competitive intensity, industry type). Note that since stakeholder perceptions of firm motivations may moderate evaluations of social responsibility initiatives, such moderating factors must be carefully controlled during empirical investigation of the relationship between CSR and firm performance.

Subjectivity in judging what constitutes socially responsible behavior: The confluence of dynamic and evolving ethical standards, varying definitions of social responsibility due to cultural differences, and differences in industry practices and norms increase the degree of subjectivity about what is deemed socially responsible. Such subjectivity is further compounded by whether a short or long term perspective is adopted. In Votaw's words, "To some it (CSR) conveys the idea of legal responsibility or liability; to others it means socially responsible behavior in an ethical sense; to still others, the meaning transmitted is that of "responsible for", in a causal mode; many simply equate it with charitable contribution." This has created problems for researchers trying to operationalize and empirically test models of corporate social responsibility.

Multiple domains of CSR: In an early essay, Carroll proposed that corporate social responsibility consisted of four components relating to a firm's economic, legal, ethical, and discretionary obligations. While this was initially meant to distinguish between mandated and voluntary action, it later formed the basis for empirical inquiry into corporate social performance. These multiple domains necessitate attention to several interrelated firm objectives and require psychometrically valid measures to capture the full dimensionality of the concept. Also, varying degrees of importance given to these domains by different stakeholders make assessment of CSR a difficult task.

METHODOLOGICAL IMPLICATIONS

The above discussion clearly underscores the need for a multidisciplinary inquiry of CSR. Next, we discuss the methodological implications of such multidimensionality and propose some solutions. The first step would involve establishing common definitions and standards for CSR and associated constructs. For this purpose, it may be useful to start with an assessment of stakeholder expectations and build up towards a collective definition of CSR. Agreement across disciplines regarding concepts and definitions is necessary for the purpose of establishing construct validity. In addition, this would help researchers develop nomological networks to differentiate CSR from associated constructs and assist in the evaluation of discriminant validity. Such agreement would also facilitate the development and use of common measures for CSR and associated constructs so that CSR performance can be reliably evaluated.

Second, the dynamism of the CSR concept highlights the need for new approaches and research designs. It necessitates longitudinal research designs to evaluate the progress of firms at various points in time. Within-industry studies would be useful for controlling the influence of context-specific norms and moderating factors. This would also enable researchers to deal with the issue of test-retest reliability. Triangulation is critical, not just of method, but also of concepts and findings. Multiple methods that simultaneously utilize perceptual and behavioral measures can help establish predictive validity. One key problem especially with self reported measures of motivation and values is social desirability bias. Developing indirect measures and triangulating studies with multiple methods would help alleviate this problem. Triangulation of results and key findings of studies would also help establish criterion validity. In conclusion, we feel that there is an urgent need for collaborative and coordinated efforts to study CSR. We hope that such multidisciplinary research will herald a new age that is succeeded by multidisciplinary teaching and practice.

CSR AND COMMUNITY DEVELOPMENT CSR

It would be no exaggeration to say that but for the sense of commitment and responsibility of some industrial groups such as the Tatas, TVS, Reliance, etc. Country could not have seen the strides that has made in many areas. Tatas and Birlas, of course, as a group undertook community work before CSR was even coined and become fashionable. As Venu Srinivasan,

CMD of TVS Motor Company, points out succinctly in an interview said, "CSR in a developing world can not be limited to saying I have paid my taxes and thus have done my duty to society, 'which is a capitalist way. CSR has to be there to get more directly to the population rather then wait. Aspiration levels have gone beyond what was there. Many large companies now issue a corporate social responsibility report along with their annual report. The CSR report concentrates on their non-financial societal activities (usually positive contributions in nature).

An approach for CSR that is becoming more widely accepted is community-based development projects. The majority of these CSR projects are established in developing countries. A more common approach of CSR is through the giving of aid to local organizations and impoverished communities in developing countries. Community Based Development (CBD) and its more recent variant, Community Driven Development (CDD), are the fastest growing mechanisms for channeling development assistance.

INDIA'S DEVELOPMENT

P. Sainath's article in The Hindu dated 24th December 2007, titled "India 2007: high growth, low development" has brought chilling statistics about the India's Development. India's falling to rank 128 in the Human Development Index of United Nation Development Programme (UNDP) from 126 last year. It means the other nations did much better then us and hence we went down to rank 128 this year.

El Salvador, which saw a bloody civil war for over a decade from the 1980s, rank 25 places ahead of us at 103; Bolivia, often called South America's poorest nation, is 11 steps above us 117. Guatemala, nearly half of whose citizens are poor indigenous people, saw the longest civil war in Central America and which saw 200,000 people killed or disappears. The nation of just 12 million, Guatemala ranks 10 places above us at 118.

In Africa, Botswana-ranked below us in 2006 HDI at 131-

climbed four places above us at 124 this time. The Occupied Palestinian Territories, with all their woes, slipped six places to 106 but still well ahead of India.

In Asian, countries like Vietnam-victim of the bloodiest conflict since World War II- rose further in the charts, to rank 105 this year. Sri Lanka, of course, is way ahead of us at 99. So are nation like Kazakhstan and Mongolia. They too have risen in the ranks and the former from 79 to 73 and the latter from 116 to 114. Our top billionaires are doing fine. "Their collective wealth has soared 27 per cent since July this year," The Times of India told us on its front page on October 8. The headline said they'd got "richer by $65.3 billion" in just three months since July. We rank fourth in superrich and 128th in Human Development Index.

THE CONTEMPORARY DEBATE

In the contemporary debate on Modern Corporation and its impact on economy, society and nation, the focus has shifted from growth with only profitability to growth with sustainable development, which includes the stakeholders. While there is considerable debate on the corporations' obligations to civil society in the Western world, in the developing countries the debate is sporadic. The subject of Corporate Social Responsibility has risen to the top on the agenda of policy makers, managers, social scientist and social activists in recent times.

The present International Conference is an effort to initiate a nationwide discourse on the concepts and practices of corporate social action in India. Keeping the organizer's ongoing (seven years completed) experience in the field of CSR (TVS Group) and community development project among the marginalized along with other stakeholders, it aims at formulating a working model. The basic methodology is Participatory approach and such efforts led us to achieve development with equity. The model will facilitate in building sustainable models of development. Hence, we are requesting the corporate to put this model into practice along with the other stakeholders.

Outcome:

- In-depth understanding of the conceptual, theoretical and practical aspects of development through equity.
- Insight into the successful development strategies and models carried out by corporates and NGO's.
- Identification of the challenges faced by the corporates, process facilitators and the beneficiaries in achieving the goal.
- Understanding the roles and responsibilities of the stakeholders including the corporates, process facilitators and the beneficiaries.
- Networking with internationally acclaimed academicians and researchers in the fields of sociology, anthropology and developmental studies.

POSITIONING STAKEHOLDER THEORY

The present-day conception of corporate social responsibility (CSR) implies that companies voluntarily integrate social and environmental concerns in their operations and interaction with stakeholders.

The European Commission defines it as "a concept whereby companies decide voluntarily to contribute to a better society and a cleaner environment." It is related to complex issues such as environmental protection, human resources management, health and safety at work, relations with local communities, relations with suppliers and consumers. The notion of CSR is one of ethical and moral issues surrounding corporate decision making and behaviour. Knowing if a company should undertake certain activities or refrain from doing so because they are beneficial or harmful to society is a central question. Social issues deserve moral consideration of their own and should lead managers to consider the social impacts of corporate activities in decision making.

Regardless of any stake- holders' pressures, actions which lead to things such as the conservation of the Earth's natural resources or bio-diversity preservation are morally praiseworthy. However, some argue that the contribution of concepts such as CSR is just a reminder that the search for profit should be constrained by social considerations. Increasingly CSR is analysed as a source of competitive advantage and not as an end in itself. In effect, the concept of CSR has evolved from being regarded as detrimental to a company's profitability, to being considered as some- how benefiting the company as a whole, at least in the long run. CSR has been conceptualised in a number of different ways which are related clearly to differing views regarding the role of business in society.

These views are often presented within the stakeholder-shareholder debate. The idea which underlies the "shareholder perspective" is that the only responsibility of managers is to serve the interests of shareholders in the best possible way, using corporate resources to increase the wealth of the latter by seeking profits.

In contrast, the "stakeholder perspective" suggests that besides shareholders, other groups or constituents are affected by a company's activities (such as employees or the local community), and have to be considered in managers' decisions, possibly equally with shareholders. The purpose of this chapter is to give an account of the concept of CSR and its evolution, based on the notion that nowadays companies engage in CSR because they can reap benefits from such engagement. Thus, it is necessary to have a CSR notion which is able to address this important feature.

The argument is that such notion should be based on a stakeholder view and should be capable of addressing both normative and instrumental aspects of CSR. This chapter argues that the stakeholder perspective has become something which is inescapable if one wants to discuss and analyse CSR. Stakeholder theory is considered as "a necessary process in the operationalisation of corporate social responsibility, as a complimentary rather than conflicting body of literature." Furthermore, it can be said to exist a "stakeholder meta narrative" which underlies the CSR debate. In fact, recent analysis of the extensive body of research on ethics and social responsibility issues show that an important number of the authors who devote themselves to these areas of study have mostly drawn on stakeholder theory.

In the following section, the different perspectives of CSR are analysed and the argument that a stakeholder view of the role of business in society is more adequate, is presented. Thereafter, follow sections on the evolution of the concept of CSR based on the stakeholder perspective, and a discussion of the debate on business and society relationships.

PERSPECTIVES ON CORPORATE SOCIAL RESPONSIBILITY

Based on Clarke and Lantos two viewpoints on the role of business in society (which lead to different views on CSR) will be distinguished? The "classical view", based on neoclassical economic theory, defines it in purely economic profit making terms, focusing on the profit of the shareholders. In contrast, the "stakeholder view", based on stakeholder theory, holds that companies have a social responsibility that requires them to consider the interests of all parties affected by their actions. Classical view Lantos has identified two perspectives in the classical view: the "pure profit-making view"; and the "constrained profit- making view". The "pure profit-making view" is exemplified by Carr's position. The distinctive feature of this author's perspective is that some degree of dishonesty is acceptable be- cause business people have a lower set of moral standards than those in the rest of society. He compared the ethics of business to those of the poker game.

The lower set of moral standards permits what he calls "business bluffing" which includes things like conscious misstatements, concealment of pertinent facts, or exaggeration. Deception is probably a necessary component of a strategy to be successful in business, and thus business people can not afford to be guided by ethics as conceived in private life.

Thus, for Carr, a company has the legal right to shape its strategy without reference to anything but its profits, so long as it stays within the rules of the game legally set out by law. The major proponent of the "constrained profit-making view" is Friedman, who believed companies should behave honestly: that is, they do not engage in deception and fraud. This economist argues that the purpose of the company is to make profits for shareholders.

The only responsibility of business is to use its resources to engage in activities designed to in- crease its profits so long as it stays within the rules of the game. Because managers are agents of the shareholders they have a responsibility to conduct business in accordance with their interest. This is generally to make as much money as possible and maximise their wealth. Under this view, because shareholders are the owners of the company and therefore the profits belong to them, requiring managers to pursue socially responsible objectives may be unethical, since it requires managers to spend money that belongs to other individuals. Asking companies to engage in social responsibility activities is considered to be harmful to the foundations of a free society with a free-enterprise and private-property system. Social problems should be left for the state to address. Although Friedman's ideas are better known, his view had a conspicuous predecessor in Levitt.

The latter also believed that companies should be concerned with improving production and increasing profits while abiding by the rules of the game, which include acting honestly and in good faith, and that social problems should be left for the state to address. The classical view also has contemporary adherents. Their arguments, which can be associated with the "constrained profit-making view", have arisen mainly in debate with stakeholder perspective proponents. However, it is important to note that not all of these authors can be shown as opposing social responsibility actions by companies. Barry argues that companies can only engage in social responsibility activities the less competitive the markets in which they operate are, and that such engagement is a form of rent-seeking by managers.

However, the central argument is that the use of companies' resources to further social goals amounts to managers' usurpation of the political function. The difficulty in making appropriate decisions when the predominant authority of shareholders is removed and the purpose of maximizing shareholder wealth is disregarded in order to take into account a variety of interests is stressed by Barry when he argues that in such conditions decision-making in a company "would resemble that of a parliamentary assembly." Barry claims that it leads "to the politicization of the company in that many groups and a number of almost certainly competing purposes must now be considered."

Therefore, Barry's assessment of the stakeholder perspective is that it "tries to make the business system operate like the political system." This is not advisable because it will "bring all the disadvantages of voting, as well as the enervating effect of pressure groups to an activity that depends on personal freedom and individual initiative to fulfill its promise." The ex-OECD Chief Economist David Henderson is another of the modern critics of CSR. Whereas Friedman focused his concern in managers adopting misguided objectives, Henderson's focus is on outside interferences with efficient resource allocation. Henderson contends that CSR adversely affects a company's performance. However, his case against CSR rests primarily on the contention that it impairs the performance of business enterprises in their primary role, and would make people in general poorer. He is an adamant opponent of overregulation, and views increased legislation in this matter to be harmful, and lead to decreased business activity.

CSR is seen as leading to ineffective markets, reduced wealth generation and increased social inequity and poverty. He does not attribute any social responsibility related function to companies. Other contemporary authors defend shareholder value maximization as the one objective function to all companies but are not necessarily against the social responsibility actions by companies. Basically these authors argue that having more than one objective creates difficulties for managers and some confusion in their decision making. On the other hand, having shareholder value maximization as objective is believed to lead managers to decisions that enhance outcomes for multiple stakeholders. Jensen, for example, considers that "200 years' worth of work in economics and finance indicate that social welfare is maximized when all companies in an economy maximize total company value." However, their basic point is that value seeking should be a company's only objective function and having as only objective making money for share- holders implies that managers should not be allowed to pursue moral goals at the expense of profitability.

These authors repeat several of their predecessors' arguments, but they are not necessarily against the social responsibility actions by companies. In the words of Sternberg, a company "cannot afford to ignore any stakeholder concern that might affect its ability to generate long-term owner value." A company's interactions with its stakeholders are recognized as affecting profitability, and "ethical executives should consider this as part of their fiduciary duties to shareholders." Social responsibility actions might even be used strategically by companies in seeking value maximization of the company. These authors seem to defend what Jensen calls "enlightened shareholder maximization" view, according to which a company cannot maximize value if any important stakeholder is ignored or mistreated, but the criterion for making the requisite tradeoffs among its stakeholders is long-term value maximization.

Even Carr, in spite of defending the pure profit-making view recognized that if a company wishes to take a long-term view of its profits, "it will need to preserve amicable relations with whom it deals. A wise businessman will not seek advantage to the point where he generates dangerous hostility among employees, competitors, customers, government, or the public at large." However, he thought that "decisions in this area are, in the final test, decisions of strategy, not of ethics." The classical view is justified mainly on the basis of neoclassical economic theory arguments using notions such as the free market, economic efficiency, and profit maximisation.

This view might be grounded in three different, but complementary, ways: - first, shareholders are the owners of the corporation, and managers have no right to act on their own preferences, to make discretionary decisions or to use company's resources to further social goals which cannot be shown to be directly related to profits; - second, companies' role is to produce wealth, and pursue socially responsible objectives may impair their performance in that role interfering with efficient resource allocation; - finally, other organizations exist to deal with the kind of function requested by socially responsible actions, such as government, and companies and managers are not equipped to per- form such role. However, some authors believe that CSR is often useful in generating long-term owner value.

For some time the arguments that have been presented for strategic CSR arise, at least in part, from the classical idea that the sole objective of business is to maximise shareholder wealth and that a company should engage in CSR activities only if it allows value to be created. This approach is synthesized by McWilliams and Siegel. They argue that decisions regarding CSR should be treated by managers "precisely as they treat all investment decisions." Some authors argue that CSR "should be considered as a form of strategic investment." Stakeholder view Stakeholder theory is based on the notion that beyond share- holders there are several agents with an interest in the actions and decisions of companies. Stakeholders are "groups and individuals who benefit from or are harmed by, and whose rights are violated or respected by, corporate actions." In addition to shareholders, stakeholders include creditors, employees, customers, suppliers, and the communities at large. Stakeholder theory asserts that companies have a social responsibility that requires them to consider the interests of all parties affected by their actions.

Management should not only consider its shareholders in the decision making process, but also anyone who is affected by business decisions. In contrast to the classical view, the stakeholder view holds that "the goal of any company is or should be the flourishing of the company and all its principal stakeholders." It is important to stress that shareholders are stakeholders and that dividing the world into the concerns of the two is "the logical equivalent of contrasting 'apples' with 'fruit'." Many interesting typologies of stakeholders have been pro- posed. Clarkson's typology of stakeholders is the most widely cited and accepted. Clarkson distinguishes primary and secondary stakeholders.

Primary stakeholders are those "with- out whose continuing participation the corporation cannot survive as a going concern" (shareholders and investors, employees, customers and suppliers, and also governments and communities "that provide infrastructures and markets, whose laws and regulations must be obeyed, and to whom taxes and other obligations may be due"),whereas secondary stake- holders are "those who influence or affect, or are influenced or affected by, the corporation, but they are not engaged in transactions with the corporation and are not essential for its survival."

Some of the problems with stakeholder theory lie in the difficulty of considering "mute" stakeholders (the natural environment) and "absent" stakeholders (such as future generations or potential victims). The difficulty of considering the natural environment as a stakeholder is real because the majority of the definitions of stakeholders usually treat them as groups or individuals, thereby excluding the natural environment as a matter of definition because it is not a human group or community as are, for example, employees or consumers. Phillips and Reichart argued that only humans can be considered as organizational stakeholders and criticize the attempts to give the natural environment stakeholder status. One way of seeing the environment as a stakeholder is through the interests of future generations.

However, it is impossible to ask the opinion of the natural environment or of future generations, and they cannot be members of a consultative committee. Thus, the problem is that only humans are capable of generating the necessary obligations for establishing stakeholder status and of the necessary volition in the acceptance of benefits of a mutually beneficial cooperative scheme. However, if among the interests of legitimate stakeholders is a concern for the natural environment, it has to be taken into account. Moreover, the interests of the environment and future generations should contemplated by "being represented in decision-making structures, whether of companies or of society as a whole."

Regarding stakeholder theory, Donaldson and Preston argue that it can be used in three different ways:

1. The descriptive/empirical, when it is used to "describe, and sometimes to explain, specific corporate characteristics and
2. The instrumental, when it is used to "identify the connections, or lack of connections, between stakeholder management and the achievement of traditional corporate objectives (e.g., profitability, growth)"; and
3. The normative, when it is used to "interpret the function" of companies and identify "moral or philosophical guidelines" that should be followed with regard to their "operation and management" (ibid.). The empirical and the instrumental uses are interrelated inextricably.

This suggests a difficulty in relating empirical and normative endeavours. Whereas the former is descriptive in nature and attempts to analyse the way things are, the latter is prescriptive and aims to prescribe how things should to be. The normative and instrumental uses probably entail the existence of two conflicting approaches to stakeholder theory. The normative approach to stakeholder theory views stakeholders as "end".

The instrumental approach is interested in how stakeholders can be considered in a way that enhances financial performance and efficiency, and thus regards stakeholders as "means". The instrumental approach to stakeholder theory views stake- holders' interests as factors to be taken into account and man- aged while the company is engaged in maximization of shareholders wealth.

The underlying argument is that stakeholders' interests are considered as means for higher level goals, such as profit maximization, survival and growth. Referring to the instrumental use, Jawahar and McLaughlin consider that a "fundamental assumption is that the ultimate objective of corporate decisions is marketplace success, and stakeholder management is a means to that end." Having established the importance of stakeholder management, a question that remains is which stakeholders managers view as most significant. This question has been addressed by Mitchell et al. (1997). They offered a theory of stakeholder identification and salience that suggests that managers' perceptions of three key stakeholder attributes (power to influence the company, legitimacy of the relationship with the company and urgency of the claim on the company) affect the degree to which managers give priority to competing stakeholder claims.

A stakeholder "may have a legitimate claim on the company, but unless it has either power to enforces its will in the relationship or a perception that its claim is urgent, it will not achieve salience for the company's managers."

Power is a stakeholder attribute that has been used to identify and prioritize stakeholders, with some authors suggesting that companies respond to the most powerful stakeholder issues. For example, Nasi et al. found that forestry companies in Canada and Sweden focused on issues that were relevant to the most powerful stakeholders rather than on those issues that were relevant from an ethical or socially responsible point of view.

The "social activist" perspective shares with stakeholder theory the notion that companies are accountable to all other stakeholders beyond shareholders. Hence, they should behave to actively promote social interests, even when it is not expected or demanded by society.

Companies should be involved actively "in programs which can ameliorate various social ills, such as by providing employment opportunities for everyone, improving the environment, and promoting worldwide justice, even if it costs the shareholders money." The question that one can legitimately pose is: in what way is the use of some kind of stakeholder management as a means to achieve marketplace success different from the classical view? If stakeholder theory does not give any primacy to one stake- holder over another, there will be times when some groups will benefit at the expense of others.

The problem that then arises is which groups would be given preferential treatment? One can say that the classical view is purely economic in nature, and presents a clear differentiation between economic and social aspects, whereas stakeholder management perspective brings together social and economic aspects. Jensen argues that what he calls "enlightened value maximization" and "enlightened stakeholder theory" may be thought of as identical. Enlightened value maximization uses stakeholder theory to consider that a company cannot maximize value if any important stakeholder is ignored or mistreated. However, it maintains as the criterion for making the requisite tradeoffs among its stakeholders long-term value maximization. Enlightened stakeholder theory considers long-term value maximization or value as the objective function of the company, thereby solving the problems that arise from considering multiple objectives, as in traditional stakeholder theory.

Proponents of stakeholder theory, such as Freeman et al., question the alternatives available for managers to create shareholder value other than "by creating products and services that customers are willing to buy, offering jobs that employees are willing to fill, building relationships with suppliers that companies are eager to have, and being good citizens in the community". What are it then that differentiates stakeholder theory from this enlightened value maximization. Freeman et al. argue that the former "begins with the assumption that values are necessarily and explicitly a part of doing business, and rejects the separation thesis", according to which ethics and economics can be separated clearly. Stakeholder theory proponents reject the separation thesis.

They see a moral dimension to business activity, because economics "is clearly infused or embedded with ethical assumptions, implications, and overtones." On the other hand, many proponents of the share- holder, single-objective view distinguish between economic and ethical consequences and values and see business as an amoral economic activity. According to Porter and Kramer, Friedman's argument has two implicit assumptions: social and economic objectives are separate and distinct; and by addressing social objectives companies do not provide greater benefit than is pro- vided by individual donors. The enlightened shareholder maximization view also has such assumptions. But the dichotomy between economic and social objectives is a false one because companies do not function in isolation from the society in which they operate. For these authors, "in the long run, then, social and economic goals are not inherently conflicting but integrally connected."

Therefore, contrary to Friedman's ideas, managers who undertake social responsibility activities do not necessarily misuse financial resources that legitimately belong to shareholders. Freeman et al. correctly consider that the shareholder, single-objective view "is a narrow view that cannot possibly do justice to the panoply of human activity that is value creation and trade, i.e., business." Whereas the shareholder view sees a unique answer, and attributes one objective function to all companies, stakeholder theory admits a wide range of answers. Freeman et al. also believe that these theories should not be considered as opposed, in the sense that even shareholder theory can be regarded as a version of stakeholder theory, because stakeholder theory admits many possible normative cores.

As a particular version of stakeholder theory, shareholder view's moral presuppositions can be seen as including "respect for property rights, voluntary cooperation, and individual initiative to improve everyone's circumstances. These presuppositions provide a good starting point, but not a complete vision of value creation." Sundaram and Inkpen recognize that decisions to enhance efficiency are made to increase shareholder value and impose costs on other stakeholders, and imply that it is an acceptable trade-off.

According to stakeholder theory as perceived in this chapter, such costs are unacceptable unless it can be proven that benefits for the society outweigh them. It is important to note that existent deviations between short run impacts of business activities and the long run alignment of business and social interests in wealth creation leave ample scope for abuse or market power and irresponsible conduct. Furthermore, "the leitmotif of wealth creation can easily lead to both moral misconduct and financial manipulation ultimately destructive of social purposes and stakeholders' welfare."

THE EVOLUTION OF THE CORPORATE SOCIAL RESPONSIBILITY CONCEPT

Frederick (1994) referred to the distinction between social responsibility and social responsiveness when he identified two stages of development in the thinking about CSR. The first stage, which he labelled CSR1, focused on CSR as an examination of companies' "obligation to work for social betterment". Around 1970, there was a shift to corporate social responsiveness, labelled as CSR2, which is "the capacity of a corporation to respond to social pressures".

Frederick further developed this analysis by adding a third stage, that of corporate social rectitude (CSR3), to include "the notion of moral correctness in actions taken and policies formulated". In a more recent work, Frederick refers to the need to enter a new stage (CSR4) "enriched by natural sciences insights". In this chapter, the distinction between social responsibility and social responsiveness is of interest and will be developed. The term "social responsibility" has been challenged as early as the 1970's. Sethi distinguishes between social obligation, social responsibility, and social responsiveness.

He argues that, like all other social institutions, companies are an integral part of society and must depend on acceptance of their role and activities for their existence, continuity and growth.

When a difference between corporate performance and social expectations for such performance occurs, a legitimacy gap is said to exist. The crucial issues in the concept of CSR are the search for legitimacy by companies and the doubts by critics about the legitimacy of companies' actions. Corporate behaviour in response to market forces or legal constraints is defined as social obligation, and is proscriptive in nature. Social responsibility implies congruence of corporate behaviour with prevailing social norms, values and expectations of performance, and it is a concept which is prescriptive in nature. The concept of social responsiveness suggests that what is important is not how a company should respond to social pressures, but what should be their long-term role in a dynamic social system.

The idea is that business orientation in any social dimension must be anticipatory and preventive. Although Sethi implied that social responsiveness could be seen as a replacement for social responsibility, later writers reject such a view. For example, Carroll holds that social responsiveness is not an alternative to social responsibility but rather "the action phase of management responding in the social sphere." Wartick and Cochran hold that both "are equally valid concepts and that both should be included as separate dimensions of corporate social involvement."

The concepts of social responsiveness and of corporate social performance can be seen as the evolution of the concept of social responsibility. In this chapter, the concept of CSR is seen as including the other two concepts. Carroll's "Three-dimensional Conceptual Model" was the initial model of corporate social performance.

It consisted of an integration of three aspects: first, a definition of social responsibility; second, an identification of the social issues to which these responsibilities are tied, such as consumerism, environment, employment discrimination, product safety, occupational safety and health; and third, the philosophy of responsiveness, that is the philosophy, mode, or strategy behind companies' response to social responsibility and social issues (reaction, defense, accommodation, and pro-action). Building on previous definitions of CSR which refer to the responsibility to make a profit, obey the law, and "go beyond" these activities, Carroll argues that CSR encompasses four categories of social responsibilities: economic, legal, ethical, and discretionary (or philanthropic).

Economic responsibilities reflect the belief that companies have an obligation to produce goods and services that consumers need and want, and to be profitable in the process. Legal responsibilities indicate that companies are expected to pursue economic responsibilities within the confines of written law. Ethical and discretionary responsibilities encompass the more general responsibilities to do what is right and avoid harm. Ethical responsibilities indicate a concern that companies meet society's expectations of business conduct that are not codified into law, but rather are reflected in unwritten standards, norms, and values implicitly derived from society. Companies' discretionary responsibilities are volitional or philanthropic in nature, in the sense that they represent voluntary roles assumed by companies for which society's expectations are not as clear-cut as in the ethical responsibilities.

Carroll (1991) argues that these four categories of corporate social responsibilities can be depicted as a pyramid, in which economic responsibilities are the foundations upon which all other responsibilities are predicated and without which they can not be achieved, and discretionary responsibilities are the apex. Notwithstanding, companies are expected to fulfill these four social responsibilities simultaneously. An important consideration regarding this perspective is that, contrary to the common belief that economic responsibility is related to what the companies do for themselves, and the other responsibilities are related to what they do for others, "economic viability is something business does for society as well." Matten et al. underline the centrality of the ethical and philanthropical areas of responsibility to the study of CSR because of the differentiation they allow to establish between voluntary corporate behaviour and mere compliance.

The CSR debate has focused on the moral and philanthropic responsibilities, giving little attention to economic and legal responsibilities. In this chapter, the term CSR will also be used to refer to ethical and philanthropically responsibilities of business. An important and recent addition to the discussion of Car- roll's model was offered by Carroll himself in Schwartz and Carroll (2003). These authors develop a three-domain approach, in which they propose the subsumption of the philanthropic or discretionary component under the ethical and/or economic components. The reasons for such proposal are related, on the one hand, to the difficulty in distinguishing between "philanthropic" and "ethical" activities on both the theoretical and practical levels, and, on the other hand, to the observation that philanthropic activities are often explained by underlying economic interests. As the authors argue, a company can engage in philanthropical activities for ethical or economic reasons or a combination of the two.

When economic motives, such as increased sales, enhanced public image or improved employee morale, underlie a company's actions in the form of strategic philanthropy, this does not constitute a distinct philanthropic obligation. Carroll provided a linkage to stakeholder theory by noting the "natural fit between the idea of CSR and an organization's stakeholders." Furthermore, the concept of stake- holder personalizes social responsibilities by specifying groups or persons to whom companies are responsible and should be responsive. Carroll's model was later extended and modified by Wartick and Cochran and Wood, Wartick and Cochran presented a "Corporate Social Performance Model" which also integrates three areas: the principles of CSR (using Carroll's four categories of social responsibilities as "principles"); the processes of corporate social responsiveness (reactive, defensive, accommodative, and proactive); and the policies developed to address social issues (social issues management).

Wood considers that the basic idea of CSR "is that business and society are interwoven rather than distinct entities; therefore, society has certain expectations for appropriate business behaviour and outcomes." She retained Carroll's four categories and identified how they relate to the CSR principles (the principle of legitimacy, the principle of public responsibility, and the principle of managerial discretion), considering that the first can be viewed as domains within which the latter are enacted. The principle of legitimacy operates on an institutional level and is based on a company's overall responsibilities to the society in which it operates, specifying what is expected of all companies. It is a proscriptive principle, "and it implies that society has available sanctions that can be used when these obligations are not met." The principle of public responsibility functions on an organizational level, stating that companies are "responsible for solving problems they have caused, and they are responsible for helping to solve problems and social issues related to their business operations and interests."

Finally, the principle of managerial discretion functions on an individual level and emphasizes managers' responsibilities to behave as moral actors and make choices about activities designed to achieve socially responsible outcomes. Wood also suggests that companies use three main kinds of processes to bring these principles into practice: environmental assessment, issues management, and stakeholder management. She then presents the outcomes of bringing principles into practice within the economic, legal, ethical, and discretionary domains, categorizing them in terms of social impacts (beneficial or negative), social programs (which refer to the actions companies take to manage their social impacts in a favourable manner), and social policies (which emerge to guide decision making). Wood and Jones use a stakeholder framework to modify Wood's definition of corporate social performance as principles, processes, and outcomes.

They redefine the outcomes as internal stakeholder effects, external stakeholder effects, and external institutional effects. They argue that stakeholders have three roles: they are the sources of expectations about what constitutes desirable and undesirable company performance, defining the norms for corporate behaviour; they experience the effects of corporate behaviour; and they evaluate the outcomes of companies' behaviours in terms of how they have met expectations and have affected the groups and organizations in their environment. From a stakeholder theory perspective, corporate social performance can thus be assessed in terms of a company meeting the demands of its multiple stakeholder groups, and companies must seek to satisfy their demands "as an unavoidable cost of doing business."

Corporate social performance is considered to refer to "the ability of the company to meet or exceed stakeholder expectations regarding social issues." Clarkson holds that a stakeholder management frame- work is more useful to the analysis and evaluation of corporate social performance than models and methodologies based on concepts of social responsibilities and responsiveness. He con- tends that it is necessary to distinguish "between stakeholder issues and social issues because corporations and their managers manage relationships with their stakeholders and not with society." However, it is vital to understand that being responsive to stakeholders' expectations implies the need to consider prevailing social norms and dominant views of corporate responsibilities.

Stakeholders' expectations of companies are intertwined inextricably with society's views or expectations of business performance which evolve over time. Thus, the distinction between stakeholder issues and social issues may not be as straight forward as it seems. Nonetheless, Hillman and Keim argue that to analyze the relationship between social performance and financial performance, it is useful to distinguish between two components of corporate social performance: stakeholder management and social issue participation. They believe that these two components of social performance have opposing relationships to financial performance. Building good relations with primary stakeholders is susceptible of leading to increased financial returns.

On the one hand, it assists companies in developing valuable intangible assets (resources and capabilities) which can be sources of competitive advantage because such assets can differentiate a company from its competitors. On the other hand, pursuing social issues that are not related directly to the relationship with primary stakeholders may not create such advantages, because participating in social issues is something which can be easily copied by competitors.

Thus, one can infer that social responsibility activities can pay off, as long as they are in the interest of a company's primary stakeholders. Hillman and Keim's conclude that whereas stakeholder management can lead to shareholder wealth creation, participation in social issues does not have the same kind of result.

The conception of CSR adopted in this chapter is based clearly on the perspective put forward by Carroll and Schwartz and Carroll and extended by Wartick and Cochran, Wood, and Wood and Jones. This perspective has evolved to incorporate stake- holder theory concepts already present in Carroll and Wood but particularly developed by Wood and Jones and Clarkson.

Carroll's model is adopted in this chapter, although the focus will be on ethical and philanthropic components. A distinctive feature of Carroll's model is that it draws attention to the importance of economic responsibilities as a fundamental concern of managers. In this chapter this is considered as an important concern for three reasons.

First, the economic responsibilities of companies are also fundamental from a social point of view, as the notion of sustainable development also stresses. Second, shareholders are stakeholders whose interests must be considered by managers. This is not only because those interests are protected by law but also because the managers' livelihood is dependent upon how shareholders evaluate their performance. Finally, the other responsibilities depend on the fulfillment of economic responsibilities in the sense that the survival of the company and availability of sufficient resources to devote to other responsibilities depends on such fulfillment. Another important aspect to consider is that the existence, survival and profitability of a company depend on the fulfillment of legal responsibilities. If a company does not comply with the law either it will be subject to things such as fines, which impair its profitability, or it will be impeded of functioning.

Therefore, CSR, as the subject of analysis of this chapter, is seen as an "obligation" to constituent groups in society other than shareholders, which extends beyond that prescribed by law and union contract and is voluntarily adopted. Thus, although economic and legal responsibilities of companies are part of their social responsibilities, they are not included in corporate social responsibilities as a subject of analysis. In this chapter, CSR is understood as a two-way relationship which involves recognition on the part of "society" both of its significance and of the efforts made by companies to gain "society's" approval of its behaviour. Therefore, CSR relates to society's constituent groups' expectations about corporate behaviour that companies have to identify and try to behave in conformity with. CSR is the concept used most widely to address the relation- ships between business and society.

However, some concepts, such as corporate sustainability and corporate citizenship, have been proposed recently to conceptualize these relations. Some authors view these three concepts as synonymous whereas others propose some distinctions between them. In this chapter such concepts are considered to address the same basic issues as CSR. They all are about companies' impacts on, relationships with, and responsibilities to, society. These three concepts also integrate the perspectives which have been discussed so far. For example, the definition of corporate citizenship "as the extent to which businesses meet the economic, legal, ethical, and discretionary responsibilities imposed on them by their stakeholders" proposed by Maignan and Ferrell incorporates Carroll's classification of four main corporate social responsibilities and acknowledges the conceptual contributions of stakeholder management literature.

CSR is used in a loose sense to embrace similar concepts such as corporate citizenship and corporate sustainability, and integrating elements of stakeholder management. However, the typology of corporate social responsibilities proposed by Lantos is considered to be a useful development of Carroll's model, because it addresses the problem of distinguishing the ethical and philanthropic components that Schwartz and Carroll stressed, and because it considers the purpose with which companies engage in social responsibility activities. Based on their nature (required versus optional) and purpose (for stakeholders' good, the company's good, or both), Lantos considers three different types of responsibilities: ethical, altruistic, and strategic. Ethical responsibilities are regarded as morally mandatory. They involve preventing or rectifying harm or social injuries, even if the company might not appear to have benefited from such endeavours. It is important to note that ethical responsibilities are required even if their fulfillment is detrimental to the company's profitability.

From this point of view, companies are considered as "morally responsible to any individuals or groups where it might inflict actual or potential injury (physical, mental, economic, spiritual, and emotional) from a particular course of action. Even when the two parties to a transaction aren't harmed other parties (stakeholders) might be." Thus, managers of a company "do not have an obligation to maximize profits for the shareholders without regard to the means used." Lantos argues that harm cannot always be avoided, but should be minimized where feasible. He offers, as an example, the decision to close or relocate a plant because the product is no longer selling or the source of raw materials has changed. Although it seems sound from a financial point of view, it entails difficulties (wishfully temporary) for some employees and their community.

Ethical CSR: morally mandatory fulfillment of a company's economic responsibilities, legal responsibilities, and ethical responsibilities. Altruistic CSR: Fulfillment of an organization's philanthropic responsibilities, going beyond preventing possible harm (ethical CSR) to helping alleviate public welfare deficiencies regardless of whether or not this will benefit the business itself. Strategic CSR: fulfilling those philanthropic responsibilities which will benefit the company through positive publicity and goodwill implies a more efficient use of resources and therefore benefits society as a whole, "it is the socially responsible thing to do so long as injuries to workers are minimized as much as reasonably possible via means such as advance notification and severance pay." Another example is the money spent by a company on product safety or pollution control that might reduce shareholders profit, but have as alternative to threaten unethically the welfare of others in society.

Altruistic responsibilities involve going beyond ethical responsibilities to address social problems that the company has not caused and regarding which it has no responsibilities for. It can thus be said that altruistic responsibilities involve the assumption of some kind of responsibility for public welfare deficiencies that have not been caused by the company. It involves actions which are not morally mandatory but are beneficial for the company's stakeholders even at "at the possible, probable, or even definite expense of the business."

Finally, strategic responsibilities imply engaging in socially responsibility activities only when they are expected to benefit both one or more stakeholder groups and the company. In the case of altruistic responsibilities, the motive is not to reap financial benefits for the company as a consequence of their fulfillment (although that could happen as a by-product).

In contrast, with strategic responsibilities, companies contribute to their stakeholders because they believe it is in their best financial interests to do so, thereby fulfilling their responsibilities to the shareholders. Lantos argues altruistic responsibilities are only legitimate when they are strategic: that is, when they also further the objectives of the company.

From the perspective of the authors of this chapter, rather than offering a definition of CSR it seems more worthwhile to agree on the following five key elements identified by Buchholz:

- Companies have responsibilities beyond the production of goods and services at a profit;
- These responsibilities involve helping to solve important social problems, especially those they have helped create;
- Companies have a broader constituency than shareholders;
- Companies have impacts that go beyond simple marketplace transactions;
- Companies serve a wider range of human values than can be captured by a sole focus on economic values.

Views on CSR are often distinguished between those who oppose it and those who favour it. It is possible to have within the same perspective those who stand for CSR and those who reject it. Following Jones, the arguments in favour and against social responsibility engagement by companies are summarized in the following two paragraphs. Arguments against social responsibility are based on the institutional function of companies or on property rights perspectives. The institutional function argument can be held from three perspectives: first, other organizations, such as government, exist to deal with the kind of function requested by social responsible actions; second, managers are not seen as having the abilities and/or time to implement such kind of public actions; finally, unlike politicians, who are democratically elected, managers should not be held accountable for their social responsibility actions.

The argument based on the property rights perspective has its roots in neoclassical economic analysis, and maintains that managers' only obligation is to maximize the shareholder value. Arguments in favour of companies engaging in social responsibility activities can be ethical or instrumental. Ethical arguments are derived from religious principles, philosophical references or prevailing social norms. They suggest that a company should behave in a socially responsible manner because it is morally correct to do so. These arguments have a strong normative flavour. The instrumental arguments in favour of social responsibility rely on calculative assumptions that it will somehow benefit the company as a whole, at least in the long run. It is possible to distinguish two contrasting cases for CSR: the normative case which searches for motivations in the desire to do good; and the business case which focuses on the notion of enlightened self-interest.

Although there is a clear difference between these two perspectives, the reasons for a company engaging in CSR activities might reflect a mixture of the two. Based on Swanson, who refers to the economic and the duty-aligned perspectives as the two dominant approaches in the business and society field, Maignan and Ralston distinguish three main types of motivations to engage in social responsibility activities. First, following the economic or utilitarian perspective, CSR can be viewed as an additional instrument used by companies to achieve traditional corporate objectives. Second, according to the negative duty view, companies engage in social responsibility activities to conform to stakeholder norms and expectations about how their operations should be conducted, thus constituting mainly a legitimacy instrument used by a company to demonstrate its adherence to such norms and expectations. Third, according to the positive duty approach, companies may be self-motivated to engage in social responsibility initiatives and actively promote social interests, even when they are not expected or demanded by society.

As Maignan and Ralston state, "both the negative duty and the utilitarian approaches suggest that CSR can be used as an impression management tool employed to influence stakeholders' perceptions of the company." Whilst the utilitarian arguments can be associated easily with the classical view of social responsibility and the negative-duty arguments with the instrumental use of stakeholder theory, the positive-duty arguments can be associated with the normative use of stakeholder theory and with the activist view of social responsibility. The first two perspectives hold that companies engage in social responsibility activities for strategic reasons. Such motivation is different to the one envisaged by the two latter perspectives. CSR is understood as a two-way relationship which involves recognition on the part of "society" both of its significance and of the efforts of companies to gain "society's" approval of its behaviour. Therefore, CSR relates to society's constituent groups' expectations about corporate behaviour that companies have to identify and try to conform with.

Stakeholders are considered to have three roles: they are the sources of expectations about what constitutes desirable and undesirable company performance, defining the norms for corporate behaviour; they experience the effects of corporate behaviour; and they evaluate the outcomes of companies' behaviours in terms of how they have met expectations and have affected the groups and organizations in their environment. Trying to meet stakeholders' expectations implies the need to consider prevailing social norms and dominant views of corporate responsibilities. There have always been widely spread assumptions about what a modern company should be and how it should behave. Then it becomes important for companies that are expected to (or want to) appear to be modern to incorporate such assumptions into their operations, or at least into their presentations.

The growing social awareness about CSR issues has come to place substantial pressures on companies to manage the social and environmental impact of their activities and to become accountable to a wider audience than shareholders. All these aspects have an ethical dimension and it is probably true that, in many cases, engaging in CSR for strategic reasons will have some ethical and moral motivations and will lead to social benefits. As argued by Post et al. (2002), the interdependencies that exist among the company and its stakeholders cannot be de- scribed in terms of simple contractual exchanges. Furthermore, it is relationships rather than transactions that are the ultimate sources of a company's wealth and it is the ability to establish and maintain such relationships within its entire network of stakeholders that determines its long-term survival and success.

Relationships imply continuity and involve on-going conflict as well as collaborative elements. Post et al. define the stakeholders of a company as the "individuals and constituencies that contribute, either voluntarily or involuntarily, to its wealth-creating capacity and activities, and who are therefore its potential beneficiaries and/or risk bearers." A company's stakeholders are seen as those who supply critical resources, place something of value "at risk," and have sufficient power to affect its performance. For example, company's competitors are not considered as stakeholders when they are competing for resources and markets but may be considered as such when they have common interests and may gain or lose status and wealth as a result of competitors' actions.

The principal means of sustaining and enhancing a company's wealth-creating capacity are the linkages between the company and its multiple constituencies. Because of their linkage with the company, these constituents have a "stake" in its operations. As a result of the companies' operations, they have the possibility either of gaining greater or lesser benefits or experiencing greater or lesser harm. The stakeholders who engage in voluntary relationships with a company and contribute directly to its operations, such as investors, employees, customers, market partners, expect to be better off as a result of the relationship. Involuntary stakeholders, on the other hand, "particularly that who may be negatively affected by externalities such as pollution or congestion, the guiding principle has to be reduction or avoidance or harm and/or the creation of offsetting benefits."

These stakeholders expect that they will be at least as well off as they would be if the company did not exist." Lantos' conception of CSR as good stewardship of society's economic and human resources are a reasonable and particularly appropriate one nowadays. Companies are seen as having an obligation to consider society's long-run needs and wants, which implies that they engage in activities which promote benefits for society and minimize the negative effects of their actions. However, the company should not be prejudiced by engaging in such activities. The mission of a company should not be restricted to the creation of profit for shareholders. Rather, it should be acknowledged as that of identifying opportunities that are beneficial both for the company and for society. Managers are not mere shareholders' agents. They are "builders of stakeholder relations".

7

Current Approaches to Funding in Social Development

The focus of the last day of the conference was twofold: to give participants the opportunity to learn about specific US and international funding sources which have supported independent living efforts and to discuss the various types of funding which currently support independent living. Additionally, recommendations were made as to how to access more funds as well as to expand the circle of funding sources.

INTERNATIONAL AGENCIES AND ORGANISATIONS

The first presenter was Janet Allem from the United States Agency for International Development. When preparing a proposal, Allem stressed the importance of insuring that the goals of the proposal coincide with those of the funder, that goals are clearly stated and specific procedures to measure how those goals will be met are also clearly articulated. She cautioned participants about the importance of financial accountability as well as the need for a plan to generate financial self-sufficiency. Allem concluded that USAID is still not committing significant funds to disability-specific projects, but retains a major emphasis on disability-prevention issues through its maternal/child health program, as well as some provisions for simple rehabilitation services such as prosthetics for those injured in war or civil conflict.

Allem listed the following projects currently receiving funds: 1) the Egypt office is providing capacity building funds to the Alexandria Rehabilitation Hospital; 2) in Guatemala the Agency works with two organizations to strengthen disability rights legislation; 3) the USAID West Bank office is providing advocacy training and capacity-building to the General Union of the Disabled; 4) USAID Kenya is providing computers and training to people blinded by the Embassy bombing in Nairobi.

In summary, she pointed out that disabled individuals are often included in larger programs without a disability component, for example micro-enterprise programs tend to be inclusive. Civil society strengthening programs also provide a mechanism for helping disability-related NGOs to develop. USAID offers technical support to assist organizations in both proposal writing and organizational planning to maintain self-sufficiency. Next, David Levin representing the United States Information Agency gave a brief overview of the agency's involvement in supporting independent living efforts.

Recent examples included sponsorship of the DPI World Council Meeting held in Washington D.C. in 1996 and the National Clearinghouse on Disability and Exchange, a five-year project being conducted by Mobility International USA. The Clearinghouse advises organizations involved in international visits and exchanges about how to make their programs more accessible and provides connections for disabled Americans interested in studying, teaching or volunteering overseas.

In addition to disability specific initiatives, USIA offers funding for Americans to study overseas by way of Fulbright scholarships, as well as to bring international visitors to the US to explore scientific and cultural aspects of American society. In recent years the number of disabled scholars awarded Fulbright support has increased. Organizational grants to US agencies working with foreign partners are also available to fund grassroots exchanges of citizens working on a number of issues including: law, media, and conflict resolution.

The final presenter was Stephanie Gottlieb representing the Ashoka Foundation. Ashoka works in 33 countries in Latin America, Asia, Central Europe and Africa. Rather than funding projects, Ashoka invests in individuals, providing three-year grants which offer financial and other support for "social entrepreneurs." Ashoka has developed criteria to assess if people who are investing their energy to create social change also meet their requirements for support. A number of those selected by Ashoka as social entrepreneurs have been people with disabilities working to change their communities, and a few of these were given support to attend the IL Summit. After these presentations, participants discussed the wide variety of mechanisms being used to fund independent living efforts throughout the world.

OTHER INTERNATIONAL AGENCIES

Some disability groups in developing countries received their initial funding for independent living efforts through the United Nations to support the International Year of Disabled Persons (1981). In 1980 the UN set up The Trust Fund for Disabled Persons and since, this entity has funded many projects in support of the Year and then the Decade of Disabled Persons. This fund has dwindled since the UN Decade concluded, but continues to support small projects in developing countries. The InterAmerican Development Bank has funded projects in both the Caribbean and in Central America. Efforts to convince both the IDB and the World Bank to fund independent living projects have born little fruit thus far.

FUNDING APPROACHES IN VARIOUS COUNTRIES

In Bosnia, disability organizations are beginning to partner with each other as well as with other international organizations to develop long-term sustainable projects. Disability-related funding has primarily targeted emergency situations and has been very short-term. Currently Threshhold, a Finnish organization is funding small projects to assist disabled Bosnians.

One of the barriers to funding IL projects in Malawi is that disability is not viewed as a human rights issue, but rather as a charity issue. All funds dedicated to empowering disabled people are raised by disabled people themselves while the government continues to allocate funds to charities which don't provide services to empower disabled people.

In Cambodia, disability organizations have located some funding by collaborating with other small groups in pursuing projects from the development agencies. Some independent living efforts are funded by the Finnish government through its development agency, FINNIDA. In Brazil, early social and athletic groups of people with disabilities often supported themselves through the selling of lottery tickets and candy, and crafts production. The goal of these income-generation projects was usually to enable their members to contribute financially to their families.

In the late 1980s the Centro de Vida Independente in Rio de Janeiro, the first independent living center to be established outside of the industrialized world, began to train workers for employers, and uses the management and administrative fees from these contracts to fund core independent living services. The CVI of Rio has developed a comprehensive work-readiness program that prepares disabled people who have never worked for jobs in the mainstream labor market. In this way, the CVI offers services that in more materially affluent societies would be provided by rehabilitation centers and state-funded social services.

The success of this model has stimulated the growth during the 1990s of an additional 15 independent living centers throughout the country.

Currently, eight cooperatives for personal assistance users exist in Sweden, administering the government-funded PAS program. Access to PAS services is seen as the mainstay of independent living, in conjunction with accessibility initiatives and anti-discrimination legislation. This model demonstrates how a disability-run entity can qualify for government subsidy of service provision. Similar to Brazil, the administrative fees charged by the cooperatives for providing a service, are utilized to pay staff and expand their service base.

Most foreign non-governmental organizations working in Vietnam are concentrating their energies on provision of basic medical, rehabilitation and training services to assist the often-isolated members of Vietnam's disabled community to participate in the family-based economy. Support for independent living oriented groups is not yet available, although recently there have been some efforts to provide jobs for disabled Vietnamese in the foreign-supported wheelchair production workshops.

Beginning in the late 1970s, independent living centers throughout the US, funded in part by Federal monies, were established through the passage of Title VII of the Rehabilitation Act of 1978. During the 1980s and 90s the availability of Federal and other support led to the establishment of more than 300 centers in all 50 states. While this Federal funding enabled the number of independent living centers to increase, some feel that this development caused the IL movement to lose its grassroots nature and to become severed from the disability rights movement.

Many independent living centers no longer have the latitude to provide advocacy and community development services because their federal funding restricts them to more outcome-measurable services. Instead of defining disability community needs from the bottom up, centers find themselves driven by federally mandated priorities and processes. Guatemala has had success approaching private US foundations, such as the Kellogg Foundation to secure funding for materials.

Networking with community leaders, such as the mayor, has resulted in material support, including free space to house programs. Other financial support has been found by taking a proactive entrepreneurial approach for example, exploring ways to bring tourist traffic to underdeveloped areas. Many countries also face the barrier that funders want to see immediate results, even though experience has taught us that in reality there must be preparation and training over time before impact becomes evident.

In Germany, large social development agencies ran the institutions, and it has been difficult for grassroots organizations to create a public identity that would attract support and funding. More recently, the grassroots organizations have been able to use the media effectively to establish their own identity and are now attracting more financial support.

In the Philippines, Kampi, a federation of grassroots disability organizations, receives some funding from Denmark. Over three years, their rehabilitation projects to assist and educate children with disabilities have been successful and grown, attracting renewed funding for the upcoming years.

For most of this century, the needs of disabled people in Russia were considered the responsibility of the state; as a result there were neither charities nor independent living organizations of people with disabilities. Following the collapse in 1990 of the Soviet system, disabled people confronted both the end of state-provided social supports and the first real opportunities for self-organization.

Since, both US and Canadian development agencies have supported efforts of the All-Russian Society of Disabled Persons and smaller regional disability groups to adopt an independent living orientation, develop public education outreach and small businesses. In the case of the US, small grants were awarded to domestic independent living organizations, including the World Institute on Disability and Whirlwind Wheelchairs International, to provide guidance and training to Russian disability groups. In 1995, the Federal Law on the Social Protection of Persons with Disabilities was enacted, requiring that assistance be provided to disability organizations, though very little of this law has been implemented.

Under apartheid in South Africa, disability benefits were four times higher for whites than for black people. In 1981, the Self-Help Association of Paraplegics in Soweto set up a factory employing primarily disabled people, capitalized by outside assistance for the physical building. The initial thirty workers received only transportation and a single meal a day for the first six months of the factory's operation.

Strategies to Increase Funding for Independent Living Programs and Projects:

1. Design awareness programs with the purpose of educating donors that disability is a social/human rights issue as opposed to strictly a health/medical issue.
2. Improve the sustainability of disability programs in developing countries by developing partnerships between disability groups and other organizations struggling for social change.
3. Recognizing that some development agencies (CIDA, SIDA, JICA, and FINNIDA) have had IL-oriented disability policies since the early 1980s, initiate an ongoing mechanism for these agencies to exchange strategies and experience with other development agencies who are interested in IL programs and projects. This mechanism should involve NGOs which have experience in implementing IL-oriented projects in other countries, so that all can benefit and learn from this process.
4. The majority of disability-related external funding provided to poor countries is earmarked for prevention projects and established charities and rarely reaches grassroots organizations of disabled people. One approach to shifting more funds to IL-oriented programs would be to reserve a specified percentage of the overall budget of development assistance agencies. A second approach, which has proven effective for increasing support for women in development programs, has been to require that women are served agency-wide through each and every program budget.
5. There are a growing number of disability-directed groups

in donor countries who now have 15-20 years of practical experience in working with governments, disability organizations and other constituencies in developing countries. They have now accumulated skills, experiences and international development strategies, comprising a unique knowledge base that should be shared with emerging international disability leaders.

The Funding for Outcomes (FfO) project arose as one response to the findings of the Community and Voluntary Sector Working Party in 2001. The Working Party identified major issues that needed to be addressed to improve the way that the government funds and enters into contracts with community, Kiwi and Maori organisations. These issues included the complex reporting requirements set by government agencies, the "siloed" approach to contracting taken by these agencies, and the inability of providers to influence contract terms. FfO was established in 2003 as a mechanism for government agencies to collaborate in contracting with community organisations and, as a consequence, to reduce contract compliance costs for providers. It is changing the culture of government contracting with not-for-profit social service providers in New Zealand.

Interdepartmental work on contracting with non-government organisations (NGOs) that began in 1997 had noted that government's segregated approach to contracting was counterproductive in delivering services to clients with complex and multiple needs. An interdepartmental committee tackling this problem in 1999 developed a programme Best Practices in Funding. This aimed to improve interdepartmental collaboration and reduce compliance costs for providers by:

- Standardizing and simplifying contract and grant application documentation
- Sharing capability assessments and information between funders, and
- Adopting a "lead funder" approach.

Grant application forms were standardised and made available via the internet. A first attempt was made at developing an integrated contract in 1999 with a provider delivering a wraparound (holistic) service to clients with complex and multiple needs. Unfortunately, as the evaluation of this pioneering attempt reveals, the contract that emerged was a compendium of the existing siloed contracts, was not simplified, and did not reflect the integrated service being delivered by the provider.

The "lead funder" approach (where one funder managed the contract on behalf of all other funders) was trialled in 1999–2001 and proved unworkable as no one government agency had the technical expertise and knowledge to advise the provider on all aspects of another government agency's business, and accountability needed to stay with the funding source. Intermittent attempts were made to share capability assessments and information between funders during the same period, but there was no structure in place to normalise and embed this approach and so enable the available funding to be used as effectively and efficiently as possible.

In April 2003 the State Services Commission and Ministry of Social Development (MSD) jointly released a report on their integrated service delivery programme called *Progress Report on Integrated Service Delivery Programme (Mosaics)*. The programme was part of a set of initiatives under the Review of the Centre that began in 2000 as a comprehensive analysis of the strengths and weaknesses of the public sector and included ongoing work to lift the performance of the public service. The Review of the Centre focused on "circuit breaker" problems - finding new ways of working to resolve specific problems in service delivery, regional coordination including removing barriers to collaboration, and enhancing evaluation of public service performance to assist in achieving desired results.

Also in 2003, Treasury released its *Guidelines for Contracting with Non-Government Organisations for Services Sought by the Crown*. This document brought more uniformity to contracting practices and dispelled common myths about what was allowable in social service contracts between government and service providers (for example, contracts could be made for three or more years not just one year as many government officials then thought). Against this background, MSD was asked to lead a "whole of government" approach to address the Government's concerns about the way government departments and agencies were contracting with non-government organisations for services sought by the Crown.

The Funding for Outcomes Project

In late 2003, the FfO project was established to:

- Speed up progress in developing and implementing a more integrated approach to government contracting with NGOs
- Reduce compliance costs for service providers
- Identify success factors in achieving improved funding practices between multiple government funders and providers beyond the life of the project.

In brief, the FfO project responded to the Ministers' directive by, first, formalising a collaborative approach through the legally mandated platform of an integrated contract. Second, the project shifted the focus of these contracts from outputs to outcomes. Because all government agencies seek the same high-level, long-term outcome for clients, multiple government agencies can use the mechanism of a single integrated contract to collectively fund each provider. Likewise, each provider can use the integrated contract to describe, deliver and report on either a holistic wraparound service for individual clients or the various different services they are funded to deliver for the same client group.

Contract advisors were initially seconded from across government to form the first FfO team· In April 2004 they began work with their government colleagues on reducing barriers to developing integrating contracts by:

- Identifying and understanding the barriers to an integrated approach to contracting
- Developing policy and operational frameworks to address barriers and issues

- Developing and refining the tools and frameworks needed to manage the contracting process
- Developing an increased facilitation and brokering presence in the regions to facilitate the design and management of integrated contracts
- Documenting and evaluating the process of integrated contract development and management to inform best practice
- Sharing best practice experience across government and NGOs on developing common outcomes and monitoring the results of service delivery
- Integrating quality assurance, audit and reporting processes
- Instituting a senior officials group representative of government departments ("Steering Group") that would provide high-level advice on the project, and confirm the decision-making process about who would be involved in the project
- Using a transparent escalation process through the project steering group when cross-government barriers arose.

In the pilot stage of the project the FfO team was tasked to work with up to 20 significant service providers (at least eight of which were Maori or Kiwi providers) and with smaller organisations requiring capacity building and support. The team was also asked to work with at least two providers of disability services, and later with providers delivering family violence prevention services.

BARRIERS TO INTEGRATED SERVICE DELIVERY

Each government funder has responsibility and accountability for services and activities in its own sphere of influence or portfolio. Each government agency contracts with the community, Kiwi or Maori organisations that will best deliver its programmes. The community, Kiwi and Maori organisations delivering these services tend to specialise in delivering particular kinds of services (such as service to prevent family violence, or to improve parenting skills) or deliver services to meet the needs of particular clients (such as teenagers who have dropped out of school or are likely to do so).

To finance this work, and pay the salaries of the professional people who deliver these services, providers seek funding from numerous sources, including various government agencies. This funding is secured through bilateral contracts for each programme or activity that the provider agrees to carry out on behalf of the funder. The programmes the provider contracts to deliver will not necessarily perfectly match the needs of all the clients with whom the provider is working. Providers may also take on contracts for work that is not their main focus so that they can use some of the funding for interventions their clients need.

Providers, therefore, often have several contracts with multiple government funders and this creates fragmented service funding. These multiple contracts mean providers work with multiple and diverse IT systems, legal requirements, payment systems and administrative processes. Providers have major problems reporting to government on their use of the money for service delivery, as their work often does not fit into the reporting template, particularly if a contract is highly specific in telling a provider what to do. They can be at risk of being censored for not doing what their contract specifies, even if their contract does not address their particular client groups' specific needs (but what they are doing does).

Providers often do not get credit or funding for the work they undertake "outside" of their contract. Providers spend considerable time breaking down their work to fit multiple report templates that do not match what they do. For some providers this task is so complex they hire a person just to write service reports. Providers also spend time providing the same information for reports and for audit purposes, but in a different format to different government agencies. While this is frustrating and costly for providers, it is also problematic for funders. Under bilateral contract arrangements each government agency focuses on its own contract and the delivery of its own particular programme or service.

The government agency may be unaware of the other services that the provider is delivering, and may not appreciate that the provider is delivering a holistic service, or that the various services delivered by the provider to the same clients could be more efficiently managed if merged into one integrated service. Funders do not have a basis for understanding the effort needed to work with clients when they only see part of the service that is being delivered. There is much scope for misunderstanding about the effectiveness of service delivery and value for money, and the government agency does not receive a clear picture of which interventions are working for the client and which are not.

Enabling Integrated Service Delivery

Integrated contracting encourages all the parties involved to think differently about how they contract with social service providers. In particular, the integrated approach has introduced two major new features to contracting:

- A collaborative approach on the part of government agencies
- An outcomes or results-based focus.

COLLABORATION

All the agencies with an interest in the service being delivered, including local authorities, district health boards and philanthropic groups, are party to the integrated contract. Agencies work collectively to ensure the programmes they are funding meet client needs. By doing this, service gaps (and the agencies that should be funding work to fill these gaps) are more obvious (so those funders can also be invited to become a party to the contract). Where possible, funders will work with each other to merge their service requirements into an integrated service. This is one of the key benefits of the integrated contract.

Multiple individual contracts for specific services cannot reflect an integrated service, whereas the single integrated contract is able to document the complexity of interventions required for wraparound or holistic service delivery. Sometimes government agencies that do not fund the service will, nevertheless, become a party to the contract by providing non-financial resources (such as data, or personnel who work alongside the provider).

As a party to the integrated contract, providers are also involved in developing the contract. This improves parity for the provider with funders.

It is also giving effect to the promise made in the *Statement of Government Intentions for an Improved Community–Government Relationship* that community organisations participate in decision-making on the delivery of services.

Collaboration through FfO integrated contracting is proving to have many advantages for all participants:

- Funders meet each other - often for the first time - and improve their knowledge of the range of work performed by providers to meet the multiple needs of clients.
- Funders also share information about their own areas of work and expertise so get a better understanding of their co-funders' core work.
- The collaborative effort means improved relationships between funders and providers, and the development of greater trust so that there can be more creativity in finding effective interventions to get the right results for clients.
- By involving the provider in the contract discussions, everyone gets a better, better-rounded picture of the work.
- Providers are, for the first time, feeling involved in the process of contract development, as opposed to being given a contract to undertake.
- Service delivery can be made more cost effective when funding is transparent and the funding that is available can be used more efficiently.

- Providers' compliance costs are falling when they are required to write fewer reports, and when reports more closely match the service being delivered.
- The increased upfront effort in drafting the results-based contract is mitigated by the certainty provided by the longer term of the contract (three years), and the greater robustness of the process.
- The capability of new contract managers is raised by the knowledge they gain from participating in integrated contract development and joint review meetings.
- All funders learn from the dialogue with providers – and this is especially apparent at review meetings.

FOCUS ON OUTCOMES (RESULTS)

By taking outcomes focus, the contracts articulate the results that the provider is seeking for clients by delivering the service, and that government is seeking for clients in funding the service. The implications are far-reaching.

- There is a better match between what providers do and what their contract says it wants to achieve.
- Funders and providers have a clearer understanding of the results sought from the services and of the clients for whom the services are designed and delivered.
- Clients have a better chance of getting the services they need.
- Reports go beyond counting the number of interventions.
- The contract articulates the changes that the clients are expected to experience and reports document these results, so are more meaningful, and also reflect the progress made in achieving the results.
- The outcomes focus builds opportunities to review trends and see whether the outcomes we are looking for, for clients, are being achieved.
- By monitoring results, providers' efforts are acknowledged and the effectiveness of policies and programmes is made transparent (whereas in the past providers may have been seen as non-performers if clients did not respond as expected).

- The results-based reports provide opportunities for performance measurement – that is reports can record how well and how quickly a service is reaching the client group, and the extent to which clients participate in the programme or service activities.
- In a collaborative situation where all the funders and the providers are collectively reviewing the reports and viewing trends, there is a richness of information-sharing and opportunities to build knowledge about what is happening for particular groups of clients.

ASPECTS OF THE INTEGRATED CONTRACT

Pre-Approved Standard Terms and Conditions

The contract instruments have been agreed for use by all the government agencies involved in the process, and their legal teams. Several government agencies (MSD, Department of Labour and district health boards among others) are now starting to use the integrated contract standard terms and conditions in their own contracts with social service providers. This practice is paving the way for a single generic set of terms and conditions to be utilised with third-party social service delivery across New Zealand – whether the long version for use with larger contracts over $200,000, or the pared-down short version for smaller contracts. Using a pre-agreed standard set of terms and conditions provides the opportunity to speed up contract negotiation and sign-off processes, thereby reducing transaction costs for all parties.

Each Funder's Accountability and Relationship

The funding from each government agency is kept separate (i.e. is separately invoiced) to give transparency to the money flow. In other words, the integrated contract enables each government agency to retain its autonomy and accountability for its own portfolio responsibilities, funding, and relationship manager while joining in funding collaborative action to address clients' needs in quite complex ways. Contract service descriptions identify which funder is paying for each activity and even when activities are jointly funded it is still clear which funder has responsibility for funding which intervention or part of it.

Clarity of Structure and Processes

Integrated contracting has a clear structure and processes so that everyone involved knows their role and what is expected of them. The process is facilitated by a Funding for Outcomes Contract Advisor whose role is unbiased and non-representative of any one funding agency.

Legal Status

The integrated contract is a legal document. This means that all parties must engage in the process and cannot make unilateral decisions or withdraw unlawfully. The process and the product are mandated, are supported by providers, and meet government quality assurance requirements.

Flexibility

Integrated contracts are flexible so that government systems can be accommodated when it would take too long to change them (e.g. payment systems that have been decreed through regulatory or legislative processes). The system can cope with fee-for-service funding as well as payments in advance or in arrears. This is particularly important because integrated contracts can accommodate the full range of Crown entities as well as non-government funders such as funders from the philanthropic sector, and non-monetary resources (like data sets, equipment, accommodation or personnel).

ACHIEVEMENTS OF THE FFO TEAM TO DATE

In developing integrated contracts the FfO team has achieved some significant milestones. It has developed new contract instruments and new processes which did not previously exist. These include:

- Provider risk assessments that were developed with the support of the Office of the Auditor-General to protect both the provider and funders (and which form the basis of the shared monitoring framework)

- A working together charter documenting expectations, roles and responsibilities of government officials participating in an integrated contract
- Standard terms and conditions drafted with input from government legal teams, some providers, and academics from the community and voluntary sector (now being used by several government agencies as their standard)
- A template for drafting the "special" terms and conditions – that is, a single document in which is recorded the results expected from the services delivered by the provider; the activities that the provider will carry out in order that the expected results will be achieved; the target group, volumes; funding amounts and payment dates for each funder
- A framework for shared monitoring
- An integrated report template (that matches the expected results) and reporting schedule (including dates of synchronised or integrated audits) which forms the basis of the collaborative review process
- An integrated contract variation template
- Collaborative integrated contract review meetings.

In implementing the integrated contract process the FfO team has worked with over 45 government agencies (including district health boards, local government and Crown entities) in main centers and several small towns across New Zealand. The work has entailed in-depth discussions with legal, financial, IT and procurement teams, contract managers, advisors and specialists, and policy staff. The FfO team has also worked with over 80 providers. From that work:

- 23 integrated contracts are operational and the team is supporting the management of review meetings
- 26 integrated contracts are under development.

This means around 250 bilateral contracts have been, or are being, pulled into 49 integrated ones.

Another 10 providers are being assessed for inclusion in the project, and there is a waiting list. The team has also worked with around 20 providers whose work did not lend itself to an integrated contract, but acted to resolve contracting issues or provide other capacity building and support. Around half of the integrated contracts are with Kiwi or Maori providers.

Current work often involves facilitation of a redraft of the results and reporting framework of existing integrated contracts. With increased experience in this work, funders are seeing the value of documenting in the contract the integrated service delivered by the provider, and can also see where the part of the service they fund fits. Review meetings also provide an opportunity for funders and providers to collectively assess whether the service being purchased is the right service, and to identify service gaps.

In 2007 the FfO team is focusing on providers of family violence prevention services. It is also working with providers of youth services, disability services, youth offending prevention, family wellbeing /whanau ora services, early childhood services, services for ethnic minorities, services for people recovering from substance abuse, paroled prisoners, and so on. As well as dealing with individuals, providers also work with families and sometimes whole communities. The integrated contract reporting framework is flexible enough to handle this diversity of clients and also addresses the tension between providers' desire to report on their whole service and each funder's requirement to know the number of clients that received the services it funded.

The team has developed and is delivering a training programme for participants in the integrated contract process. This aims to:

- Bring everyone up to speed with changes in documentation
- Ensure each government funder's contract manager understands his or her role and responsibilities in managing the integrated contract, and
- Give participants practice in developing a results-based contract.

IMPACT AND VALUE OF INTEGRATED CONTRACTING

The process of integrating contracts is shifting the culture of contracting across government from micro-management to a client-focused relational approach built on trust. The strong emphasis on collaborative reviews of the provider's work provides a robust, risk-aware, supportive service delivery environment.

The reviews emphasize continuous improvement through adoption of "best" practice. Funders have a better understanding of what they are purchasing, the cost of service delivery and gaps in service delivery become more transparent, and the myriad tensions between providers' and funders' agendas are explored and addressed.

The earlier difficulties encountered in developing integrated contracts are being overcome with the development and refinement of tools and processes. As government funders become increasingly familiar with these processes and with the results framework introduced by Mark Friedman (2005), the speed with which integrated contracts can be developed is increasing. In 2006 an evaluation was carried out on the first two years' operation of integrated contracts. Despite the newness of the process at that time, the evaluation found that both providers and funders supported integrated contracting and wanted to continue with the process.

Benefits identified included:

- Better service development and planning
- Increased capacity and transparency in the delivery of holistic services
- Greater capacity to meet the needs of clients and focus on achieving longer-term outcomes
- Providers experiencing improved operating effectiveness
- More transparent accountability
- Greater certainty of funding through longer-term contracts
- A range of transaction benefits resulting from a reduction

in the number of reports required a reduction in the number of separate provider-funder meetings, improved understanding of funders of the services being funded, and the focus on results of service delivery for clients.

The evaluation identified that results-based integrated contracts are introducing a new contracting culture. The FfO project has acted as an important catalyst for ongoing evolution of contracting processes that are collaborative and outcomes focused. Under these evolving processes funders and providers are being involved, often for the first time, in collective contract negotiation. Providers value this changing culture of contracting for a range of reasons.

- They feel they have a better understanding of funders' requirements.
- Their participation is beginning to be on a more equal footing with funders.
- Funder-provider relationships are valued.
- The nature of their services is more accurately reflected in contracts.
- Their achievements are more identifiable in the reporting frameworks.

Funders feel that they have a better understanding of the operational and policy contexts in which their co-funders work and a better idea of how to work with and support providers individually and collectively in ways that are leading to better service delivery and better outcomes for clients.

DESCRIPTION OF THE PROGRAM

The Social Development Partnerships Program (SDPP) works in partnership with social not-for-profit organizations to help improve life outcomes for people with disabilities, children and families and other vulnerable populations. People with disabilities, children and families, and other vulnerable populations have unique social development needs that are compounded by physical, economic and social pressures. As a result, they may experience a diminished quality of life, with limited ability to participate in the workplace or to contribute to their communities.

Objectives

The objectives of the Program are to:

- Support the development and utilization of effective approaches to address social issues and barriers;
- Develop, exchange and apply knowledge, tools and resources that sustain social inclusion for individuals, families and communities;
- Foster collaborations, partnerships, alliances and networks to address existing and emerging social issues; and
- Recognize and support the ability of not-for-profit organizations to identify and address social development priorities.

Individuals, families and communities continue to be a priority of the Government of Canada. In the 2007 Speech from the Throne, the Government of Canada reiterated its commitment to work to invest in Canadian families and people with disabilities through an array of programs. The SDPP plays an important role in Human Resources and Skills Development Canada (HRSDC) and is consistent with the Department's vision and overall government priorities with respect to individuals and families, namely, "a strong and competitive Canada that enable individuals to make choices that help them to live productive and rewarding lives."

The link between the SDPP and the Department's Management, Resources and Results Structure is further documented in the HRSDC Program Activity Architecture, which highlights the importance of individuals, families and communities in the Department's mission. In particular, "the Department develops policies that make Canada a society in which all can participate and that ensures that individuals can use their talents, skills and resources to benefit the entire country. The Department creates programs and supports initiatives that help Canadians invest in themselves and move through life's transitions - from families with children to seniors, from school to work, from one job to another, from unemployment to employment, and from the workforce to retirement - and delivers citizen-centered service with integrity, commitment and excellence."

By contributing to the enhanced well-being of individuals, families and communities, the SDPP supports the Department in achieving one of its strategic objectives:

- Income security, access to opportunities and well-being for individuals, families and communities.

Outcomes

SDPP funded activities are expected to lead to the development and sharing of knowledge of existing and emerging social issues; the creation of collaboration, partnerships, alliances and networks; and the development of approaches to respond to existing and emerging social issues. Over the long term, SDPP support for these activities will help the not-for-profit sector and partners be more effective in addressing existing and emerging social issues, and will help target populations have access to information, programs and services.

Government social policies and programs will also be informed of the needs of target populations. Recipients of grants and contributions will be expected to report on the achievement of results in relation to the SDPP's objectives. The precise expected results and outcomes are indicated in the Program's Accountability, Audit and Risk Framework.

Program Authority

The Social Development Partnerships Program (SDPP) is developed under the authority of the *Department of Social Development* Act which provides in subsection 5(1) that the powers, duties and functions of the Minister "extend to and include all matters over which Parliament has jurisdiction relating to the social development of Canada which are not by law assigned to any other Minister, department, board or agency of the Government of Canada."

The *Act* also provides in subsection 5(2) that the Minister shall exercise the powers and performs the duties and functions assigned by subsection (1) with a view to promoting social well-being and income security. Section 7 provides that the "Minister may, in exercising the powers and performing the duties and functions assigned by this *Act*, establish and implement programs designed to support projects or other activities that contribute to the social development of Canada, and the Minister may make grants and contributions in support of the program." The SDPP is a program that relates to the mandate of the Minister.

Interpretation

The phrase "social not-for-profit sector" includes a wide range of not-for-profit organizations working to advance the goals of social development. The phrase "other vulnerable or excluded populations" refers to those groups facing systemic barriers to their full participation in Canadian society.

CORPORATE SOCIAL RESPONSIBILITY

Corporate Social Responsibility (CSR) is the continuing commitment by business to behave ethically, contribute to economic development, improving quality of life of workforce, their family, local community and society, build a meaningful relationship between the corporate sector and the rest of the society. Business has to adopt practices that ensure ethical, legal, commercial and public expectations. It must be the integrated part of day to day business engaging all stakeholders, strategies to support individual managers to make socially responsible decisions conforming ethical behaviour and law.

- Companies are obliged to comply with law, give the community a variety of financial and non-financial ways and take into account the environment and social context in which the business operates.
- Shrinking of government resources, distrust of regulations, demand for greater disclosures, increased customer's interests, investors' pressure, competitive labour markets

etc are some of the driving forces of CSR.

- The concept of CSR involves voluntarily adopted behaviour going beyond legal obligations, practices intrinsically connected to sustainable development and culture incorporated into core business strategies.

Accountability, transparency, conduct in conformity with laws, business ethics, good workplaces and labour relations practices, affirmative actions / good practices, customers loyalty and satisfaction, environmental benefits and company involvement with community are some of the components of CSR. Triple Bottom line reporting on resources and market reputation, improved ability to understand business performance and risks, attract quality employees, greater profile for raising capital are few benefits of CSR.

Corporate Social Responsibility (CSR) is on the rise all over the world and in India also. Civil Societies, consumers and other actors have increased pressure on companies to adhere to social and environmental standards and this pressure has impacts on the business in India. Limits of regulatory initiatives, changing nature of judicial activism, government's greater relevance on private enterprises, etc. places greater responsibility on voluntary approaches as an alternative means of building social rights. Voluntary initiatives for environmental protection have been restricted to large firms. CSR is often guided by the commitment of the top management.

With compliance and enforcement slack, employee's care is just employers' benevolence, environment care and total quality management are driven by market forces and legislation, CSR is considered as an additional activity of Human relation and public relation department. Democratic institutions need to be strengthened for steady movement, towards strengthening of enforceable regulation. Space to be created for various actors to operate, provide, support and resistance as required government need to be re-engineered so that civil society vigilance can reinforce its regulating and monitoring roll. Re-engineering of government requires active defense or advocacy of constitutional rights from court to civil society.

A new initiative, Corporate Responsibility for Environmental Protection (CREP) was initiated by the Government of India. Four years ago, Reliance Industries Ltd. launched a countrywide initiative known as "Project Drishti", to restore the eye-sights of visually challenged Indians from the economically weaker sections of the society. This project, started by one of India's corporate giants has brightened up the lives of over 5000 people so far. Corporate Social Responsibility (CSR) defined as "the ethical behavior of a company towards the society," manifests itself in the form of such noble programs initiated by for-profit organizations. CSR has become increasingly prominent in the Indian corporate scenario because organizations have realized that besides growing their businesses it is also vital to build trustworthy and sustainable relationships with the community at large.

This is one of the key drivers of CSR programs. Another reason fuelling this rapid adoption of CSR is the state of the Indian society. Though India is one of the fastest growing economies, socio-economic problems like poverty, illiteracy, lack of healthcare etc. are still ubiquitous and the government has limited resources to tackle these challenges. This scenario has opened up several areas for businesses to contribute towards social development. CSR is not a new concept in India. Corporates like the Tata Group, the Aditya Birla Group, and Indian Oil Corporation, to name a few, have been involved in serving the community ever since their inception. Many other organizations have been doing their part for the society through donations and charity events.

Today, CSR in India has gone beyond merely charity and donations, and is approached in a more organized fashion. It has become an integral part of the corporate strategy. Companies have CSR teams that devise specific policies, strategies and goals for their CSR programs and set aside budgets to support them. These programs, in many cases, are based on a clearly defined social philosophy or are closely aligned with the companies' business expertise. Employees become the backbone of these initiatives and volunteer their time and contribute their skills, to implement them. CSR Programs could range from overall development of a community to supporting specific causes like education, environment, healthcare etc.

For example, organizations like Bharath Petroleum Corporation Limited, Maruti Suzuki India Limited, and Hindustan Unilever Limited, adopt villages where they focus on holistic development.

They provide better medical and sanitation facilities, build schools and houses, and help the villagers become self-reliant by teaching them vocational and business skills. On the other hand GlaxoSmithKline Pharmaceuticals' CSR programs primarily focus on health and healthy living. They work in tribal villages where they provide medical check-up and treatment, health camps and health awareness programs. They also provide money, medicines and equipment to non-profit organizations that work towards improving health and education in under-served communities.

Many CSR initiatives are executed by corporate in partnership with Non-governmental organizations (NGOs) who are well versed in working with the local communities and are experts in tackling specific social problems. For example, SAP India in partnership with Hope Foundation, an NGO that works for the betterment of the poor and the needy throughout India, has been working on short and long-term rebuilding initiatives for the tsunami victims. Together, they also started The SAP Labs Center of HOPE in Bangalore, a home for street children, where they provide food, clothing, shelter, medical care and education. CSR has come a long way in India.

From responsive activities to sustainable initiatives, corporates have clearly exhibited their ability to make a significant difference in the society and improve the overall quality of life. In the current social situation in India, it is difficult for one single entity to bring about change, as the scale is enormous. Corporates have the expertise, strategic thinking, manpower and money to facilitate extensive social change. Effective partnerships between corporates, NGOs and the government will place India's social development on a faster track. Corporate social responsibility is not a new concept in India. However, what is new is the shift in focus from making profits to meeting societal challenges. Now-a-days, employees are actively participating in the social activities even on holidays. This is mainly because employees feel a sense of pride when they are involved in such activities.

Moreover, companies are having dedicated departments for CSR. Giving a universal definition of Corporate Social Responsibility is bit difficult as there is no common definition as such. However, there are few common threads that connect all the perspectives of CSR with each other; the dedication to serve the society being most important of them. Most ideal definition of Corporate Social Respon-sibility (CSR) has been given by World Business Council for Sustained Development which says, "Corporate Social Responsibility is the continuing commitment by business to behave ethically and contribute to economic development while improving the quality of life of the workforce and their families as well as of the local community and society at large".

Thus, the meaning of CSR is two fold. On one hand, it exhibits the ethical behavior that an organization exhibits towards its internal and external stakeholders (customers as well as employees). On the other hand, it denotes the responsibility of an organization towards the environment and society in which it operates. Firms can no longer continue to exploit environmental resources and escape from their responsibility by acting as separate entities regardless of the interest of the society. Organizations, now, are realizing the need to shift their focus on the interest of society. The sense of being socially responsible has to come from within. CSR involves various voluntary efforts in which companies engage themselves in order to give something back to the society. It involves providing innovative solutions to societal and environmental challenges. Organizations generally believe that acting in a socially responsible manner will create value for them.

The fact that an organization is committed to social causes, also gives employees a sense that the company would also be committed to the welfare of its employees as well. In India, CSR has evolved to encompass employees, customers, stakeholders and sustainable development or corporate citizenship. The spectrum of CSR includes a number of areas as human rights, safety at work, consumer protection, climate protection and caring for the environment, and sustainable management of natural resources. From the perspective of employees, CSR activities include providing health and safety measures, preserving employee rights and discouraging discrimination at workplace. This helps in fostering a healthy environment within the company. For example, after 1945, TATA implemented social welfare provisions for its employees that have since become the legislative norm. From the perspectives of customers, CRS activities may include commitment to product quality, fair pricing policies, and so.

CSR taken up by various genres of companies primarily focuses on poverty alleviation, environmental protection and sustained development. Companies are taking initiatives for developing infrastructure in rural areas, e.g., TATA Motors provides desks, benches, chairs, tables cupboards, electrical fittings and educational and sports material to various primary schools in Singur. The company has also planned similar programmes to upgrade school infrastructure and is also planning to set up a computer laboratory in one of the high schools. Similarly, TVS Electronics was involved in CSR during the Tsunami to provide relief measures to the victims. They have also participated with the government to improve sanitation in a village called Tiruvidenthai.

Such initiatives will help in improving the conditions of rural people. Satyam Foundation of Satyam Computer Services Ltd., Infosys Foundation of Infosys Technologies Ltd., and GE Foundation of the General Electric Company are exemplary instances of the philanthropic commitment of the corporate sector in India. Irrespective of the profits they make, these foundations are aiming at uplifting of the poor and enhancing the standard of life in the rural sector. Corporate social responsibility offers manifold benefits both internally and externally to the companies involved in various projects. Externally, it creates a positive image amongst the people for its company and earns a special respect amongst its peers. It creates short term employment opportunities by taking various projects like construction of parks, schools, etc.

Working with keeping in view the interests of local community bring a wide range of business benefits. For example, for many businesses, local customers are an important source of sales. By improving the reputation, one may find it easier to recruit employees and retain them. Businesses have a wider impact on the environment also. Plantation and cultivation activities taken up by Intel India are a step towards the same. Recycling used products also acts as a step towards minimizing wastes. Internally, it cultivates a sense of loyalty and trust amongst the employees in the organizational ethics. It improves operational efficiency of the company and is often accompanied by increases in quality and productivity. More importantly, it serves as a soothing diversion from the routine workplace practices and gives a feeling of satisfaction and a meaning to their lives.

Employees feel more motivated and thus, are more productive. Apart from this, CSR helps ensure that the organization comply with regulatory requirements. Even though companies are taking serious efforts for the sustained development, some critics still are questioning the concept of CSR. There are people who claim that Corporate Social Responsibility underlies some ulterior motives while others consider it as a myth. Is CSR really a stalking horse for an anti-corporate agenda? The reality is that CSR is not a tactic for brand building; however, it creates an internal brand among its employees. Indulging into activities that help society in one way or the other only adds to the goodwill of a company. An essential component of our corporate social responsibility is to care for the community. We endeavor to make a positive contribution to the underprivileged communities by supporting a wide range of socio-economic, educational and health initiatives.

Many of the community projects and programs are driven by active participation from our employees. Our commitment to address important societal needs extends throughout our philanthropic outreach programs driven by the Zensar Foundation. Established for the purpose of improving, guiding and inspiring the lives of the underprivileged, the Foundation facilitates programs and gives direct assistance and resources to individuals, families and other charitable organizations. Nurturing experiences and personal opportunities are also provided for those in the community who have little or no access to any assistance. The Zensar Foundation has taken up several initiatives to improve living conditions of the underprivileged and make a positive difference in their lives.

The Foundation has adopted Ambedkar Nagar, a small community near the Zensar Campus for sustained community development programmes. Health and education have been identified as the primary objectives in the community development process. The foundation works relentlessly to ensure improvement of general health and spread of non-formal education among all members in the community. A number of focused initiatives have been implemented to bring about general health awareness and improve the level of education.

Bibliography

AAmba-Rao, Sita C. 1993. "Multinational Corporate Social Responsibility, Ethics, Interactions and Third World Governments: An Agenda for the 1990s." *Journal of Business Ethics* 12: 553-572.

Arnoldo C. Hax and Nicolas S. Majluf. 1996. *The Strategy Concept and Process*, 2nd Edition. Prentice-Hall.

Arthur Thompson, Jr., and A. J. Strickland III. Irwin. 1996. *Strategic Management: Concepts and Cases*, 9th Edition.

Benjamin Tregoe and John Zimmerman. 1980. *Top Management Strategy*. Simon & Schuster.

Collins, Marylyn. 1993. "Global Corporate Philanthropy - Marketing Beyond the Call of Duty?" *European Journal of Marketing* 27 (2): 46-59.

Faulkner, J. Hugh. 1995. "Public-Private Partnerships in Sustainable Development." *Review of European Community & International Environmental Law* 4 (2): 133-137.

Fogarty, Michael, and Ian Christie. 1990. *Companies and Communities: Promoting Business Involvement in the Community*. London: Policy Studies Institute.

Gratias, F.X. Alan, and Melanie Boyd. Summer 1995. "Beyond Government: Can the Public Sector Meet the Challenges of Public-Private Partnering?" *Optimum* 26: 3-14.

H. Igor Ansoff. 1965. *Corporate Strategy*. McGraw-Hill.

Hood, John. 1997. *The Heroic Enterprise: Business and the Common Good*. New York: Free Press.

Horkan, Kathleen, and Patricia Jordon. July 1996. *Endowments as a Tool for Sustainable Development*. USAID. Center for Development Information and Evaluation. Washington. (PN-ABY-616)

Independent Task Force on Community Action for Social Development. 1995. *Partnerships for Community Development.* Franklin, WV: Future Generations.

Kenneth Andrews. 1980. *The Concept of Corporate Strategy.* Richard Irwin.

Korton, David. 1995. *When Corporations Rule the World.* West Hartford: Kumarian Press.

Larkin, G. Richard. Winter 1994. "Public-Private Partnerships in Economic Development: A Review of Theory and Practice." *Economic Development Review* 12: 7-10.

Lewin, Arie, et al. February 1995. "Corporate Citizenship in Japan: Survey Results From Japanese Firms." *Journal of Business Ethics* 14: 83-101.

Logan, David; Delwin Roy; and Laurie Regelbruge. 1997. *Global Corporate Citizenship: Rationale and Strategies.* Washington: Hitachi Foundation.

McCarthy, Kathleen, et al. 1992. *The Nonprofit Sector in the Global Community: Voices from Many Nations.* San Francisco: Jossey-Bass Publishers.

Mooers, Donald L. "Volunteers in Overseas Cooperative Assistance European Northern Tier: Guide for Program and Project Development in the Region."

Mullen, Jennifer. Summer 1997. "Performance-Based Corporate Philanthropy: How 'Giving Smart' Can Further Corporate Goals." *Public Relations Quarterly* 42: 42.

Patten, John. "Government, Business and the Voluntary Sector: A Developing Partnership." Fall 1994. *Policy Studies: The Journal of Policy Studies Institute* 12: 4.

Paul, Karen. 1995. "Corporate Philanthropy in South Africa: Lessons for Local Development Initiatives." *Voluntas* 6 (1): 67-83.

Peterson, George, and Dana Sundblad. 1994. *Corporation as Partners in Strengthening Urban Communities.* Conference Board.

Reder, Alan. Winter 1995. "The Wide World of Corporate Philanthropy." *Business and Society Review* 92: 36-42.

Reilly, Bernard, and Kyj Myron. Summer 1994. "Corporate Citizenship." *Review of Business* 16: 37-43.

Reilly, Bernard, and Kyj Myron. 1990. "Ethical Business and the Ethical Person." *Business Horizons.* 23-27.

Reilly, Bernard, and Kyj Myroslaw. "The Social Conscience of Business." *Business and Professional Ethics Journal* 7 (3/4): 81-101.

Russell Ackoff. 1981. *Creating the Corporate Future: Plan or be Planned For.* John Wiley.

Ruzica, Miroslav. 1994. "The Eastern European Initiative in Philanthropy." *Philanthropy Matters.* 10-20.

Schmidheiny, Stephan. 1992. *Changing Course: A Global Business Perspective on Development and the Environment.* Boston: MIT Press.

Shanker, Amy, and Len Rodman. April 1996. "Public-Private Partnerships." *Journal of the American Water Works Association* 88: 102-142.

Sidel, Mark. 1997. "The Emergence of a Voluntary Sector and Philanthropy in Vietnam: Functions, Legal Regulation and Prospects for the Future." *Voluntas* 8 (3): 283-302.

Simon, Francoise L. 1995. "Global Corporate Philanthropy: A Strategic Framework." *International Marketing Review* 12: 20-37.

Smith, Craig. May-June 1994. "The New Corporate Philanthropy." *Harvard Business Review.* 105-115.

Somaya, Shilpi. "Non-Philanthropic Corporate Involvement in Community Development." *Business and Society Review*: 32-38.

Velasco, Gisela T. 1996. "Corporate Philanthropy in Asia:

The Philippine Case." CUNY Graduate Center. New York.

Waddell, Steve. 1997. "Market-Civil Society Partnership Formation: A Status Report on Activity, Strategies and Tools." Institute for Development Research. Boston, MA.

William King and David Cleland. Van Nostrand Reinhold. 1987. *Strategic Planning and Management Handbook.*

Williams, Nancy. Summer 1991. "Community Agenda for the 1990s: A Corporate View." *Economic Development Review*: 26-31.

Williams, Nancy. Winter 1994. "Partnerships that Redefine the Corporate Role in Community Economic Development." *Economic Development Review*: 10-11.

Index

G

H

I

K

L

M

N

P

Q